INTRODUCTION TO ḤADĪTH

SECOND EDITION

DIRĀYAT AL-ḤADĪTH

by

Al-Shahīd al-Thānī

followed by

INTRODUCTION TO ḤADĪTH

by

ʿAbd al-Hādī al-Faḍlī

Translated by
Nazmina Virjee

British Library Cataloguing-in-Publication Data
A catalogue record for this book is available from the British Library.

ISBN: 978-1-904063-47-6 (pbk)

First edition, 2002
Second edition, 2011

ICAS Press
133 High Road, Willesden, London NW10 2SW
www.islamic-college.ac.uk

CONTENTS

Translator's Preface vii

Translator's Introduction xi

DIRĀYAT AL-ḤADĪTH

Preface 3

Introduction 5

1. Classification of *Ḥadīth* 10
2. Those Whose Transmission Can Be Accepted and Those Whose Transmission is Rejected 18
3. The Modes of Receiving and Transmitting Traditions 21
4. Terminology Pertaining to the Names and Generations of Reporters 25

INTRODUCTION TO ḤADĪTH

Introduction 29

1. Introduction to the Principles of *Ḥadīth* 31
2. History of the Principles of *Ḥadīth* 41
3. General Terminology in *Ḥadīth* Studies 49
4. Sources of *Ḥadīth* 53
5. Components of the Tradition 76
6. The *Mutawātir* Report 79
7. The *Āḥād* Report 91
8. Evaluating Narrators 131

9. The Fabricated (*Mawḍūʿ*) Tradition 148

10. Who Can Relate *Ḥadīth*? 185

11. General Authentications 201

12. Manner of Receiving and Transmitting *Ḥadīth* 220

Glossary 227

Bibliography 233

Index 239

TRANSLATOR'S PREFACE

In the Name of Allah, the Most Beneficent, the Most Merciful, who has endowed us with all our faculties to be able to understand his Revelation and His Will, through the Words and Actions of His beloved Prophet Muḥammad (S) and his purified family, the Ahl al-Bayt (A).

The field of *ḥadīth* is a vast sea that encompasses various fields of knowledge and numerous sciences within its depths, such as the science of jurisprudence, biographical studies, the principles of jurisprudence, history of Islam and the spread of Islam, and interpretation of the Qurʾān, to mention but a few. The *ḥadīth* is in fact the embodiment of the Sunnah, the words and actions of our Prophet (S) and his purified family, the Ahl al-Bayt, whom we are obliged to follow in all matters of faith, and social and religious conduct, as stated by Allah's command in the Holy Qurʾān: 'O you who believe! Obey Allah and obey the Apostle and those in authority from among you.'

The study of the origin, development, and criticism of *ḥadīth* literature as we have it today is essential because it serves as a copious source of information about the history of pre-Islamic Arabia, early Islam, the development of Arabic literature and Islamic law, as well as serving to establish a common source of legislation for the whole Muslim world after the Qurʾān. The science itself is extremely interesting for it gives the reader insight into the thought processes and endeavours of early Islamic scholars, as well as into many of the key theological, political, and cultural movements that developed in the Muslim world throughout its history.

There is an undoubted lack of English resources at present in the field of *ḥadīth* sciences written from a Shīʿa Muslim viewpoint, especially as several of the *ḥadīth* works available represent Orientalist and mainstream approaches to *ḥadīth* scholarship, which is not at all representative of the normative Shīʿa Muslim viewpoint, not to mention the true state of affairs. Because there is no exhaustive

English study that focuses on achieving this aim, this humble translation of an Arabic contribution to the field will *insha'allah* be a step forward in this regard, though it must be noted that, within Arabic scholarship, the author's contribution is invaluable, for he has quoted the opinions and rulings of many renowned scholars within the field to give as objective a view of the science as possible, without detracting from the subject. At the same time, he presents the views of both classical scholars as well as modern scholars in the field, resulting in an effective overview of the science of *ḥadīth*.

He quotes the opinions of both Akhbārī (traditionalist and literalist scholars) scholars such as al-Amīn al-Astarābādī, al-Fayḍ al-Kāshānī, and al-Mīrzā Ḥūsayn Nūrī, and Uṣūlī scholars such as al-Shaikh al-Baḥrānī, al-Sayyid al-Khū'ī, and al-Shaikh al-Ṭūsī, whose accomplishments came to dominate Islamic scholarship and led to the extinction of the Akhbārīs two centuries ago. The main difference between the two Shīʿa legal tendencies in Akhbārism and Uṣūlism was the validity of reason in connection with religious matters, although many other points of disagreement existed at the time. This was mainly embodied in the scholars' acceptance or non-acceptance of solitary traditions (*āḥād*) that did not generate certitude of their sound origin. Where the Akhbārīs accepted these traditions without any process of legal investigation or rational proof, the Uṣūlīs relied firmly on general Qur'ānic principles and on widely transmitted (*mutawātir*) traditions, analysing sources rationally and systematically. All this will be explained in greater detail during the course of the book.

The foundations of this science have been established by the author in this work, without unnecessary elaborations and futile debates into controversial matters, but simply equipping the student with the necessary tools and background to delve as deeply as he wants thereafter.

It must be noted here that Arabic is a very complex and rich language, whose vocabulary encompasses much more than the meanings of singular words but also includes the very mindset and psychology of the Arabic people and their culture. Arabic that expresses religious terminology or vocabulary is even more complex, for a single word can hold a very specific meaning that can be known only through thorough understanding of the religious matter, as opposed to mere knowledge of the Arabic language.

In translating this particular work, I have come across many such specific technical terms that express characteristics of a chain of transmission or circumstances of a reporter. Therefore, words are often not translated according to their lexical meaning but according to their significance within this technical field. For example, as the reader will note, the word *ʿādil* in jurisprudence is used to describe a person of righteous moral conduct, whose transmission of reports is reliable and who is generally a trustworthy and law-abiding person. However, the lexical English translation for this does not express this juristic significance at all, having been translated as 'just', 'fair', 'equitable', 'upright', 'honest', 'straightforward', 'righteous'.[1] Although all these words may signify dependability, they do not express oral honesty. Moreover, 'honest' and 'veritable' do not necessarily refer to overall physical moral conduct. This is why I have chosen to translate *ʿādil* as 'veracious', because it denotes oral as well as practical honesty and equity in a person, though this is by no means conclusive.

There are similar technical terms that cannot be expressed accurately with a single English term, such as the word *mutawātir*. Its lexical translation is 'continuous', 'unbroken', 'consecutive'. Within the science of *ḥadīth*, it refers to a type of report that has been narrated and handed down through generations in a consecutive manner so many times that is conventionally impossible for it to have been intentionally fabricated. Although various translators have translated it as 'celebrated report', 'consecutive narration', or – as I have at times rendered it in the text of the book – 'multiple successive transmission', none of these truly expresses its technical significance. 'Celebrated' does not tell us anything about the nature of the chain of transmission and is synonymous with 'famous', which is not the meaning intended at all; 'consecutive' does not express the multiplicity of its transmission in every generation; and 'multiple successive' is not a singular expression. Because it is paramount that the reader understand the exact significance of this widely used term, I have resorted to using the Arabic word itself, with frequent explanations of the term in English, reminding the reader of its specific meaning.

[1] See *The Hans Wehr Dictionary of Modern Written Arabic.*

Regarding the word '*ḥadīth*' itself, I have left it as *Ḥadīth* (with a capital '*Ḥ*') when referring to the concept, the science and the literature of traditions. An individual *ḥadīth* is referred to as either 'tradition' or 'report' interchangeably.

Where in brackets I have written '(S)', this is an abbreviation of the Arabic for 'peace be upon him and his family' (traditionally used for the Holy Prophet (S)), and (A) is an abbreviation of the Arabic for 'peace be upon him/her/them', used in connection with the names of the Holy Household of the Prophet (S).

I have italicized most of the Arabic terms within the text and explained their significance in footnotes and brackets throughout the book, as well as in the glossary. I have compiled the glossary by combining my own translations of words with technical terms that have already been coined in the English language in other Orientalist and Muslim works, such as 'solitary report' (*khabar al-wāḥid*). The English meanings suggested for the Arabic technical terms are by no means exhaustive and have been concluded from my own personal experience within the depths of the English language and how it can best convey the meaning of multifaceted Arabic words, along with my understanding of the technical terms in this field from reading around the subject.

All Praise is due to Allah, and all Knowledge belongs to Him. There is no Power or Strength except Allah's, the Mighty the Great. May His Peace and Blessings be upon his chosen and purified guides on this earth, the Ahl al-Bayt.

NAZMINA VIRJEE

TRANSLATOR'S INTRODUCTION

With the grace of the Almighty, the Islamic College has undertaken the translation and publication of the oldest Shīʿa *ithnā ʿasharī* text written on the science and contextual study of *ḥadīth* – *Dirāyat al-Ḥadīth* ('the contextual study of *ḥadīth*') – by the great and renowned scholar and jurist from the tenth century after *hijrah*, al-Shahīd al-Thānī.

This work is a short treatise on the science of *ḥadīth*, which although brief in length, was a pioneering and essential work in its time, by virtue of which this science came to be recorded in the first place, and which paved the way for all subsequent works. The work documented the basic principles and terminology of *ḥadīth* in a systematic manner, giving a valuable outline of the various topics in such a way that the student can easily and rapidly glean all that he/she needs to know.

Shaikh Zainuddīn, better known as al-Shahīd al-Thānī (the second martyr), is among the greatest Shīʿa legal theorists. He was born in 911 AH in Jabal ʿĀmil, but he must have lived in Ṭūs for a considerable time, as he occasionally signed his name 'al-Ṭūsī al-Shāmī'.

He was a widely travelled man, having visited Egypt, Syria, Hijaz, Jerusalem (*bayt al-muqaddaṣ*), Iraq, and Constantinople. Always in pursuit of knowledge, he studied under great Shīʿa scholars and some twelve Sunni scholars of *fiqh*, among whom were Shihāb al-Dīn Aḥmad al-Ramli (a great Shāfiʿī jurist) with whom he studied the celebrated Shāfiʿī works such as the *Minhāj* nd other Sunni texts of *uṣūl al-fiqh* and legal theory. He also studied *Ṣaḥīḥ al-Bukhāri* and *Ṣaḥīḥ Muslim* under the Ḥanafī scholar of Damascus, Shams al-Din ibn Tūlūn al-Ḥanafī, and under other great scholars of *tafsīr* such as Shaikh Nāsir al-Dīn al-Milqānī he studied the celebrated Sunni work of al-Bayḍāwi.

Apart from his proficiency in *fiqh*, he was educated in *uṣūl*, philosophy, *ʿirfān*, medicine, and astronomy. He was a man of piety, known for his austere way of life. His students have recorded in his biography that Shahīd maintained his family by cutting wood at night and selling it, and then sat down to teach during the day. While in Baʿlbak, he conducted classes in *fiqh* according to five schools – Jaʿfarī, Ḥanafī, Shāfiʿī, Mālikī, and Ḥanbalī. His most famous work is the commentary on *al-Lumʿah*, written by al-Shahīd al-Awwal (the first martyr). This commentary, *Sharḥ Lumʿah*, forms a part of the curriculum in almost every Shīʿa educational establishment even today. He studied under Muḥaqqiq Karaki before the latter migrated to Iran. Al-Shahīd al-Thānī was martyred in 966 AH/1559 CE by the Turkish sultan Selmi.

According to his prominent student Ibn al-ʿAwdī, he was born on 13 of Shawwāl 911 AH and was executed in Rajab. By the time he was ten years old he had already completed his study of the Qur'ān. After that he studied jurisprudence and Arabic language under his father, a well-known and respected scholar who died in 925 AH. Still only a teenager, he then migrated to Mes, a village in the province of Ṭūs, to continue his studies in Islamic law, ethics, and principles of jurisprudence. He studied under Shaikh al-Jalīl (ʿAlī ibn ʿAbd al-ʿAlī al-Karkī) from 925 to 933 AH. During this period he was introduced to the research methods and *ijtihād* in the study of Islamic legal theory.

He left Mes for Karkuk where he met Sayyid Ḥasan ibn al-Sayyid Jaʿfār, who was the author of the famous book *Mahajjat al-Bayḍā'* and under whom he studied philosophy, theology, grammar, literature and linguistics.

After travelling across the Muslim world studying under prominent Shīʿa and Sunni scholars, he began to dedicate his life to Islamic scholarship. Among his many works were:

- *Al-Rawḍat al-Bāhiyyah fī Sharḥ al-Lumʿah al-Dimashqiyyah.* This is a commentary on the book on Islamic law written by al-Shahīd al-Awwal.
- *Rawḍat al-Janān fī Sharḥ Irshād al-Adh-hān.* This work focused on the laws of ritual purity (*ṭahārah*) and regular prayer (*salāh*). It was published in Iran together with the work *al-Mazīd*, also written by al-Shahīd, in 1307 AH. According to his student and biographer, Ibn al-ʿAwdi, this is perhaps his first book on Islamic legal thought.
- *Masālik al-Afhām fī Sharḥ Sharāʿi al-Islām. Tawḥīd al-Qawāʿid al-Uṣūliyyah wa al-ʿArabiyyah.* This work is divided into two parts. The first part deals with a hundred general principles of law and

the second part discusses the hundred general laws of the Arabic language. It is a dialogue between language and law in Islam.

- *Ḥāshiyat al-Irshād.* An edited and annotated work containing very insightful and important notes.
- *Ḥāshiyat ʿala al-Irshād.* This is a summarized version of the above work, which has been published in two volumes.
- *Al-Tanbīhāt al-ʿĀliyah ʿala Waẓaʾif al-Ṣalāh al-Qalbiyyah.* This is a very small treatise on the secrets of *ṣalāh.*
- *Muniyat al-Murīd fī Adab al-Mufīd wa al-Mustafīd.* Another small book dealing with Muslim educational ethics.
- *Maskan al-Fawāʾid ʿind Faqd al-Aḥibbah al-Awlād*
- *Jawābāt al-Masāʾil*
- *Natāʾij al-Afkār fī Ḥukm al-Muqīmīn fī al-Asfār*
- *Shurūḥ al-Alfiyyah*
- *Al-Fawāʾid al-Miliyyah fī al-Nafliyyah*
- *Kitāb al-Ijārāt*
- *Ḥaqāʾiq al-Imān*
- *Ḥāshiyat al-Qawāʿid al-Aḥkām*
- *Al-Dirāyah wa Sharḥuha*
- *Al-Bidāyah fī Sabīl al-Hidāyah*
- *Jawāhir al-Kalimāt*
- *Risālah fī ʿAsharat ʿUlūm*
- *Ghunyat al-Qāṣidin fī Maʿrifat Iṣtilāḥāt al-Muḥaddithīn*
- *Mansak al-Ḥaj wa al-ʿUmrah*
- *Kitāb al-Rijāl wa al-Nasab*
- *Kashf al-Raybah ʿan Aḥkām al-Ghībah*
- *Wujūb al-Ṣalāt al-Jumʿah*
- *Manāzil al-Qāṣidīn fī Asrār Maʿālim al-Dīn*
- *Al-Iqtiṣād wa al-Irshād*

These are just some of his many works on various aspects of Islamic law, theology, philosophy, language, ethics, astronomy, and other matters.

Albeit long overdue, the present work is the first translation undertaken of this important sourcebook, which will no doubt be an invaluable contribution to *ḥadīth* scholarship in the English language and which will give students a fuller insight into the developments in the documentation of the science of *ḥadīth* from its beginning embodied by this very book.

DIRĀYAT AL-ḤADĪTH

THE CONTEXTUAL STUDY OF ḤADĪTH

by the Ḥadīth scholar and jurist

Zayn al-Dīn ibn ʿAlī al-ʿĀmilī
(al-Shahīd al-Thānī)

911-965 AH

Translated by

Nazmina A. Virjee

PREFACE

In the Name of Allah, the Most Beneficent, the Most Merciful

We begin this contextual study of traditions with Your Praise O Allah, and we request Your special care and attention towards us until the end, and we ask You to bestow Your ever-abundant blessings on Your Prophet Muḥammad, the saviour from deviation and our leader on the path of Divine guidance, and on his family and companions.

This is a synopsis of the contextual study of *Ḥadīth* criticism, which concisely outlines the technicalities within the science. The book consists of an introduction and four sections.

INTRODUCTION

The contextual study and terminology of *ḥadīth* comprises several topics, which we will go on to elucidate:

1. The *Ḥadīth* (often referred to as 'tradition') and the *Khabar* (often referred to as 'report')

The words *ḥadīth* and *khabar* have the same meaning within the contextual study of *ḥadīth*, whose technical meaning is 'a statement carrying the speech, action or tacit approval of a *maʿṣūm* (infallible person)'.[1]

The word *ḥadīth* may be used specifically to denote the statement issued by a *maʿṣūm*, whereas the word *khabar* may also be used for statements by other people. The word *athar*[2] is the most general term.

2. The Text and the Chain

The text (*matn*) is the wording of the tradition, indicating its content.

The chain (*sanad*) is the path of the tradition, i.e. the chain of reporters who transmitted the tradition.

The supported chain (*isnād*) is a chain of transmission that can be traced all the way back to the Prophet, Imam or anyone else who uttered it.

3. Categories of Reports

The report, as an entity in itself, may be either true or false,

[1] According to the Ahl al-Sunnah, the word *khabar* is used to refer to the speech of the Prophet (S) as well as that of his Companions and their Followers.

[2] *Athar*: report of a companion, although the Shīʿa do not accept these as *ḥadīth*, so it is used synonymously with *khabar*.

regardless of the honesty or dishonesty of the person who utters it. The truth or falseness of a report can be identified by means of external factors, where:

- The truth in the report is decisively and automatically known, such as the *mutawātir* report; or it is known by virtue of the actual existence of whatever it is narrating, such as the existence of Makkah.
- The truth of the report is decisively known, though not automatically but through investigation and acquisition of information such as the Word of Allah in the Qur'ān, or other statements of the Prophet and the Imams, such as the tradition that is *mutawātir* in meaning, and the report that is linked to associated evidence proving its sound origin. The same goes for ascertaining the falseness of a report.

The report may equally be both true and false, where the truth or falsehood in it is not decisively known, as is the case with most reports.

4. Another Classification

A report invariably fits into either of two categories, regardless of whether it is known to be true or not.

The *mutawātir* is a report that has so many narrators that it is conventionally impossible for them all to have agreed upon its fabrication. This multitude must be fulfilled on all the levels or generations of reporters, in such a way that the beginning of the chain is the same as its end, and the middle of the chain is congruous with the two ends. The number of reporters has not been stipulated or restricted to an exact figure, as some people believe, but rather it serves to generate certitude if it fulfils all the following conditions:

- That the listener be previously unaware of the content of the report that he is hearing, for if he were it would be tautological.
- That the listener's mind be free of any suspicion about the report that may cause him to reject the multiple and successive nature of it.
- That the reporters' narration be based on personal perception, rather than presumption or logical deduction.

Multiple successive transmission (*tawātur*) in wording is often achieved in fundamental legal rulings, such as the obligatory nature of the daily prayers, the number of units in them, fasting, *ḥajj* (pilgrimage), etc. It is seldom achieved in traditions of a specific nature, although their meaning may have come down in multiple successive transmission.

The tradition *'All actions will be judged according to one's intention'* is not technically *mutawātir*, even though at present the number of people who have transmitted it exceed by several times the number required for it to be considered *mutawātir*. The reason for this is that multiple successive transmission in this particular tradition started in the middle of the chain and continued until the present era, whereas the condition of congruity and multitude must be fulfilled on all the levels (not just in later times). Most of the reports claimed as *mutawātir* are of this type.

The *khabar al-wāḥid* ('solitary report') is the report that does not attain multiple successive transmission, and is divided into:

- The *mustafīḍ* ('extensively narrated') report, which is a report that has been narrated by more than two or three reporters on every level. This is also termed *mashhūr*, or 'famous'. Sometimes a distinction is made between *mustafīḍ* and the *mashhūr*, namely that *mustafīḍ* can be said of whatever fulfils the requirements of the *mustafīḍ* at its beginning and end, and *mashhūr* is more flexible and broader.
- The *gharīb* ('rare') report is one that has been narrated by only one reporter.
- The *maqbūl* ('accepted') report is one that the scholars have implemented and have come to accept.
- The *mardūd* ('rejected') report is one that the scholars have rejected because of a discrepancy in the narration of the reporter or distortions in the text of the tradition.
- The *mushtabah* ('suspect') is a report whose circumstances are dubious and whose reporter is suspect.

5. The Number of Extant Reports

The number of extant reports is not restricted to a specific figure, for people may have had traditions in their possession that have not come down to us. Those people who do restrict it to a set number, such as some of the Ahl al-Sunnah, do so according to the reports that have come down to them.

The early scholars compiled all that they had heard by way of reports on the authority of our Imams (A) into four hundred books entitled *uṣūl*[3] which were reliable source collections, such as the *aṣl* of Jamīl ibn Darrāj, the *aṣl* of Zurārah, etc.

Some of our classical scholars collected and arranged the contents of these source collections into special compilations in order to make them accessible to all. The best of these books are those known as the Four Books, which are pivotal and on which enormous reliance is placed today. They are:

1. *al-Kāfī* (*The Sufficient*), by Muḥammad ibn Yāʿqūb al-Kulaynī (d. 329 AH), in which he categorized traditions of all subjects
2. *Man Lā Yaḥḍuruhu al-Faqīh* (*Every Man His Own Lawyer*), by Abū Jaʿfar Muḥammad ibn ʿAlī ibn Bābawayh al-Qummī (d. 381 AH), a compilation of all the traditions that have to do with legal rulings.
3. *al-Tahdhīb*[4]
4. and *al-Istibṣār* (*Insights into Disparities of Reports*), both by al-Shaikh Abū Jaʿfar Muḥammad ibn al-Ḥasan al-Ṭūsī (d. 460 AH), who compiled, in the two works, traditions on specific legal rulings.

6. Text and Significance of the Tradition

The text and significance of the tradition are rarely investigated within this science; rather the strength or weakness in the chain is investigated, along with other characteristics that correspond with the circumstances of its reporters, such as their veracity, accuracy, faith, etc., or with its chain, such as whether it is a consecutive chain

[3] *Uṣūl* (sing. *aṣl*): In *ḥadīth* terminology of the school of the Ahl al-Bayt, an *aṣl* was a book in which a reporter would compile all the traditions that he himself had reported on the authority of the *maʿṣūm*, or those that an intermediary reporter had narrated to him. These did not include any traditions quoted from textual sources. The prevalent opinion is that there were four hundred such *uṣūl* written by Companions of Imam Jaʿfar al-Ṣādiq (A), though some say by both the companions of Imam al-Ṣādiq as well as those of Imam Mūsā al-Kāẓim (A).

[4] Also known as Tahdhīb al-Aḥkām (Refinement of Laws).

or a broken chain of narrators, or whether it is a hurried chain or a confusing chain, among other things. This in turn necessitates study into the following areas:

- Classifications of traditions into *ṣaḥīḥ* ('authentic'), *ḥasan* ('good'), *muwaththaq* ('dependable'), etc.
- Expressions of disparagement and authentication of reporters
- Modes of receiving and transmitting traditions undertaken by reporters, such as *samāʿ* ('hearing'), *ijāzah* ('permission'), etc.
- Technical terms with regard to the classification of reporters and their generations.

These topics will be dealt with in the following four sections:

Section 1: Classification of *Ḥadīth*
Section 2: Those Whose Transmission Can Be Accepted and Those Whose Transmission is Rejected
Section 3: The Modes of Receiving and Transmitting Traditions.
Section 4: Terminology Pertaining to the Names and Generations of Reporters.

CLASSIFICATION OF *ḤADĪTH*

There are four fundamental categories of *ḥadīth*, to which all the rest relate.

1. *Ṣaḥīḥ* ('Authentic')

[This is] the tradition whose chain of transmission is consecutively linked to the *maʿṣūm*, narrated by one veracious (*ʿādil*)[1] *imāmī*[2] to another, on all the levels.

Therefore, a tradition that has a broken chain of transmission – wherever the break may be – cannot be termed 'authentic', even if all the reporters in its chain are veracious *imāmīs*.

The *ṣaḥīḥ* tradition, according to the Sunni definition of it, is a tradition that is consecutively transmitted from one reliable, accurate reporter to the next, although it must be noted that according to them it suffices for the reporter to be veracious to the extent that there be no outward sign of immorality in him and that he calls himself a Muslim by his apparent conduct. This results in an abundance of 'authentic' traditions in Sunni *ḥadīth* literature.

It must also be noted that people such as al-Sayyid al-Murtaḍā, who do not implement solitary reports at all, investigate only the circumstances of *mutawātir* reports. Similarly, those who do implement solitary reports have no cause to doubt the correctness of implementing an 'authentic' report, since the prerequisite for its reporters to be veracious *imāmīs* has been fulfilled.

[1] *ʿĀdil* ('veracious') lexically means just, equitable and reliable. In jurisprudence, this designates a person of irreproachable reputation and veracity whose testimony is valid. (See Introduction and Chapter 8 for a detailed explanation.)

[2] *Imāmī*: Shīʿa Ithna ʿAsharī or a follower of the twelve Imams, who adheres to the Jaʿfarī school of jurisprudence.

If an 'authentic' report is *shādh* ('unusual') or contradicts other 'authentic' reports, then it is not implemented, and the preponderant report is sought out and used instead.

2. *Ḥasan* ('Good')

Ḥasan is the tradition whose chain of transmission is consecutively linked to the *maʿṣūm* by commendable *imāmīs* whose reliability has not been affirmed. This must be the case on either all the levels or on some; and it takes only one reporter in the chain to be a commendable *imāmī* to render the whole report *ḥasan* ('good'), even though the rest of the reporters may be veracious *imāmīs*.

If the chain contains a single reliable non-*imāmī*, then the tradition is classified as *muwaththaq* ('dependable'), and if it contains a single weak reporter, then the whole tradition is classified as *ḍaʿīf* ('weak').

The tradition, therefore, is classified according to the lowest characteristics of its reporters.

Scholars have differed with regard to implementing the 'good' report. There are some who implement it absolutely, as they would as 'authentic' report, such as al-Shaikh al-Ṭūsī – may Allah have mercy on him – from what we can see from his works. All scholars who deem veracity to be an outward manifestation of Islam in a person implement the 'good' report.

There are many scholars who have absolutely rejected it, necessitating both veracity and faith (i.e. *imāmī*) as a prerequisite for acceptance, such as al-ʿAllāmah al-Ḥillī in his books on the principles of jurisprudence.

Others, such as al-Muḥaqqiq in his *al-Muʿtabar* and al-Shahīd in his *al-Dhikrā*, have singled out and accepted certain 'good' reports, as well as 'dependable' reports and sometimes even 'weak' reports, provided that they are well known to have been implemented by previous scholars. These scholars rely on this renown so much so that they sometimes accept a 'renowned' weak report in preference to an 'authentic' report whose implementation is not renowned among scholars.

3. *Muwaththaq* ('Dependable')

Muwaththaq has also been termed *qawī* ('strong'). It refers to that tradition narrated by reporters who are deemed reliable by the classical scholars, although they adhere to a corrupt school of thought, such as sects opposing the Shīʿa Ithnā ʿAsharī school, even from other Shīʿa sects.

The rest of the chain must not contain any other weakness, otherwise it is regarded as a weak tradition, based on the fact that the weakest characteristic always predominates.

The term *qawī* ('strong') may also be given to a report narrated by an *imāmī* who has been neither commended nor disparaged.

Scholars have differed with regard to the implementation of the 'dependable' report. As with the 'good' report, some have accepted it absolutely, others have rejected it and still others have differentiated it according to its renown or lack thereof.

4. *Ḍaʿīf* ('Weak')

Ḍaʿīf is a report that does not fulfil any of the conditions from the above three categories, because its chain comprises a reporter who has been defamed because of his immorality, etc. or because he is unknown or because he is a fabricator.

There are varying degrees of weakness according to how far the report is from fulfilling the prerequisites of authenticity: the further the report is from attaining that level, the weaker it is, and similarly the more weak and defamed reporters there are in the chain, the weaker it is.

In the same way, the degrees of 'authentic', 'good' and 'dependable' also vary according to the predominant characteristics of their reporters. So, the report narrated by a reliable pious and accurate *imāmī* jurist such as Ibn Abī ʿUmayr is more authentic than the report of one who lacks some of these qualities, and so on down to the lowest degree of authenticity.

Similarly, the narration of a reporter who has been much commended, such as Ibrāhīm ibn Hāshim, is better (more 'good') than the report of someone who has not been so highly commended.

The same goes for the 'dependable' report, for reports whose chains of narration include reporters such as ʿAlī ibn Faḍāl and Abān ibn ʿUthmān, are stronger than other dependable reports, etc.

The strength or weakness of reports is especially significant when reports contradict each other, in which case the stronger of two disparate traditions would be implemented. Most scholars hold that it is absolutely impermissible to implement a 'weak' report, although others have allowed it if it has been reinforced by its own renown, that is, that it has been recorded and narrated numerous times in the same wording or in different wordings implying the same meaning – or by previous scholars' legal verdicts in accordance with it in their books of jurisprudence.

5. Another Classification of *Ḥadīth*

Traditions also have additional characteristics to those mentioned above, which may either be characteristics alongside the above categories or which may be specific to the weak report.

The categories common to all reports are:

musnad ('supported'): This describes a tradition supported by a consecutive unbroken chain of narration that can be traced all the way back to the *maʿṣūm*.

muttaṣil ('consecutive'): This type of tradition is also referred to as *mawṣūl* 'connected' and is used to describe the tradition that is consecutively handed down from the *maʿṣūm* or someone else, where each reporter would have heard it directly from whoever is above him in the chain, or would have received it by other such means.

marfūʿ ('traced'): This refers to a report describing the *maʿṣūm*'s speech, action or tacit approval with words to the effect of 'He (S) said... or did...', etc.

muʿanʿan: This is the report whose chain of narration contains the word *ʿan* ('on the authority of') between every reporter, i.e., 'on the authority of x, on the authority of y, on the authority of z', without any indication of the mode of transmission in each case, as to whether it was narrated, dictated or heard.

muʿallaq ('suspended'): This is when the names of one or more reporters are omitted from the beginning of the chain of transmission, and these omitted names would be known to be reliable, for example, al-Shaikh al-Ṭūsī in *al-Tahdhīb* and *al-Istibṣār* merely mentioned 'Muḥammad ibn Yaʿqūb al-Kulaynī' or someone else as his source and then, at the end of the book, listed the names of all the people included in the chain of Muḥammad ibn Yaʿqūb and all other such suspended chains. In this case, it is as if the omitted names were mentioned and are investigated within the chain, and the same standards of evaluation of authenticity and strength are applied to it. If, however, the omitted names are not known, then the tradition is considered to be *mursal* ('hurried') (see 'Categories of Reports').

mufrad ('exceptional'): This is used to describe a report that has been narrated only by a specific individual or by particular people from a specific location, for example Baṣrā or Kufa.

mudraj ('interposed'): This is a report in which the statement of one of its reporters has been interposed, which may lead the whole text to be considered as being from a *maʿṣūm*.

mashhūr ('famous'): This is a report that is renowned among the *ḥadīth* scholars in that it has been narrated by many people.

gharīb ('rare'): This is a report that has been narrated by one reporter only. It is also known as *shādh* ('unusual').

muṣaḥḥaf ('misspelt'): Spelling errors often occur with respect to reporters' names, where the diacritical dots on letters are misplaced, such that *Ḥarīz* is changed to *Jarīr*, and *Barīd* to *Yazīd*, etc., as well as in the actual text of the tradition.

ʿālī al-sanad ('short-chained'): This is a report that is consecutively narrated from the *maʿṣūm* but has very few intermediaries in between. The shortness of the chain safeguards the tradition from possible shortcomings in its transmission.

shādh ('unusual'): This report is narrated by a single reliable individual, in opposition to what the majority have narrated. If the narrator of the contrasting tradition is more accurate or has a better memory or is more reliable, then the unusual tradition is rejected; if not, it is accepted.

musalsal ('sequential'): This is used to describe a tradition that contains a succession of common observances or attributes concerning the reporters, in the similarity of a statement or action, for example if most of the reporters say, 'By Allah!' before their narration, until the end of the chain, or if they all follow a same practice before or during narration, such as, 'x narrated to us crossing his fingers', and so on until the end of the chain; or saying, 'x informed us while he was reclining on...', and so on until the end of the chain.

mazīd ('added'): This refers to a tradition that contains an addition, in contrast to other similar traditions. The addition may sometimes be in the text, such as the addition of an extra word that is not present in other traditions, or it may be in the chain, for example if it contains four reporters instead of the usual three.

mukhtalaf ('disparate'): This is when two traditions contradict each other in their apparent sense. Their significance is derived by combining them as much as possible, even if it is quite far-fetched. This is one of the most important facets in the science of *ḥadīth* and can be undertaken only by scholars who possess a certain insight and are skilled in jurisprudence and *uṣūl* (principles of jurisprudence).

nāsikh ('abrogative') and *mansūkh* ('abrogated'): This is where a tradition would abrogate the legal ruling suggested by a previous tradition, in which case the abrogated tradition is called *mansūkh.* Abrogation is known through textual stipulation, the transmission of a companion, history or legal consensus.

al-gharīb al-lafẓī ('strangely worded'): This is when the text of the tradition contains words that are ambiguous or difficult to understand.

maqbūl ('accepted'): This is used to describe a tradition whose content has been accepted and implemented by the scholars without any regard to whether it falls into the category of 'authentic', 'good', or 'dependable', such as the tradition of ʿUmar ibn Ḥanẓalah about the disparate reports.

6. Categories of a Weak Report

There are eight characteristics that render a report weak and are specific to a weak report.

mawqūf ('stopped'): This is the tradition about a statement or an action, narrated on the authority of the companion of a *maʿṣūm.* This type of tradition is not authoritative, even if the chain of transmission is sound, because its origin is one who has been instructed and whose statement is not authoritative.

maqṭū[3] ('broken'): This refers to the tradition narrated on the

[3] *Tābiʿī* (pl. *tābiʿūn*) 'Follower' or 'Successor' – refers to the second generation of Muslims who came after the Companions, who did not know the Prophet (S)

authority of a *tābiʿī* (Follower). It too is not authoritative.

mursal ('hurried'): This is a report narrated on the authority of the *maʿṣūm*, without mention of the names of the intermediary reporter(s) in between, because the subsequent reporter has forgotten them, omitted them or been unsure of them. For example, he may say, 'The Prophet (S) said...' or 'On the authority of a man' or 'On the authority of some of our associates'. The 'hurried' report is not authoritative because of the omission of the names.

muʿallal This is used to describe a tradition that contains subtle, hidden justifications for the legal ruling in it, which impairs the soundness of the report, even though it may appear sound. An expert jurist would be able to discern this through the paths of its transmission and its text.

mudallas ('deceptive'): This is when the reporter has tried to conceal the flaw in a tradition by giving the impression that he is relating it from someone whom he has met, when he has not in fact done so but only pretends that he has done so. He may say, for example, 'x said...' or 'On the authority of x', rather than explicitly saying 'x related to me', which would be a downright lie as opposed to a deception. This is a deception that occurs in the chain. There is also another type of deception that occurs amongst shaikhs: if a reporter heard a tradition from a shaikh whose name he does not want to mention, for reasons of his own, he may refer to him by a name or a title by which he is not usually known.

muḍṭarib ('conflicting'): This is when a reporter is inconsistent in his narration of a particular tradition, be it in the text or in the chain. He may relate it one way the first time and the opposite way the next time. A tradition, however, can be labelled as 'conflicting' only when there are at least two traditions that support the opposite view. If this is not the case, then unless one of the conflicting traditions gains preponderance over the other because it is more accurate or sounder, it cannot be called conflicting.

maqlūb ('altered'): This is a tradition whose original chain of transmission has been altered into a better chain, in order to increase the chain's popularity. This may sometimes occur among

---

but knew his Companions.

scholars when they are trying to test each others' accuracy and memory.

mawḍūʿ ('fabricated'): This is an invented and forged tradition, and is the worst category of weak reports. It is not permissible to relate it, except with a view to pointing out the fabrication in it. Fabrication is ascertained by the fabricator's own admission of it, by reference to the poor quality of its wording or through investigation into it. There are various types of forgers and fabricators, the worst of whom are people who adhere to principles of asceticism and good conduct but have no knowledge and thus forge traditions in order to attain nearness to Allah and entice others to do good deeds. People readily believe their fabrications because they trust them from their outward conduct.

THOSE WHOSE TRANSMISSION CAN BE ACCEPTED AND THOSE WHOSE TRANSMISSION IS REJECTED

Knowledge of this subject is very important, for this is the way that one is able to distinguish between authentic reports and weak reports. Because of this, investigation into the circumstances of reporters has been permitted, even though it may entail calumnizing a Muslim, for the sake of preserving the pure Islamic law. Of course, the scholar must be careful and cautious in his investigation, so that he does not slander a blameless person with what he believes to be a flaw. This subject entails eight points of discussion.

1. The *ḥadīth* scholars are in unanimous agreement that the requirements of a reporter are that he be a Muslim and that he possess maturity (in the legal sense) and reason. The majority of scholars also stipulate veracity (*ʿadālah*) as a condition, i.e. that he be of sound conduct and free from vices of corruption and immorality. They have also stipulated accuracy, in that if he is narrating a tradition from memory, he must possess a good memory, and if he is narrating from a book, he must be accurate in his writing of it and aware of any possible mistakes that may distort the meaning. Masculinity is not a prerequisite, nor freedom, nor prior knowledge of jurisprudence or Arabic, nor sight. Most people also hold that faith (i.e. Shīʿa Ithnā ʿAsharī) is a prerequisite and have laid it down in their books on the principles of jurisprudence, in spite of their awareness of extant 'dependable' and 'weak' reports in matters of jurisprudence, which they justify using the reinforcement of their renown.

2. The veracity of a reporter is ascertained by the testimony of two veracious individuals, by his widespread repute, according to popular opinion or by the evidence given by a single veracious person.

3. The prevalent opinion is that the authentication (*taʿdīl*) of a reporter is acceptable, even if there is no reason given for it, since a person may be deemed reliable for numerous reasons that cannot all be listed. As regards disparagement (*jarḥ*) of a reporter, it is not acceptable unless the reason for disparaging him is supplied, because people differ among themselves about what is blameworthy and what is not, so a reporter whom one person deems blameworthy may not be found to be so by another.

4. The prevalent opinion as regards defamation is that the evidence of a single individual suffices, as was the case with ascertaining the veracity of a reporter, and since number had no consequence in the initial acceptance of the report, it should have no consequence in the subsidiary investigation. If there are both statements defaming a reporter as well as attesting to his veracity, the defamatory statements are taken to be more correct, even though there may be many people attesting to his veracity. This is because the person commending him is doing so as a result of what he can see from his outward conduct, whereas the person defaming him is acting on the basis of information that would otherwise be concealed and unknown to the other. In spite of all this, if the defamatory and commendatory statements conflict with each other, it must be investigated further until one gains preponderance over the other.

5. If a veracious reporter says, 'A reliable person related to me', his statement is not sufficient for us to implement his report if he does not mention the name of the reporter, for it may well be that *he* may consider him reliable but others do not.

If a veracious reporter narrates a tradition from a man whom he names, his action does not vouch for the authentication of that person, just as the jurisconsult's legal verdict according to a tradition does not automatically mean that the tradition is trustworthy and his rejection of it does not automatically depreciate the tradition.

6. The expressions used to attest to the veracity of reporters are: equitable (*ʿadl*), reliable (*thiqah*), competent authority (*ḥujjah*), narrates authentic traditions (*ṣaḥīḥ al-ḥadīth*) and other such phrases denoting veracity.

The expressions used to defame reporters are: weak (*ḍaʿīf*), liar (*kadhdhāb*), fabricator (*waḍḍāʿ*), extremist (*ghāl*) and other such phrases.

7. If a reporter deviates into folly, madness, corruption or immorality after having been in a previous state of righteousness, whatever he has related before his deviation is accepted and everything after it is rejected. This was the case with the Wāqifiyyah at the time of Imam Mūsā al-Kāẓim (A) and the Faṭḥiyyah at the time of Imam al-Ṣādiq (A), who deviated after having been righteous.

8. If a reliable person narrates a tradition on the authority of another reliable person, which the original speaker of the tradition denies, then if the speaker determinedly asserts his denial, saying, 'I did not narrate this', the tradition must be rejected. If however, he says, 'I don't know it' or 'I don't remember it', then it does not detract from the more authentic report, but rather the speaker is allowed to narrate it on the authority of whomever he has subsequently heard it from, saying, 'x told me on my authority that I narrated to him that...'. This type of thing may occur when old people have forgotten their traditions after having transmitted them.

THE MODES OF RECEIVING AND TRANSMITTING TRADITIONS

1. Competence in Reception

A reporter must be able to distinguish the report he is transmitting if he hears it, i.e. he can differentiate between the report he confirms having transmitted and other reports.

Neither Islam nor maturity is a prerequisite for the reception of traditions, since we have come across narrations from Companions of the Prophet (S) before they had attained maturity, such as Imam Ḥasan and Imam Ḥusayn (A), ʿAbdallāh ibn ʿAbbās, Ibn al-Zubayr and others.

It is incorrect to fix a specific age for maturity, such as ten years or five or four, because people differ in their degrees of perception and distinction. Similarly, there is no requirement for the speaker to be older than or superior in position to the narrator.

2. Modes of Reception

There are seven modes of reception.

2.1. Samāʿ: hearing the tradition from the shaikh's[1] utterance of it. This is the mode that the majority of scholars deem most esteemed, because the reporter would say, 'I heard x saying...'. In the same way, this expression is the best at denoting *samāʿ*, followed by 'x narrated to me/us', because this may also imply reception through the shaikh's reading of the tradition or through his having given *ijāzah* (permission) to transmit on his authority. Following this expression is the phrase 'x reported to me', and then 'x informed me'.

[1] 'Shaikh' here simply denotes 'teacher' or someone from whom a student would receive traditions.

2.2. Qirāʾah: reading back a tradition to the shaikh. This mode is also referred to as *ʿarḍ* (presentation), because the receiver presents what he has understood by reading it back to the shaikh, whether he reads it from memory or from a book. The reporter would narrate it, saying, 'I read to shaikh x', or 'The tradition was being read back to the shaikh while I was also there and the shaikh acknowledged it'. The phrase 'x narrated to us/informed us of his reading' is less esteemed than the above.

2.3. Ijāzah: permission to transmit on someone's authority. This is allowing someone to transmit on one's authority, whereby the person giving authority would say, 'I gave him permission to transmit tradition x on my authority'. A better phrasing is when the name of the person is specifically mentioned along with the name of the book, as in, 'I have permitted you to transmit book x on my authority'. Or he may use the following phrase, which is less esteemed: 'I allow you to transmit the traditions I have heard on my authority'. Unspecified permissions, such as 'permission to all Muslims' or to 'permission to everyone from this era' are even lower in ranking.

2.4. Munāwalah: handing over a book of traditions. This is higher in ranking than *ijāzah* because it does not need the oral permission of the reporter, whereas *ijāzah* does require it. *Munāwalah* is of two types:

a. *Munāwalah* along with permission to transmit from it, if for example the book is handed over as a possession to keep, whereupon the one passing it over may say, 'These are traditions that I have heard from x, so narrate them on my authority' or 'I permit you to narrate these on my authority.
b. *Munāwalah* without explicit permission to transmit from it, where the person would hand over the book and say merely, 'These are traditions that I have heard/narrated'. The correct opinion is that transmission from it is not allowed.

2.5. Kitābah: writing down. This is of two types:

a. *Kitābah* along with permission to transmit from it, where the person conveying the work would say, 'I permit you to transmit my writings on my authority'.
b. *Kitābah* without permission to transmit from it. The prevalent opinion is that transmission from it is allowed because permission is implied within it. Of course, the author's handwriting would

also be examined in order to ensure that it has not been fabricated.

2.6. Iʿlām: declaration. This is when the shaikh declares to his student that a particular book or tradition is the result of what he has heard or narrated, without actually saying, 'Transmit on my authority' or 'I permit you to transmit on my authority'. There are two opposite opinions with regard to whether transmission from such a declaration is allowed or not.

2.7. Wijādah: finding traditions. This is when a reporter finds the traditions of a person in his handwriting, without actually having heard them from him, in which case he may say, 'I found...written by x'.

3. Modes of transmission

The best transmission is when the reporter has heard the tradition himself from the narrator, whereby it is safeguarded from alteration and change. Transmitting from someone's book is allowed and is sounder in safeguarding from alteration. Transmitting the meaning of a tradition is allowed, provided that the original wording of the tradition is preserved and has not been distorted in any way.

4. Disconnection of traditions[2]

Scholars hold differing opinions with regard to the permissibility of disconnecting traditions (i.e. if a tradition deals with various different subjects). Some scholars have allowed it, provided that the rest of the tradition is quoted somewhere else or that it is quoted in full somewhere else.

It is more likely to be permissible for an author of a *ḥadīth* compilation to disconnect a tradition within his book in order to allocate each part to its respective subject.

A tradition cannot be quoted from a reader (who reads back to the shaikh) who makes grammatical errors or does not pronounce his words properly. Instead one must be aware of the correct

[2] Disconnection of traditions refers to the cases in which later scholars would quote parts of a long tradition that dealt with various issues, under respective topics of jurisprudence, and hence disconnect the long tradition.

pronunciation of words, so that if an error does occur in what he is narrating, he knows the correct version, and can say, 'This is the correct version of the tradition' or 'This is the distorted version and this is the correct version of it'.

When a reporter narrates a tradition on the authority of two or more people who have narrated the same thing in meaning, though not in wording, and he has combined their reports into a single chain, he should clarify which of his sources the wording of the tradition came from, saying, 'x and y informed me of..., and this is x's wording of it'.

If there are numerous traditions that have come down with the same chain of transmission, then the transmitter should quote the chain for every tradition he transmits, or he should at least mention it in the first tradition, and then for the second and subsequent traditions he should say, 'and with the same chain' or 'and with it (i.e. the previous chain) also'.

If a reporter hears part of a tradition from one person and part of it from another, he should transmit them as one, pointing out at the same time that part of it was from one person and part of it from another, so that the tradition is then ascribed to both. In this instance, if both of them were veracious, then the tradition is implemented, and if one of them is disparaged, then no part of it is accepted.

TERMINOLOGY PERTAINING TO THE NAMES AND GENERATIONS OF REPORTERS

A *ṣaḥābī* (pl. *ṣaḥābah*), or 'Companion', is someone who met the Prophet (S), believed in him and died a Muslim. A *tābiʿī* (pl. *tābiʿūn*), or 'Follower', is someone from the second generation of Muslims who succeeded the Companions.

If the reporter of a tradition is the same age as the narrator who handed it to him, or if they both received the tradition from the same scholars, then the narration is termed *riwāyah al-aqrān* ('narration between contemporaries'). If each of these two narrates on the authority of a third person, then it is termed *mudabbaj* ('prestigious'), for it is as if each of them has given the third person the prestige of the tradition's being on his authority.

If a reporter narrates a tradition from someone younger than himself or lower in importance, then it is termed *riwāyah al-akābir ʿan al-aṣāghir* ('narration of elders on the authority of youngsters'). Narrations of fathers from sons is a case in point.

If two people who share the same name both transmit on the authority of a shaikh, and one dies before the other, he is known as the former (*sābiq*) and the other as the latter (*lāḥiq*).

If there is a similarity in the names of the reporters, though their fathers' names merely resemble each other in writing, for example Muḥammad ibn ʿAqīl and Muḥammad ibn ʿUqayl, then the tradition is termed *mutashābih* ('similar'), for the first Muḥammad is Nīsābūrī, and the second is Faryābī.

If the names of both reporters as well as their fathers' names are the same, the tradition is termed *muttafiq wa al-muftariq* ('same yet different'), i.e. they have the same names, but are different people. An example of this is the tradition on the authority of al-Shaikh al-Ṭūsī and other shaikhs before him, on the authority of Aḥmad ibn

Muḥammad. This name is common to a large number of people including Aḥmad ibn Muḥammad ibn ʿĪsā, Aḥmad ibn Muḥammad ibn Khālid, Aḥmad ibn Muḥammad ibn Abī Naṣr and Aḥmad ibn Muḥammad ibn al-Walīd. The way in which they are distinguished from one another when the chain mentions only Aḥmad ibn Muḥammad is to look at their contemporaries from that time period. So if the narrator in question appears near the beginning of the chain as a contemporary of al-Shaikh al-Ṭūsī, then it is Aḥmad ibn Muḥammad ibn al-Walīd. If he appears at the end of the chain, from among the contemporaries of Imam al-Riḍā (A), then it is Aḥmad ibn Muḥammad ibn Abī Naṣr al-Biẓanṭi, and if he appears in the middle of the chain, then it is most probably Aḥmad ibn Muḥammad ibn ʿĪsā, although it could be someone else.

If the names of the reporters resemble each other in their spelling but differ in their pronunciation, then it is termed *al-mu'talif wa al-mukhtalif* ('matching yet different'). An example of this is the similarity in the names Jarīr and Ḥarīz (in their Arabic spelling without diacritical dots), where the first is Jarīr ibn ʿAbdallāh al-Bajalī, and the second is Ḥarīz ibn ʿAbdallāh al-Sijistānī. Their names as well as their fathers' names are spelt the same, and the only thing that distinguishes one from the other is their time period.

Knowledge of these things, as well as of the generations of reporters and their dates of birth and death, is very important in this field, for these data enable us to safeguard the tradition from the infiltration of impostors and from false claims of having met a particular narrator.

This has been a short treatise outlining the objectives of this science. Any reader wishing to investigate further and discover more examples of each topic should refer to more detailed works.

INTRODUCTION TO ḤADĪTH

by

ʿAbd al-Hādī al-Faḍlī

Translated by

Nazmina A. Virjee

INTRODUCTION

All Praise is due to Allah, and may His peace be upon His chosen worshippers.

It is well known that the science of *Ḥadīth*[1] comes at the forefront of the Islamic sciences, and has been laid down by Muslim scholars as one of the means of understanding Islamic thought in general, and particularly Islamic law.

The science of *Ḥadīth* is one of the Islamic sciences on which *ijtihād*[2] relies, and on the basis of which the process of deriving legal rulings from their sources is carried out. This is why it is important and necessary to study the science of *Ḥadīth*, especially for those studying the science of jurisprudence (*fiqh*). For this reason, I included the subject '*Dirāyat al-Ḥadīth*'[3] as part of the curriculum in the Islamic Legal Faculty's study programme at the International College for Islamic Studies. I prepared this treatise to cover the details of the curriculum when I had to teach the subject to second-year students in the college.

Within a rational framework, I have tried to rearrange the subject found in our *Ḥadīth* books, so that it be more practical rather than theoretical, because this science, as we know, is a comparative science, and its field of application, according to us, is the Shīʿa Ithna ʿAsharī *Ḥadīth* books.

I have omitted, on the basis of research that has been carried out previously in books on the study of *Ḥadīth*, whatever material does

[1] *Ḥadīth* (pl. *aḥādīth*): The traditions of the Prophet (S) and the infallible *maʿṣūm* Imams (A), i.e. their sayings, actions or tacit approval, or narrations of these. Throughout the course of this book, I have used the word '*ḥadīth*' to refer to the bulk of tradition literature and the general concept, and the word 'tradition' or 'report' to refer to individual narrations.

[2] *Ijtihād*: independent jurisprudential investigation when deducing legal rulings from Sharīʿah sources

[3] *Dirāyah*: contextual study and criticism of the text of traditions.

not exist in our *Ḥadīth.* And I have added whatever material is present in our books, though not to be found in previous books on *Ḥadīth.* Similarly, I have slightly changed the division of chapters so that interconnected subjects are placed together, where the former leads on to the latter. I have tried to be as clear and concise as possible in my elucidations and expressions, with the aid of examples and proofs. I have also tried to be brief in matters that do not need elaboration, and have elaborated on whatever I felt was necessary.

Finally, this paper is, if not an investigation, then an attempt at one. And neither investigation nor attempt is free of mistakes or weaknesses, so I hope that the scholars and professors concerned with similar research will correct any mistakes and strengthen any weaknesses.

Allah – the High and Exalted – is the One who bestows success, and He is the ultimate goal.

ʿAbd al-Hādī al-Faḍlī
al-Dammam, Darat al-Ghariyīn
3 Jamada al-Thaniyyah 1413 AH

CHAPTER ONE

INTRODUCTION TO THE PRINCIPLES OF *ḤADĪTH*

1. Title

This science has been referred to by more than one term and given more than one title, the most famous of which are:

- ʿIlm al-Ḥadīth – The Science of *Ḥadīth*
- Dirāyat al-Ḥadīth[1] – Contextual Study of *Ḥadīth*
- Muṣṭalaḥ al-Ḥadīth – Terminology of *Ḥadīth*
- Qawāʿid al-Ḥadīth – Precepts of *Ḥadīth*
- Uṣūl al-Ḥadīth – Principles of *Ḥadīth*

All these mean the same thing, because a science, in the most correct sense of the word, means a group of general principles or comprehensive precepts brought together within a single context.

Therefore, calling it 'Precepts of *Ḥadīth*' or 'Principles of *Ḥadīth*' would both imply the required meaning; and as 'contextual study' is linguistically synonymous with the word 'science', the title 'Contextual Study of *Ḥadīth*' also offers considerable clarity. These titles all come to signify 'a group of comprehensive precepts or general principles that come together under one title', denoting the science being formed, in this case the science of *Ḥadīth*. So calling it 'Science of *Ḥadīth*', 'Contextual Study of *Ḥadīth*', 'Precepts of *Ḥadīth*' or 'Principles of *Ḥadīth*' is a methodological process that accords well with the nature of scientific terms.

It is true that the question may arise about the use of the title 'Terminology of *Ḥadīth*', since terminology is acknowledged as being part of a science, and not the whole science itself. However, if we consider this title from the point of view of its historical origin, we

[1] *Dirāyah*: see Glossary.

notice that there is also a scientific aspect to it, for 'terminology' was the term first used for 'Divisions of *Ḥadīth*', because of their sheer quantity, as we shall see. This ever-increasing number of *Ḥadīth* divisions, compared with the rest of the information in this legal science, ended up being the whole science and was consequently designated 'Terminology of *Ḥadīth*', meaning 'Science of *Ḥadīth*', i.e. using the part to refer to the whole.

The title could also be expanded to 'Science of *Ḥadīth* Principles' or 'Science of the Precepts of *Ḥadīth*', in order to differentiate between the legal science, in which the general information is dealt with exclusively, and the principles and fundamentals, in which the whole criteria specific to the science of *Ḥadīth* come into play.

The title 'Science of *Ḥadīth* Terminology', which is self-explanatory, could also be given. The title 'Science of Contextual Study of *Ḥadīth*', however, may be quite obscure because if 'contextual study' is synonymous with 'science', the possessive construction in this title becomes 'x of the x', which is logically impossible.

The word 'contextual study' has itself ended up signifying 'the science of the science' and thus become fathomable. Subjective differences such as these can be syntactically corrected and justified.

It seems to me, however, that the term '*dirāyah*' (contextual study) came into use in contrast to '*riwāyah*' (narration), in that narration signifies the mere transmission of *ḥadīth*, whereas contextual study signifies its critical and contextual study, by means of which it can be determined to whether its transmission originated from a *maʿṣūm*[2] or not. The choice of these words may have something to do with the fact that they rhyme in Arabic (*dirāyah* – knowledge and *riwāyah* – narration).

In any case, our title *Uṣūl al-Ḥadīth* (*Principles of Ḥadīth*) signifies 'Science of *Ḥadīth*'.

2. Definition

The oldest Shīʿa Ithna ʿAsharī text that we have on the subject is

[2] *Maʿṣūm*: infallible – referring specifically to the Prophet (S) and the Imams (A).

Kitāb al-Dirāyah by al-Shahīd al-Thānī (d. 966 AH). And the oldest definition of this science is the one he gives in his introduction:

> A science in which the text of the tradition is investigated, with its chains of transmission, from the authentic to the faulty to the weak, along with all that is needed to distinguish the acceptable from the unacceptable.[3]

The second definition we have is probably that of al-Shaikh al-Bahāʾī (d. 1040 AH) in his book entitled *al-Wajīzah*: 'A science in which the chain of a tradition is investigated, along with its text, its modes of reception, and the rules of its transmission'.

All definitions that came afterwards used these two as a basis; some merely passed them on, while others added a note or explanation and still others suggested flaws within them.

The most recent definition we have of this science is that of al-Shaikh al-Ṭihrānī in *al-Dharīʿah*, namely:

> The science that deals with the conditions and circumstances attached to the tradition's chain of transmission; i.e. the way in which the composition of a text is achieved, whereby various authorities are arranged in order of transmission, where the first receives the text of the tradition from whoever reported it to him, transmitting it in turn to whoever is after him, until it reaches us in that manner. A single chain made up of these transmitters can be exposed to various circumstances affecting the way in which the chain is regarded, such as its being 'consecutive' (*muttaṣil*) or 'broken' (*munqaṭiʿ*), 'supported' (*musnad*) or 'hurried' (*mursal*), '*muʿanʿan*'[4] or 'rare' (*ʿazīz*), 'authentic' (*ṣaḥīḥ*), 'good' (*ḥasan*), 'dependable' (*muwathhaq*) or 'weak' (*daʿīf*),[5] and other such circumstances, which must be considered when looking at the chain of transmission and which are researched within the science of *Ḥadīth* studies.[6]

If we bear in mind that the definition of a legal science depends on the subject of the science being studied and researched, and if we try to compare the above definitions in this light, we can examine which of them are closest to the actual science from a methodological point

[3] Third edition 1409 AH.
[4] See Glossary.
[5] These technical terms will be explained in detail later in the book.
[6] Vol. 8, p. 54.

of view. This brings us to the following conclusions:

- Al-Shahīd al-Thānī restricted this science to the chain of transmission and the text of the tradition.
- Al-Shaikh al-Bahāʾī expanded the field of study in this science to include the modes of reception of the tradition and the method of its transmission.
- Al-Shaikh al-Ṭihrānī restricted the field of study by limiting it to the study of the conditions and circumstances found in the chain of transmission.

In his *Dirāyah* al-Shahīd al-Thānī implies that this science concerns itself only with investigating the chain of transmission, saying,

> Bear in mind that the text of the *ḥadīth* can only rarely be taken into consideration, and that a *ḥadīth* takes on the characteristics of strength or weakness, etc., depending on the characteristics of its reporters, such as their trustworthiness or lack thereof, and on whether it is a consecutive chain or a broken chain of narrators, or whether it is a hurried chain or a confusing chain, among other things.

And in order to discern which one of these definitions is better than the others in terms of discerning what the actual science is, we have to refer back to the books written in this field and analyse their contents, in order to see whether the study of the text of the tradition forms a scientific aspect of the subject matter, in which case it can be considered as being the actual science, or whether the study of it is required only as a precursor to the actual science.

The contents of al-Shahīd al-Thānī's *al-Dirāyah* are as follows:

Chapter 1: Categories of *ḥadīth*
Chapter 2: Those whose reports can be accepted and those whose reports are rejected
Chapter 3: The reception of the *ḥadīth* and methods of its transmission
Chapter 4: The names and generations of reporters.

And the contents of al-Māmaqānī's *al-Miqbās* are as follows:

❋ Introduction to the true nature of the Contextual Study of *Ḥadīth*
Chapter 1: Clarification of terminology used in the Contextual

	Study of *Ḥadīth*
Chapter 2:	Defining the report and its types
Chapter 3:	Classification of the report into *mutawātir* (multiple successive)[7] and *āḥād* (solitary)[8]
Chapter 4:	The different types of solitary reports with regard to the circumstances of the reporters
Chapter 5:	Other terms used by *Ḥadīth* scholars
Chapter 6:	Those whose reports can be accepted and those whose reports are rejected
Chapter 7:	The dignity of the Science of *Ḥadīth*, the modes of reception and the methods and rules of transmission
Chapter 8:	The names and generations of reporters.

Contents of other books are barely more extensive than this, and differ from *al-Dirāyah* and *al-Miqbās* only in length or depth. They may sometimes contain something to do with the text such as distortions in spelling and phonetics, but this is not significant enough to be considered as a scientific aspect of the subject and thus a main part of the study.

Hence, the definition proffered by al-Shaikh al-Ṭihrānī is the most sound from a methodological point of view and the one that adheres most to the nature of the subject matters within this science. So, in light of this, we can offer our own definition of the Principles of *Ḥadīth*:

> A science in which the specifics of the chain of transmission are analysed, along with the standards of its admissibility.[9] In other words, it is the study of the degree of validity of the chain of transmission.

[7] *Mutawātir*: a tradition from the Prophet (S) or an infallible Imam, repeatedly and widely narrated in an uninterrupted sequence, through successive reliable narrators. In the absence of a single English word to express this very specific meaning, I will continue to refer to this type of multiple successive tradition as *mutawātir*.

[8] *Āḥād* or *khabar al-wāḥid*: Although termed 'solitary report', this refers to any report that is not *mutawātir*. We will refer to this as a 'solitary report', although these categories and terms will be explained in further detail in their respective chapters.

[9] Its admissibility for the purpose of deriving legal rulings.

To clarify this definition in terms of the relation between the Science of *Ḥadīth* and biographical studies,[10] we can say that where both of them are devoted to researching the chain of transmission, biographical studies analyse the individual reporters in the chain, whereas the Science of *Ḥadīth* looks at the actual chain as a whole. Put another way, biographical studies look at the status of the reporter in terms of trustworthiness or otherwise, and the science of *Ḥadīth* looks at the status of the report in terms of its validity or invalidity.

3. Subject Matter

On the basis of this definition, we are able to discern the subject matter of this science: it is 'the chain of transmission' in terms of the standards of validity it attains; or it is 'the narration', i.e. the path of transmission of a tradition from its source.

Within this science, the chain of transmission is first distinguished and then divided into categories that are defined in turn. Then its scope of validity or invalidity is set out. Similarly, the modes of reception and methods of transmission of the tradition are researched, along with all that the methodology of investigating this science necessitates.

4. Benefits of Studying the Principles of *Ḥadīth*

The Noble *Ḥadīth* represents the Noble Sunnah, and the Sunnah is the second source of Islamic legislation after the Holy Qur'ān. The Sunnah is greater in quantity and broader in terms of legislative detail than the legislative verses of the Holy Qur'ān. Because *ḥadīth* relies first on oral narration and then on written reports for its reception and transmission, and differs from the Qur'ān's mode of transmission, which relies solely on the successiveness and frequency of transmission (as these are not stipulated conditions for the transmission of *ḥadīth*), most traditions are is transmitted only once or by one narrator only. Furthermore, as established and stipulated in

[10] Known as *'Ilm al-Rijāl'* in Islamic legal terminology – the science in which the circumstances of reporters are analysed and classified.

the science of the principles of jurisprudence, one cannot know for certain that a tradition originated from a *maʿṣūm* (infallible one),[11] unless it is directly linked to something proving it as such. However, most traditions are not linked in this manner, so it is essential that we study the chain of transmission, i.e. the path by which the tradition reached us, in order to confirm and authenticate the soundness of its origin being a *maʿṣūm*. For this purpose, scholars laid down the principles of the sciences known as 'biographical studies' and 'the Science of *Ḥadīth*'.

Therefore, the study and learning of the sciences of *Ḥadīth* and reporters are considered fundamentals and precepts for the study of jurisprudence, especially in the field of *ijtihād*[12] and deriving practical legal rulings from the eminent Sunnah.

5. Relation to the Legal Sciences

The term 'legal sciences' here refers to those Islamic sciences that contribute to the legal process of independent jurisprudential investigation (*ijtihād*) and deduction of legal rulings from the eminent Sunnah, and these are:

- biographical studies
- the science of the principles of jurisprudence
- the science of jurisprudence.

a. Relation to biographical studies

We previously stated that the science of *Ḥadīth* and biographical studies both contribute to the study of the chain of transmission, though they differ in their approach to or treatment of the subject. Biographical studies deal with the credibility or lack of credibility of the narrators, by means of which it furnishes the specific facts to which the general principles of the science of *Ḥadīth* are then applied.

Therefore, if we wanted to evaluate a specific tradition in terms of

[11] *Maʿṣūm*: infallible – referring specifically to the Prophet (S) and the Imams (A).

[12] *Ijtihād*: independent jurisprudential investigation used when deducing legal rulings from Islamic sources of legislation.

its chain, we would refer to the biographical dictionaries of reporters to find out the status of each reporter in this particular chain; and if all of them are veracious (*ʿādil*)[13] and *imāmī*,[14] for example, then the chain is said to be of an authentic tradition[15] by virtue of applying the corresponding principle from the science of *Ḥadīth*, which states that: every chain in which all the reporters are veracious and *imāmī* is an authentic chain.

If we wanted to fit this into a logical syllogism, we would say:

> The reporters of this chain are veracious *imāmīs* + Every chain whose reporters are veracious *imāmīs* is an authentic chain = This is an authentic chain.

Then we would form another syllogism to establish its validity and authority, which we acquire from the *science of the principles of jurisprudence*:

> This is an authentic chain + Every authentic chain is valid = This chain is valid.

An example of the application of the general principles of *Ḥadīth* is the report of al-Shaikh al-Kulaynī in his *al-Kāfī* in the chapter on the virtue of good favours:

> ʿAlī ibn Ibrāhīm reported from his father, who reported from ʿUmayr, who reported from Muʿāwiyah ibn ʿAmmār:
>
> Abū ʿAbdallāh (A) said, 'Do good favours for people, if they are worthy of it. And if they are not, then you are worthy of doing them anyway.'

So, in order for us to know the standard of this report, we refer first to the biographical dictionaries to find out the evaluation of each reporter in the chain of this eminent tradition:

[13] The Arabic legal term for this is *ʿādil*, meaning 'just', 'equitable', and 'reliable'. In *fiqh*, this designates a person of irreproachable reputation and veracity whose testimony is valid. We will continue to refer to *ʿādil* as 'veracious'. (See Introduction and Chapter 8 for a detailed explanation.)

[14] *Imāmī*: a follower of the twelve Imams or Shīʿa Ithna ʿAsharī, who adheres to the Jaʿfarī school of jurisprudence.

[15] Termed '*ṣaḥīḥ*' in Islamic legal terminology. See glossary for a full explanation.

- ʿAlī ibn Ibrāhīm al-Qummī: veracious *imāmī* (see the biographical dictionary of al-Najāshī)
- Ibrāhīm ibn Hāshim al-Qummī: veracious *imāmī* (see biographical dictionary of *ḥadīth* reporters of al-Khūʾī)
- Muḥammad ibn Abī ʿUmayr: veracious *imāmī* (see the biographical dictionary of al-Najāshī)
- Muʿāwiyah ibn ʿAmmār al-Dahnī: veracious *imāmī* (see the biographical dictionary of al-Najāshī).

After referring to the biographical dictionaries we come to the conclusion that all the reporters of this tradition are veracious *imāmīs*.

Next we refer to the *science of Ḥadīth*, one of the principles of which states that the chain in which all the reporters are veracious *imāmīs* is an authentic and valid tradition. By applying this principle to the chain of the aforementioned *ḥadīth*, we ascertain that it is an authentic tradition.

b. Relation to the science of the principles of jurisprudence

What is researched in the *science of the principles of jurisprudence* is the authoritativeness of the sources of Islamic legislation and the way in which a legal ruling is logically derived from them.

Among these sources of legislation is the eminent Sunnah, which is represented by the *ḥadīth*. A tradition, as previously mentioned and established, is of two kinds:

- The *mutawātir* (multiple successive) report whose source, being a *maʿṣūm*, is certain; and the solitary report linked to associated evidence definitely proving its origin to be a *maʿṣūm*.
- The report whose source is conjectured to be a *maʿṣūm*.

In order to establish that the *ḥadīth* is a Sunnah that can be used as an authority to derive rulings, we must establish the authority of the 'certainty' (*ʿilm*) of the first kind of report and the conjecture or speculation (*ẓann*) of the second. This can be done through only the *principles of jurisprudence*.

If we refer back to the previously quoted report, it is a solitary report, which is not linked to any evidence definitely proving that its source is a *maʿṣūm*, and this is therefore conjectured.

It has been asserted in the *science of the principles of jurisprudence* that a solitary report whose origin is conjectured to be a *maʿṣūm* can be used as an authority from which to deduce rulings and on which to rely. Therefore this tradition is one that can be relied on and which can be used as a legal proof.

If we were to put this as a syllogism, it would be:

> This is a solitary report whose origin is conjectured to be a *maʿṣūm* + Every solitary report whose origin is conjectured to be a *maʿṣūm* is an authority = This report is an authority.

Therefore, the relation of the *science of Ḥadīth* to the *science of the principles of jurisprudence* rests in the application of the precepts in the *principles of jurisprudence* to the *precepts of ḥadīth*, which are equivalent to its details and particulars.

> In *biographical studies*, therefore, the reporters are evaluated.
> In the *science of Ḥadīth*, the report is evaluated.
>
> In the *science of the principles of jurisprudence*, the authority of the report is evaluated.

c. Relation to the science of jurisprudence

To define this more clearly, the relation between the *science of Ḥadīth* and the *science of jurisprudence* rests in the implementation of independent jurisprudential investigation (*ijtihād*) and the process of deriving legal rulings; since the *science of jurisprudence* is the last stage from which the *mujtahid* undertakes to know the legal ruling. After having confirmed the authoritativeness and validity of the report for deducing legal rulings, the jurist uses it as legislative source to help him in deriving the required ruling in the light of the other legal sources he has at his disposal for this purpose.

CHAPTER TWO

HISTORY OF THE PRINCIPLES OF *ḤADĪTH*

1. Growth and Development

The oldest record we have on *Ḥadīth*-orientated thought is contained in al-Shaikh al-Kulaynī's book *al-Kāfī*: on the authority of ʿAlī ibn Ibrāhīm who reported from his father, who reported from Ḥammād ibn ʿĪsā, who reported from al-Yamānī, who reported from Abān ibn Abī ʿAyyāsh, who reported from Sulaym ibn Qays al-Hilālī, who said:

> I told Amīr al-Mu'minīn (A): 'I have heard from Salmān (al-Fārsī) and al-Miqdād (ibn al-Aswad al-Kindī) as well as Abū Dharr al-Ghaffārī something on the interpretation of the Qur'ān and the traditions of the Prophet of Allah, which are different from what is known among the general public. Then I heard you confirm what I have heard from them (Salmān, al-Miqdād and Abū Dharr). Also I have noticed many things that people believe about the interpretation of the Qur'ān as well as the traditions of the Prophet of Allah which you disagree with, and all of which you believe to be void. Are you of the opinion that people intentionally lie against the Messenger of Allah (S) and interpret the Qur'ān according to their own opinion?
>
> Hearing this query, ʿAlī (A) turned towards me [the narrator] and observed: 'As you have raised the questions you must now understand the answer. Verily, whatever people have is true as well as false, right as well as wrong, abrogative as well as abrogated, general as well as specific, exact as well as analogous and rightly remembered as well as fancied. Even in the lifetime of the Holy Prophet, people attributed false statements to him to such an extent that he himself stood up and addressed the people: "O people, those who attribute false statements to me are in great numbers. Whoever intentionally attributes any false statement to me has taken his seat in Hell." Then the people went on attributing false statements to him after his death. Whatever

traditions you (people) have received are from four categories of narrator. There is no fifth category.

'The first is a hypocrite who poses as a believer and is actually an artificial Muslim. He does not consider it a sin to attribute false statements to the Prophet intentionally, nor does he mind such an attribution. Were the people to know how false and hypocritical he is, they would never accept a word from him, nor would they corroborate his statements. It was this type of man about whom people started saying, "This is the one who was honoured by the company of the Prophet and who has actually seen and heard the Prophet". People accepted traditions from him without knowing his credentials. Allah the Almighty has told his Prophet all that was to be told about the hypocrites and has detailed all the characteristics that were to be described, saying: "When thou seest them, marvel at their persons; and if they speak listeneth unto their speech" (al-Munāfiqūn, 63:4). Such people remained there after the Prophet as well. Then they became intimate with the leaders who misguided and seduced people towards the fires of Hell with their fabrications, falsehoods and slander, and who entrusted them with important jobs and positions. These rulers forced the people to obey them and exploited the situation through them. All, except for the few whom Allah saved, allied themselves with the rulers and the life of this world...All this is the description of one of the four categories.

'Into the second category falls the person who actually heard something from the Prophet but was not able to retain it in his mind and fell into doubt. He never intentionally told lies but he started speaking, practising, and propagating what he remembered incorrectly and sketchily, at the same time claiming, "I have heard the Prophet say so." If the Muslim community had known that he was in error they would never have accepted his words. And if the man himself had known that he was mistaken, he himself would have rejected his own version.

'The third category is of the person who has heard the Prophet ordering something to be done, but who is unaware that the Prophet later forbade the same. Or he has heard the Prophet forbidding something but is unaware that the Prophet late made it permissible. Thus the man knew of the abrogated but not of the abrogative. If he had been aware that the precept had been abrogated he himself would have withdrawn his narrated tradition. If Muslims had known that the Prophet had abrogated

> what the man had related (on the authority of the Prophet), they would have rejected his version.
>
> 'The fourth and the last is the category of person who has never attributed false statements to the Prophet and who hates false statements because of his fear of Allah and reverence for the Prophet. He never forgets anything he has heard from the Prophet and always relates exactly what he has heard without adding anything to or subtracting anything from it. He knows both what abrogates and also what has been abrogated. Hence, he acts according to what supersedes, leaving aside the superseded. Verily, the commands of the Prophet are also like the verses of the Qur'ān that consisted of the abrogative and the abrogated, the general and the specific, the exact and the analogous. Like the Qur'ān, the Prophets' wordings also had two aspects, that is, the general and the specific. As Almighty Allah Himself has said, "And whatever giveth you the Apostle, accept it, and from whatever preventeth he, stay away from it" (al-Ḥashr, 59:7). Thus, one who was not aware of all these "complications" would fall into doubt and would not understand what Allah and His messenger exactly meant.
>
> 'It was not necessarily a fact that all the Companions of the Prophet had the capability of either asking the Prophet a question or of understanding his answers. There were some who used to put a question to the Prophet but could not understand his answer. There were also others who asked the Holy Prophet a question but did not ask him to explain it until they had fully understood it, such as Bedouins or wayfarers who would come and ask the Prophet some questions just so that they could have a chance to be enlightened by the Prophet's answer.'[1]

This noble report was the conscious beginning of the study and propagation of *Ḥadīth* thought.

There are a few general principles laid down by Imam ʿAlī (A) for dealing with reports, which are considered to be the pioneering beginnings of *Ḥadīth* thought. He said:

> When you hear the report, comprehend it with a sense of care and not with a sense of narration, for the narrators of knowledge are many whereas the keepers of it are few.

[1] *Al-Kāfī*: Chapter on Disparate Traditions, vol. I, no. 191.

> If you hear a report from us that you do not understand, leave it to us, do not pursue it further, and surrender until the truth becomes clear to you; and do not be hasty talebearers.[2]

Ibn al-Nadīm has recorded in his *Fihrist* (p. 308) that Abān ibn Taghlib (d. 141 AH) wrote a book called *al-Uṣūl fi al-Riwāyah ʿAlā madhhab al-Shīʿah* (*The Principles of Narrating According to the Shīʿa School*), which may be considered one of the earliest *Ḥadīth* works.

We can see *Ḥadīth* thought from that early era in the following reports:

- That of Muḥammad ibn Muslim al-Ṭāʾifī, saying, 'I said to Abū ʿAbdallāh (A), "I hear the tradition from you, and then (while quoting it to others), I add to it and subtract from it." The Imam replied, "It does not matter, if you intend to convey the meaning of the tradition."'
- That of Zurārah, saying, 'If there are two contradictory reports issuing from you (the Imams), which one should we take?' He said, 'Take the one that is more prevalent among your companions, and leave aside the unusual rare report.' He replied, 'What if both are equally prevalent?' He said, 'Take the one that seems more authentic and trustworthy to you.'

Among the first works to be written on the ideology of *Ḥadīth* thought is *Ikhtilāf al-Ḥadīth* (*Disparity of* Ḥadīth) by Muḥammad ibn Abī ʿUmayr al-Azdī (d. 217 AH). Among the works to do with the history of the principles of *Ḥadīth* are the biographical dictionaries, of which some of the oldest are:

- *Kitāb al-Rijāl,* ʿAbdallāh ibn Jablah al-Kanānī (d. 219 AH)
- *Kitāb al-Mashyakhah,* al-Ḥasan ibn Maḥbūb (d. 224 AH)
- *Kitāb al-Rijāl,* al-Ḥasan ibn Faḍāl
- *Kitāb al-Rijāl,* ʿAlī ibn al-Ḥasan ibn Faḍāl
- *Kitāb al-Rijāl,* Muḥammad ibn Khālid al-Barqī.

Also to do with the history of the principles of *Ḥadīth* are the source books of *ḥadīth* compilations (*al-Kutub al-Arbaʿah*, 'The Four Books'). They contain several precepts of this science such as:

- The precept of preponderance (*tarjīḥ*) between two disparate reports.

[2] *Biḥār al-Anwār*, vol. IV, 2: 189.

- The precept of reliability and unreliability of the reporters.

These and others like them paved the way for the entrance of *Ḥadīth* thought into the realm of legal thought.

The oldest record we have of the methodology of this science in books on the principles of jurisprudence is the research of al-Shaikh al-Mufīd (d. 413 AH) in his book entitled *Uṣūl al-Fiqh* (*Principles of Jurisprudence*). This is the oldest book we have that deals with principles of *Ḥadīth* thought. In it, he carries out an investigation entitled 'The Report', which considers various categories and the issues of authority and admissibility. On pages 40 and 41, he says, 'Authoritative proof in traditions is that which is denoted by the certitude attained from analysing the validity of the reporter, by removing any doubt and suspicion regarding him.' Every report that does not attain validity with respect to the genuineness of its reporter has no authority in religion, and cannot impose any act at all.

The reports that legal science must consider are of two types:

- What has been narrated successively and in multiple transmissions – the *mutawātir* tradition – to the extent that it could not possibly have been fabricated without mutual collusion or unanimous agreement with regard to it
- The solitary report (*āḥād*) linked to associated evidence furnished by the *mutawātir* report for proving the veracity of reporters and removing any falseness or corruptness therein.

The *mutawātir* report is that which considerable numbers of people present in widely prevailing reports, so much so that it would be impossible for them all to have agreed upon fabricating it, since it may be conceivable for two people coincidentally to report something wrongly but not for so many of them to do so. This is the conventional distinction that everyone recognizes.

It may be that a group of people fewer than the number cited produce a report, such that through their own attestation of their narration, the articulation of their words, their apparent facial expressions, and what can be seen of their comportment, it becomes clear that the reason they were not in agreement is because mutual acquaintance and consultation were impractical. Therefore, knowing their situation in these respects is proof of their honesty and removes any obscurity from the report, even if the reporters are not as numerous as previously cited.

The decisive solitary report is that to which some kind of evidence is linked informing the observer that the reporter is of sound repute. This evidence could be a logical proof, a testimony of customary practice or unanimous consensus.

When a solitary report is devoid of any such evidence asserting the authenticity of the report, then it is neither authoritative for proving anything, nor can it denote certitude or impose actions under any circumstances.

After al-Mufīd's *Uṣūl al-Fiqh*, his student al-Sharīf al-Murtaḍā dealt with the subject of reports in his book *al-Dharīʿah ilā Uṣūl al-Sharīʿah* (*The Means to the Principles of Jurisprudence*) in the chapter entitled 'Chapter Discussing the Reports', which he divides into the following subsections:

- Defining the report and understanding its rules
- The use of the solitary report for denoting certitude
- The categories of the report
- Authorizing acts of worship by means of the report
- Attributes of the reporter who receives the tradition and the one from whom he receives it, and the mode of wording the narration, etc.

In the book *Maʿārij al-Uṣūl* by al-Muḥaqqiq al-Ḥillī (d. 676 AH) there is a separate chapter dedicated to reports, which he divides into the following subsections:

- *Mutawātir* reports
- Solitary report
- Investigations to do with reporters
- Investigations to do with reports
- Preponderances between contradictory reports.

History tells us that al-Sayyid Aḥmad ibn Mūsā ibn Ṭawūs al-Ḥillī (d. 673 AH), who was a contemporary of al-Muḥaqqiq al-Ḥillī and author of the book *Ḥall al-Ishkāl Fī Maʿrifat al-Rijāl* (*Resolving Ambiguity in Biographical Studies*), was the first to classify reports into the four divisions: *ṣaḥīḥ* (authentic),[3] *ḥasan* (good),[4] *muwaththaq* (depen-

[3] *Ṣaḥīḥ*: a tradition in which all the transmitters in its chain are *imāmī* and veracious. This is the highest grade of *ḥadīth*. We shall hereafter refer to *ṣaḥīḥ* as 'authentic'.

dable),[5] and *ḍaʿīf* (weak).[6] Perhaps when he was criticized for this classification, both positively and negatively, it was an incentive for independent recording within the principles of *Ḥadīth.*

2. Related Works

The oldest Shīʿa work in this field is the book *Sharḥ Uṣūl Dirāyat al-Ḥadīth* (*Explaining the Principles of the Critical Study of* Ḥadīth) by al-Sayyid ʿAlī ibn ʿAbdal-Karīm ibn ʿAbdal-Ḥamīd al-Najafī al-Nīlī, who was a student of al-ʿAllāmah al-Ḥillī, among the scholars of the eighth century AH.

He was probably influenced by the issues raised and mentioned by al-Sayyid Aḥmad ibn Ṭawūs, who was his own teacher's teacher.

The works of al-Shaikh Zayn al-Dīn al-ʿĀmilī – also known as 'al-Shahīd al-Thānī' – appeared in the tenth century AH, by virtue of which this science came to be recorded, and from which sprang all that followed.

The book '*Ḥall al-Ishkāl fī Maʿrifat al-Rijāl*' by al-Sayyid ibn Ṭāwūs might have had an influence on al-Shahīd al-Thānī's work, for it is mentioned that al-Shahīd al-Thānī had a copy of some of Ibn Ṭāwūs's writings in his possession.

The students and colleagues of al-Shahīd al-Thānī from among the scholars of the Ahl al-Sunnah were also influenced by him, especially on a technical level.

3. Most Famous Works on the Principles of *Ḥadīth*

Al-Shahīd al-Thānī's works on the science of *Ḥadīth* are:

---

[4] *Ḥasan*: a tradition in which all the transmitters in its chain are *imāmī* and veracious, or some of them are *imāmī* and commendable and the rest are non-*imāmī* but commendable. We will hereafter refer to *ḥasan* as 'good'.

[5] *Muwaththaq:* a tradition in which some or all of the transmitters in its chain are non-*imāmī*, but it has been established that they are dependable. We will hereafter refer to *muwatthaq* as 'dependable'.

[6] *Ḍaʿīf:* a tradition that does not fit into the categories of authentic, good, or dependable. It is therefore a 'weak' tradition. These terms will be explained in more detail during the course of the book.

- *Al-Bidāyah fī ʿIlm al-Dirāyah* (*Introduction to the Contextual Study of Ḥadīth*) – printed with its commentary in Tehran in 1310 AH.
- *Al-Riʿāyah fī ʿIlm al-Dirāyah* (*Commentary on the Introduction to the Contextual Study of Ḥadīth*) – finished in 959 AH and printed with the original work in 1310 AH.
- *Ghinyat al-Qāṣidīn fī Maʿrifat Iṣṭilāḥat al-Muḥaddithīn* (*Asset for Those Seeking to Know the Terminology of the Ḥadīth Scholars*). He referred to this work in the conclusion of his Sharḥ, saying, 'Whoever wants to investigate this matter deeply, and discover clear examples of what he is investigating, should refer to my book *Ghinyat al-Qāṣidīn fī Maʿrifat Iṣṭilāḥat al-Muḥaddithīn* for it achieves this purpose.'

Other renowned and published works following these are:

- *Wuṣūl al-Akhyār Ilā Uṣūl al-Akhbār* (*The Best People's Attainment of the Principles of* Ḥadīth) by al-Shaikh Ḥusayn ibn Aḥmad al-ʿĀmilī (d. 984 AH)
- *Al-Wajīzah fī ʿIlm al-Dirāyah* (*Summary of the Contextual Study of* Ḥadīth) by al-Shaikh Baha' al-Dīn al-ʿĀmulī (d. 1030 AH)
- *Al-Rawāshiḥ al-Samāwiyyah* by al-Sayyid al-Dāmād (d. 1041 AH)
- *Jāmiʿ al-Maqāl fī mā Yataʿallaqu bi Aḥwāl al-Ḥadīth wa al-Rijāl* (*Collection of Theses Related to the Circumstances of* Ḥadīth *and Reporters*) by al-Shaikh Fakhr al-Dīn al-Ṭarīḥī (d. 1085 AH)
- *Miqbās al-Hidāyah fī ʿIlm al-Dirāyah* (*Ember of Guidance for the Contextual Study of* Ḥadīth) by al-Shaikh ʿAbdallāh al-Māmaqānī (d. 1351 AH). Printed in Najaf 1345 AH, then edited by his grandson al-Shaikh Muḥammad Riḍā al-Māmaqānī and reprinted in Beirut in 1411 AH
- *Nihāyat al-Dirāyah* (Commentary of *al-Wajīzah* by al-Shaikh al-Bahā'ī) by al-Sayyid Ḥasan al-Ṣadr (d. 1354 AH). Printed in India in 1324 AH, then reprinted in Sidon, Lebanon, in 1331 AH
- *Dirāsāt fī al-Ḥadīth wa al-Muḥaddithīn* (Studies about *Ḥadīth* and *Ḥadīth* Scholars) by al-Sayyid Hāshim Maʿrūf (d. 1401 AH)
- *Qawāʿid al-Ḥadīth* (*Precepts of* Ḥadīth) by al-Sayyid Muḥy al-Dīn al-Gharīfī (d.1412 AH)
- *Uṣūl al-Ḥadīth wa Aḥkāmuhu fī ʿIlm al-Dirāyah* (*The Principles of* Ḥadīth *and its Rulings in the Science of* Ḥadīth) by al-Shaikh Jaʿfar Subḥānī. Printed in Qum in 1412 AH.

CHAPTER THREE

GENERAL TERMINOLOGY IN *ḤADĪTH* STUDIES

The *Ḥadīth* scholars have adopted certain general terms within this science, and explained their meanings in the Arabic language. The terms they use are *ḥadīth*, *khabar*, and *athar*.

1. *Ḥadīth*, *Khabar*, and *Athar*

From all that has been researched about these terms and the indicative relationships between them, we can conclude that the relation between *ḥadīth* and *khabar* is as follows.

i. Lexically, *ḥadīth* and *khabar* are virtually synonymous, both meaning a speech that occurs outside the timeframe of the event to which it refers, whether it actually correlates with the event or not. This is the lexical meaning of *khabar*. In English we may refer to *khabar* as 'report'. In this technical context, *khabar* is a general term encompassing the words of the Prophet (S), as well as the Imams (A) and the Companions and the Followers, etc.[1]
ii. *Ḥadīth*, however, is specific in this context, in that it refers to what has come down from a *maʿṣūm* (i.e. the Prophet or the Imams), whereas the *khabar* is general and includes what has come down from a *maʿṣūm* as well as others. Therefore, the relation between them is that of general and specific, where every *ḥadīth* is a

[1] 'Companion' refers to the Companions of the Prophet (S), termed *saḥābī* (pl. *ṣaḥābah*) in Arabic. In earlier times the term was restricted to his close friends who had close contact with him. Later the term was extended to include the believers who had seen him, even for only a brief moment or at an early age. 'Follower' refers to the second generation of Muslims who came after the Companions, who did not know the Prophet (S) but knew his Companions. The Arabic term for this is *tābiʿī* (pl. *tābiʿūn*).

khabar, but not every *khabar* is a *ḥadīth*, though some of them may be.

iii. *Ḥadīth* and *khabar* are very different in their technical (not lexical) meaning, in that *ḥadīth* is used specifically for what comes from a *maʿṣūm*, and *khabar* refers to what comes from anyone other than a *maʿṣūm*.

The relation between *ḥadīth*, *khabar* and *athar* and the different opinions about them are:

- *Ḥadīth* is what comes from a *maʿṣūm*.
- *Athar* is what comes from a Companion.
- *Khabar* is the term given to the most general of the above two, in that it refers to what comes from a *maʿṣūm*, from a Companion or from anyone else.
- The *athar* is more general than the *ḥadīth* and the *khabar*: the *ḥadīth* is specific to what has been narrated from a *maʿṣūm*; the *khabar* is specific to what has been narrated from a non-*maʿṣūm*; and the *athar* is the term for what has been narrated from a *maʿṣūm* as well as a non-*maʿṣūm*. Therefore *athar* is definitely the most general of all of the terms.
- *Athar* is the same as *khabar* in all of its meanings in spite of their differences.

It seems that this difference of opinion regarding the meanings occurs as a result of the confusion among linguists and lexicographers in dealing with words and their meanings, for they do not differentiate between the lexical and the technical usage of the words. What is needed is a methodical way of differentiating between these two levels.

If we try to shed some light on these three terms with regard to the way the scholars and jurists use them in their speech and their books, i.e. from the point of view of their technical usage, we find that all three are used to mean one thing, which is the narration of the Sunnah (practice of the Prophet and the Imams) in its three forms: speech, actions and tacit approval. This is because they are all taken from the statements '*Ḥaddatha fulān*' (i.e. x narrated – hence the word *ḥadīth*), '*Khabbara fulān*' (i.e. x reported – hence the word *khabar*), and '*Athara ʿan fulān*' (it has been related from x – hence the word *athar*).

When we say that this is one of the terms used in the science of

Ḥadīth, we mean that the scholars of this science determined the technical usage of the word. A good way of determining this usage is to examine the scholars' usage of the technical term within their field. And through investigation of the usage of these three words in the language of the Shīʿa *Ḥadīth* scholars and jurists, we find that they are all used in the sense of 'a narration of the eminent Sunnah'.

If we want to use them in a way other than the meaning mentioned above, within the *Ḥadīth* field, they are then restricted according to their respective meanings. Therefore, *ḥadīth*, *khabar* and *athar* all indicate one meaning, namely, the Sunnah. It may narrate the speech of a *maʿṣūm*, or report on an action or deed of theirs, or refer to tacit approval of something.

According to what Shīʿa authors have said, the science of *Ḥadīth* according to the Shīʿa and the science of *Ḥadīth* according to the Ahl al-Sunnah have become confused, in that some of the Ahl al-Sunnah regard what has been emitted by a Companion as Sunnah – al-Shāṭibī in *al-Muwāfaqāt* is probably the most famous proponent of that view. From here came the whole differentiation of *athar* and *ḥadīth* among some of them, where *athar* – as a technical term – is specific to the practice (Sunnah) of a Companion, and *ḥadīth* is specific to the practice (Sunnah) of the Prophet (S). However, we Shīʿa do not consider the practice of Companions to bear weight as Sunnah anyway, so we have no need to differentiate between the two.[2]

2. *Riwāyah*

Riwāyah in the Arabic language means transmission. According to *ḥadīth* terminology, however, it means transmission of a tradition with its chain of narration. This refers to the act of narration itself.

The term is also used as a noun meaning 'the transmitted tradition along with its chain'. Sometimes it may simply refer to the tradition, with or without chain.

In books of jurisprudence that deal with deducing legal rulings, especially those of the most recent Shīʿa jurists such as al-Shaikh Muḥammad Ḥasan al-Najafī, al-Shaikh Yūsuf al-Baḥrānī, al-Sayyid

[2] Translator's Note: I have used the word 'report' to mean any of these terms indicating narration of the Sunnah.

Muḥsin al-Ḥakīm, al-Shaikh Ḥusayn al-Ḥillī, al-Sayyid ʿAlī Shabar and al-Sayyid Abū al-Qāsim al-Khuʾī, this term is given to the tradition that has not yet been verified as being authentic, good or dependable.

Further inquiry into this can be done through deductive jurisprudence works such as *al-Jawāhir*, *al-Ḥadāʾiq*, *al-Mustamsik*, *al-Dalīl*, *al-ʿAmal al-Abqā*, *al-Tanqīḥ* and others.

3. *Rāwī* and *Rāwiyyah*

The word *rāwī* is one of the words used by Arabs on a cultural level to denote a bearer and transmitter of a piece of poetry. It is recorded historically that every Arab poet from the well-known pre-Islamic poets had a *rāwī*, who would memorize his poetry by heart and transmit it to others. Hence, within their cultural milieu, transmission of poetry came to be known as *riwāyah*. This term was then applied to the transmission of *ḥadīth* from the Prophet (S) and, therefore, one who transmitted *ḥadīth* from him (S) was called a *rawi* – literally, 'reporter' or 'narrator'.

Therefore, lexically a *rāwī* of *ḥadīth* or poetry is defined as a person who memorizes and transmits it. Its plural is *rāwūn* or *ruwwāh*.

Rāwiyyah denotes one who has transmitted many narrations or reports.

CHAPTER FOUR

SOURCES OF *ḤADĪTH*

1. The Transmission of *Ḥadīth*

The Arab Muslims went about transmitting traditions from the Prophet (S) in two ways: oral transmission and written transmission.

a. Oral transmission

This was the widespread and usual custom among them in transmitting their culture. Transmission of poetry in the pre-Islamic and early Islamic periods is the most distinct proof of this phenomenon.

Oral transmission relies on two fundamental pillars, which are hearing and memorization – hearing the tradition from the narrator, then learning it by heart.

The Prophetic *Ḥadīth* or Prophetic Sunnah comprised not only the speech of the Prophet (S), which relies on hearing, but also his actions and tacit approval, i.e. all his unspoken actions and his unspoken approval of others' actions. Because these latter two do not fall within the scope of what can be fathomed by hearing, witnessing and observation takes the place of listening and hearing.

In the first case, i.e. narrating the speech of the Prophet (S), the reporter would say, 'I heard the Prophet (S) saying...' or 'the Prophet (S) said...'.

In the second instance, i.e. transmitting reports about the actions or approval of the Prophet (S), the reporter would say, 'I saw the Prophet (S) doing...' or 'I saw him (S) approve of x's doing...' or 'x did such-and-such in front of the Prophet (S) and he did not censure him for it'.

The narration, therefore, is transmitted by the first reporter who is the one initially to report the eminent Sunnah, directly from the Prophet (S), without any intermediary between himself and the Prophet. The undertaking and bearing of the eminent Sunnah rely on hearing or sight and memorization.

In the case of transmitting it to others, it relies on oral transmission.

b. Written transmission

This is when the reporter writes down the sayings, actions and tacit approvals of the Prophet (S). This writing down is considered undertaking and bearing the eminent Sunnah. If he wanted to transmit it, he could transmit it to others orally or in written form, in which case they would receive it from him or copy it from him.

Because the phenomenon of writing and recording was not as prevalent and widespread as the tradition of oral transmission among the Arabs of that time, the reporters of *ḥadīth* resorted to oral transmission more than written transmission.

2. Recording of *Ḥadīth*

In spite of the fact that written transmission was not prevalent, it has been mentioned in history and attested to by the Sunni *Ḥadīth* scholars that some Companions wrote down the *ḥadīth* of the Prophet (S) during his lifetime, and the Prophet (S) approved of this act of theirs, which in itself counts as Sunnah and was thereby used as permission to write and record *ḥadīth*.

The most famous such works are:

- *al-Ṣaḥīfah al-Ṣādiqah*,[1] by ʿAbdallāh ibn ʿAmr ibn al-ʿĀṣ
- *al-Ṣaḥīfah al-Ṣaḥīḥah*, transmitted by Ḥammām ibn Munabbih on the authority of Abū Hurayrah on the authority of the Prophet (S)
- *Ṣaḥīfah* of Samrah ibn Jundab
- *Ṣaḥīfah* of Jābir ibn ʿAbdallāh al-Anṣārī.

The Prophet's (S) approval at writing down his *ḥadīth* during his lifetime and his attitude concerning this matter are evident from what ʿAbdallāh ibn ʿAmr ibn al-ʿĀṣ said:

> I was writing down everything that I heard the Prophet (S)

[1] *Ṣaḥīfah* literally means 'journal' or 'manuscript', and here refers to these small personal *ḥadīth* collections.

> saying, but the Quraysh were forbidding me from doing so, saying, 'You are writing everything that the Prophet (S) is saying, while he is just a mortal who speaks in anger as well as in pleasure,' so I stopped writing, and mentioned this incident to the Prophet (S), who pointed to his mouth with his finger, saying, 'Write! For by The One who has power over my soul, nothing but the truth comes out of it (my mouth).'[2]

Just as this report states that the Prophet (S) allowed and authorized writing about him, and refuted the assumption that the Quraysh had made about him, so it also points to the fact that there were some Companions who did forbid the recording of the *ḥadīth* of the Prophet (S) during his lifetime.

The caliph ʿUmar ibn al-Khaṭṭāb is renowned for his prevention and prohibition of it, which al-Ḥāfiẓ ibn Ḥajar[3] attributes to two reasons: first, that the Companions had forbidden it initially – as confirmed in *Ṣaḥīḥ Muslim* – for fear that it would get confused with parts of the Qurʾān.[4]

[2] *Maʿālīm al-Madrasatain*, vol. II, p. 42, taken from *Sunan al-Dārimī*, vol. I, p. 125, from the chapter on Authorization to Write Down, and from *Sunan Abī Dāwūd*, vol. II, p. 126, from the chapter on Recording of Knowledge, and from *Musnad Aḥmad*, vol. II, pp. 162, 207 and 216, and from *Mustadrak al-Ḥākim*, vol. I, pp. 105–06, and from *Jāmiʿ Bayān al-ʿIlm wa Faḍlihi*, vol. I, p. 85.

[3] *Al-Ḥāfiẓ* is a term that recurs throughout the book, usually prefixed or suffixed to someone's name. It literally means 'memorizer' and is used as a title in *ḥadīth* terminology to describe a scholar who has an excellent memory and has memorized a great number of traditions.

[4] He points to what Muslim said in his collection of traditions, that the Prophet (S) said, 'Do not write anything on my authority. And whoever writes anything down from me apart from the Qurʾān, he must eliminate it.' Al-Shaikh Manāʿ al-Qaṭān has commented on this in his book *al-Tashrīʿ wa al-Fiqh fil al-Islam* (p. 94) as follows:

> This is the tradition that has authentically come down from the Prophet (S) about prohibiting the recording of the Sunnah... and there is dispute concerning the meaning behind this prohibition, for it is said: this concerns one whose memorization is reliable, and for whom it is feared that by writing down he will become dependent on the recording... not on those traditions that come with authorization for one whose memory is not reliable.
>
> It is said that the tradition prohibiting the writing down of the Sunnah has been abrogated by these types of traditions, and that they were prohibited only during the time when it was feared that they would get mixed up with the Qurʾān, but when this factor ceased to be, writing down was allowed. It is also said that the

Al-Harawī quotes an extract in the book '*Dhamm al-Kalām*' from al-Zuhrī, saying,

> 'Urwah ibn al-Zubayr informed me that 'Umar ibn al-Khaṭṭāb – may Allah be pleased with him – wanted to write down the practices of the Prophet, and consulted the Companions of the Prophet (S) with regard to it, and most of them indicated this as possible; so 'Umar remained a whole month asking Allah for the best in this matter about which he had doubts. He awoke one morning and Allah had determined his course of action for him, so he said, 'I had mentioned to you about writing down the Sunnah, as you know; then I remembered that when someone from the People of the Book before you had written something else alongside the Book of Allah, they had devoted themselves to it and abandoned the book of Allah, and I – by Allah – do not want to obscure the Book of Allah with anything.'[5]

---

writing down of *ḥadīth* in the same book as the Qur'ān was prohibited, so that they would not get mixed up, as it would be confusing for the reader to read both these things in one book. When most of the Qur'ān had been revealed, and the majority of people had memorized it to an extent where it was safe from being confused with anything similar, the Prophet (S) gave some of his Companions special permission to write down the *ḥadīth*, in order to enhance their accuracy if it was feared that they would forget or if their memory was not reliable. It is possible that this special permission was given to certain people who were the most accurate and those with the best memories.

This resolves the contradiction between the texts that refer to the prohibition of writing down *ḥadīth* and those that mention its permissibility. The sayings of the period after the first phase of Islam all allow the writing down of *ḥadīth*.

Ibn al-Ṣalāḥ says in his introduction (see *al-Taqyīd wa al-Īḍāh*, p. 203), 'It has been reported to us from Abī Sa'īd al-Khudrī that the Prophet (S) said, "Do not write anything but the Qur'ān on my authority, and whoever writes anything down from me apart from the Qur'ān, he must eliminate it."' (Quoted by Muslim)

Those from whom we have reports about the permissibility of writing down are 'Alī, his son Ḥasan, Anas, 'Abdallah ibn 'Umar and 'Abdallah ibn 'Amr ibn al-'Āṣ, among others from the Companions and Followers (may Allah be pleased with all of them).

And one of the authentic traditions of the Prophet that indicates the permissibility of writing down is the *ḥadīth* of Abī Shāt al-Yamānī. He requested the Prophet (S) to write down something that he had heard from his address in the year of the conquest of Makkah, and the Prophet (S) said, 'Write down for Abī Shāt...'

[5] Al-Ashqar, *Tārīkh al-Fiqh al-Islāmī* (History of Islamic Jurisprudence), p. 72, according to *Tanwīr al-Hawālik*, vol. I, p. 4.

It is clear from this text that ʿUmar was exercising his independent judgment and reasoning here, which was affected by the way the Jews treated the Torah and their attitude towards it, not – as said previously – because he based it on the report about the prohibition of writing from the Prophet (S), because he does not indicate any such thing. The independent reasoning he was exercising, however, was in opposition to the text that commands writing down.

In spite of this, he insisted on and enforced his own judgement, and sent written orders to the capital cities; and it has been narrated on the authority of Yaḥyā ibn Juʿdah that ʿUmar ibn al-Khaṭṭāb wanted to write down the Sunnah; then it occurred to him that he should not write it, so he sent written orders to the capital cities saying, 'Whoever has written down anything should eliminate it.'[6]

It seems that ʿUmar was well acquainted with the Arabic language, for it is said that after he made his decision to prohibit the writing down of *ḥadīth*, he gathered all the written traditions that the Companions had in their possession over the period of a month; then he burnt it all, saying, '*Mishna* like the *Mishna* of the People of the Book'.

The *Mishna* is the Jewish text of the Talmud, the latter being a collection of Jewish legislation that was transmitted orally and annexed to commentaries by religious men. It is divided into two parts: the *Mishna*, which is the actual text, and the *Gemara*, which is the commentary.

Now if the prohibition to write down *ḥadīth*, as mentioned, had indeed issued from the Prophet (S), the Companions who did embark upon writing down would not have done so, such as ʿAlī and Ḥasan; and the Prophet (S) would not have ordered ʿAbdallāh ibn ʿAmr ibn al-ʿĀṣ to write; in the same way, he would not have ordered writing down for Abī Shāt, and ʿUmar ibn al-Khaṭṭāb would have adhered to this prohibition, rather than following the Jewish example.

All this points to the fact that ʿUmar simply exercised his independent reasoning in this matter and did not base it on the available text. And it seems to me that he did this so that the virtue of the Ahl al-Bayt with regard to their propagation of *ḥadīth* would not be widespread, and so that ʿAlī's right to the caliphate would not be

[6] *Majallāt al-Fikr al-Jadīd*, 3rd issue: *ʿUlūm al-Ḥadīth* by al-Gharbāwī, taken from *Kanz al-ʿUmmāl*, vol. X, p. 294.

revealed by way of the tradition of Ghadīr or other such traditions.

Al-Sayyid Hāshim Maʿrūf says in his book *Dirāsāt fī al-Ḥadīth wa al-Muḥaddithīn*:[7]

> It has been said of him [ʿUmar] that when Ubay ibn Kaʿb narrated about Jerusalem and its features, ʿUmar ibn al-Khaṭṭāb scolded him, and was about to beat him, so Ubay called on a group of the Anṣār to bear witness that they had heard the tradition from the Prophet (S), and when they bore witness, he left him. Then Ubay ibn Kaʿb said to him, 'Are you accusing me with regard to the *ḥadīth* of the Prophet of Allah (S)?!' So he replied, 'O Abū Mundhir, by Allah I was not accusing you, but I hated to think that the *ḥadīth* of the Prophet was becoming manifest.'
>
> Apart from that, there are many other reports that affirm that the caliph did not use the Prophet as a basis for prohibiting writing down, and that he was the only one to behave in such a way in his ardent desire for the Book of Allah.
>
> However, the report that stipulates that he scolded Ubay ibn Kaʿb for narrating the tradition about Jerusalem, and what he said at the time – 'I hated to think that the *ḥadīth* of the Prophet was becoming manifest' – shows that he was determined not to let the *ḥadīth* of the Prophet (S) spread, in spite of knowing that the *ḥadīth* of the Prophet complemented and executed legislation, expounded on the generalizations of the Qur'ān and specified the specific and general applications of verses, as well as making obligatory many moral, social and pedagogical issues.
>
> If we were to investigate such an ardent desire to keep the Sunnah secret, we should not find any cause giving him the right to behave in such a manner, although the notion that he feared the spread of the Prophet's *ḥadīth* on the virtues of ʿAlī and his sons (A) is not far from the truth.
>
> The report of ʿAbd al-Raḥmān ibn al-Aswad on the authority of his father confirms this. He reports, "ʿAlqamāh brought some books from Yemen or Makkah which included a collection of traditions on the virtues of the Ahl al-Bayt (A), so we went to ʿAbdallāh ibn Masʿūd's house, and we entered after having asked permission, and he handed him the books. He [ʿAbdallāh] called the servant girl and sent for a basin with water in it. So we said to

[7] Pp. 21–22.

him, "O ʿAbdallāh, have a look at them as there are authentic traditions among them", but he did not pay attention, and started to dissipate them in the water, saying, "We narrate to you the best of narrations, by Our revealing to you this Qur'ān".[8] The hearts are vessels, so fill them up with the Qur'ān.'

ʿAbdallāh ibn Masʿūd was one of the ones to turn away from ʿAlī (A) and allied himself with those who abandoned him, as these historical texts confirm.

3. Recording of *Ḥadīth* by the *Ahl al-Sunnah*

This state of affairs was continued by the Ahl al-Sunnah in accordance with ʿUmar ibn al-Khaṭṭāb's reasoning, up until the caliphate of the Umayyad ʿUmar ibn ʿAbd al-ʿAzīz, when the last generation of Companions ended, and writing of *ḥadīth* was implemented at the orders of ʿUmar ibn ʿAbd al-ʿAzīz.

The writing down of *ḥadīth* according to the Ahl al-Sunnah went through three phases: the phase of compiling, the phase of the *masānīd* works,[9] and the phase of the *ṣiḥāḥ*[10] works.

a. Compilation

Abū Nuʿaym says in his *al-Ḥilyah*:

> The leaders of the third generation of Muslims undertook to record legal rulings in the middle of the second century.'
>
> Al-Imām Mālik compiled *al-Muwaṭṭa'*, including in it the current practice of the people of Hijaz, considered strong, and blended it with the sayings of the Companions, and legal opinions of the Followers.
>
> Ibn Jurayj compiled a work in Makkah, al-Awzāʿī in Sham, Sufyān al-Thawrī in Kufa, Ḥammād ibn Abī Sulaymān in Basra, Hushaym ibn Wāsiṭ, Maʿmar in Yemen, Ibn Mubārak in Khurasan

[8] Qur'ān 12:3.

[9] *Masānīd* (sing. *musnad*): refers to works of *ḥadīth* categorized according to the first narrator in the chain after the Prophet (S), i.e. a Companion.

[10] *Ṣiḥāḥ* (sing. *ṣaḥīḥ*): refers to works of *ḥadīth* compiled to include authentic traditions from the Prophet (S) only.

and Jarīr ibn ʿAbd al-Ḥamīd in Ray.

All of these people were contemporaries, so it is not known who preceded whom. Many of the people of their time followed in their footsteps.[11]

b. *Masānīd* works

These works contained traditions of the Prophet (S) only.

Ibn Ḥajar says in *Fatḥ al-Bārī*:

> Some of the leading scholars, at the beginning of the 3rd century, felt that the traditions of the Prophet (S) should be singled out, so the Kufan ʿUbaydallāh ibn Mūsa al-ʿAbasī compiled a *musnad* work, as did the Basran Musaddad ibn Musarhad, Asad ibn Mūsa al-Umawī and the Egyptian Naʿīm ibn al-Ḥammād al-Khuzāʿī.
>
> Then the religious scholars followed in their footsteps, such that the few scholars who had traditions memorized went about compiling them into *musnad* works, such as al-Imām Aḥmad, Isḥāq ibn Rāhawayh, ʿUthmān ibn Shaybah and other distinguished scholars.[12]

c. *Ṣiḥāḥ* works

This is the phase when the authentic traditions of the Prophet (S) were compiled separately from the rest of the traditions from him.

The first to set this trend was al-Bukhārī. Ibn Ḥajar says,

> When al-Bukhārī saw these works, transmitted as a single collection comprising both the authentic and the good, and many of them even had weak traditions in them, he endeavoured to collect all the authentic traditions into one. The words of his teacher Isḥāq ibn Rāhawayh, when he was talking to a group among whom al-Bukhārī was present, strengthened his ambition: 'If only you had compiled a concise book comprising the authentic traditions of the Prophet (S)...' Al-Bukhārī said, 'This touched my heart, and I began collecting the Comprehensive *Ṣaḥīḥ*.'[13]

[11] Al-Ashqar, Tārīkh al-Fiqh al-Islāmī, p. 96.
[12] Ibid.
[13] Ibid., p. 97.

The most important and most famous works of *ḥadīth* of the Ahl al-Sunnah are:

- *Muwaṭṭa'* of al-Imām Mālik ibn Anas
- *Musnad* of al-Imām Aḥmad ibn Ḥanbal
- *Al-Jāmiʿ al-Ṣaḥīḥ* of Abū ʿAbdallāh Muḥammad ibn Ismāʿīl al-Bukhārī (d. 256)
- *Al-Jāmīʿ al-Ṣaḥīḥ* of Muslim ibn al-Ḥajjāj al-Qushayrī (d. 261)
- *Al-Sunan* of Abū Dāwūd Sulaymān ibn al-Ashʿath al-Sijistānī (d. 275)
- *Al-Sunan* of Muḥammad ibn ʿĪsā al-Tirmidhī (d. 279)
- *Al-Sunan* of Aḥmad ibn Shuʿayb al-Nasā'ī (d. 302)
- *Al-Sunan* of Muḥammad ibn Yazīd ibn Mājah al-Qazwīnī (d. 273).

4. Recording of *Ḥadīth* by the *Ahl al-Bayt*

As for the Ahl al-Bayt, the situation was completely the opposite, in that they adhered to and maintained the Sunnah of the Prophet (S), by recording and writing down the *ḥadīth* in small manuscripts,[14] and then in larger comprehensive books.

The previous tradition quoted by al-Kulaynī gives us a clear picture of this, as it is continued with the following words of Imam ʿAlī (A):

> Verily, I was the person who had access to the Prophet [at least] once every day and once every night when I used to be alone with him. On such occasions I had the honour of talking with him on whichever subject he was inclined to talk. The Companions of the Prophet were aware that to no other person did the Prophet extend such a privilege [of proximity] as he did to me. Sometimes I was at my house and the Prophet used to come to see me; indeed, this was more common.
>
> Whenever I entered any of his [the Prophet's] rooms to see him, he used to ask for the room to be vacated for the sake of privacy with me. In clearing the room, even his wives were not spared and there would be none with him besides myself. But when it was the Prophet's turn to visit my house for private conferences, he would not exclude Fāṭimah (my wife) or any of my sons (A)

[14] These manuscripts are termed *ṣaḥīfah* in Arabic (pl. *ṣuḥuf*).

> from this conference. On such occasions, he would reply to my queries and when I had exhausted my queries and fell silent, he would himself initiate further discussions. Never was there any case of revelation of any of the verses of the Qur'ān, which the Prophet (S) did not recite and dictate to me and which I did not write down with my own hand. Further, he informed me of their meanings, with complete elucidations, indicating the verses that were abrogative and the verses that were abrogated, the clear verses and the ambiguous ones, as well as the general verses and the specific ones.
>
> Then the Prophet prayed to Allah to bestow upon me its understanding and its unfailing memory. Ever since the Prophet prayed for me, I never forgot a single verse from the Book of Allah, nor did I forget the knowledge that the Prophet had imparted to me and that I had taken down in my own hand. Nothing of what was revealed to the Prophet, the lawful and the unlawful, nothing of the divine imperatives and the prohibitions, nothing of what has been and what would be, and nothing of the books revealed previously to any of the prophets regarding divine obedience and disobedience did the Prophet omit to teach me. I had fully grasped it and forgot not a word from it. Then the Prophet put his hand over my chest and prayed to Allah to fill my heart with knowledge and understanding, wisdom and enlightenment. I then inquired, 'O Prophet of Allah, may my parents be sacrificed for you, I have never forgotten anything ever since you have prayed for me; nor did I forget what I had not noted down. After all this, are you still afraid of my being forgetful?' Hearing this, the Prophet replied, 'No I am never afraid of your being either forgetful or ignorant.'

The first *ḥadīth* book of the Ahl al-Bayt (A) to be written on the authority of the Prophet (S) is *Kitāb ʿAlī* (the Book of ʿAlī). Mention of it has come down to us by people referring to it and quoting from it in the biographical dictionaries and in volumes on *ḥadīth*, *fiqh*, etc. Al-Shaikh al-Ṭihrānī calls it by the title *Amālī Sayyidinā wa Nabiyyinā Abī al-Qāsim Rasūlallāh (S): Amlaʾahu ʿalā Amīr al-Muʾminīn (A) (Dictations of our Master and Prophet Abū al-Qāsim the Messenger of Allah (S), which he dictated to Imam ʿAlī (A))*, which he wrote with his own hand.

This is the first book to be written by any man noting down the dictations of the Prophet, and is in Imam ʿAlī's handwriting. It is a large work, in scroll form, which can be opened and read, according to the traditions of the Ahl al-Bayt.

We shall quote one tradition regarding it here, which al-Najāshī has quoted in his book, from the translation by Muḥammad ibn ʿAdhāfir, ascribing it to ʿAdhāfir ibn ʿĪsā al-Ṣayrafī, who said,

> I was with al-Ḥakam ibn ʿUyaynah at Abū Jaʿfar al-Bāqir (A)'s house, when al-Ḥakam began asking him questions, to which Abū Jaʿfar kindly obliged, until they differed concerning an issue, and Abū Jaʿfar said, 'O my son, go and fetch the Book of ʿAlī (A),' so he took out a great scroll, opened it and began looking in it until he found the required issue. Abū Jaʿfar (A) said, 'This is ʿAlī's handwriting of the Prophet's (S) dictation'; then he handed it to al-Ḥakam, saying, 'O Abū Muḥammad, go with Salamah and Abū Miqdām, wherever you want, right or left, for by Allah, you will never find any knowledge more thorough than this, with any people upon whom Jibraʿīl descended.'

A part of this very *Dictation* has survived until today in the Shīʿa books – by the Grace of Allah – and al-Shaikh Abū Jaʿfar ibn Bābawayh al-Ṣadūq has quoted it in the 66th session of his own book of dictations. It comprises many morals, practices and rulings of *ḥalāl* and *ḥarām*, and it has around 300 lines. He narrated it, ascribing it to Imam Jaʿfar al-Ṣādiq (A), who himself narrated it from his noble forefathers; and al-Ṣādiq says at the end of it, 'This is gathered from the book that is a dictation from the Prophet (S), written by ʿAlī ibn Abī Ṭālib (A).'[15]

5. Recording of *Ḥadīth* by the Shīʿa

The recording of *ḥadīth* according to the Shīʿa went through two phases – the phase of small collections and the phase of large collections. (See shaded boxes on page 64 and 67.)

6. *Al-uṣūl al-arbaʿumiʾah* – the four hundred source collections

Al-uṣūl al-arbaʿumiʾah are the four hundred source collections, to which the name *uṣūl* (lit. 'principles', 'fundamentals' or 'roots') has

[15] *Al-Dharīʿah*, vol. II, pp. 306–7.

been given, to indicate that they are a primary source for scholars to refer to and rely upon. These collections are unique, according to the scholars, because of the following characteristics:

i. Their distinctive style of composition, whereby the traditions recorded in them are either reported by the author directly from the Imam or reported directly by the author from the person narrating it on the authority of the Imam.
ii. Commendation of their authors by the classical scholars, which inevitably shows the authenticity of their content.

The Phase of Small *Ḥadīth* Collections

We can call this the phase of early and direct reports, because the way in which these collections and those that *Ḥadīth* scholars refer to as '*al-uṣūl*'[16] are written is based on the author's narration directly from the Imam, or through only one intermediary narrator between the author and the Imam; i.e. the author would narrate the *ḥadīth* from the one who reported it to him on the authority of the Imam.

There were as many as four hundred such collections, the reason for this large number being: the great number of Shīʿa narrators reporting from the Imams (A); and the large number of traditions that the Imams (A) narrated on the authority of the Prophet (S). I have elucidated in my book *Tārīkh al-Tashrīʿ al-Islāmī* (*History of Islamic Law*) that the traditions of the Ahl al-Bayt (A) were in superabundance and covered the whole field of Islamic law comprehensively, providing all the legal textual requirements of the jurist for deducing legal rulings.

Among these collections there are some that do not fulfil the condition of direct narration from an Imam, but the traditions found in them go back to the historical periods of the respective Imams and are therefore counted as early reports.

All the *ḥadīth* material found in these four hundred *uṣūl* (source collections) and in the other aforementioned books derive from an Imam, and the traditions have been narrated on the authority of each Imam, who would, in turn, be narrating it on the authority of his own father or grandfathers, on the authority of the aforementioned Book of ʿAlī.

The veracity of the chain of transmission from an Imam all the way up to Allah – the High and Exalted – is well known among both Sunni and Shīʿa *Ḥadīth* scholars as the 'golden chain' because of its purity, sanctity and the sublimity of its narrative value.

[16] *Uṣūl* (sing. *aṣl*) is the Arabic term for books in which Shīʿa *Ḥadīth* scholars at the time of the Imams recorded the *ḥadīth* directly received by them. See detailed definition in subsection to follow.

Al-Shaikh al-Ṭihrānī says in his book *al-Dharīʿah*:[17]

> Al-Shaikh al-Bahāʾī has listed in his book *Mashriq al-Shamsayn* the factors that convinced the classical scholars to regard these traditions as authentic, of which some are:
>
> - that the tradition could be found in many of the famous and widespread four hundred source collections;
> - that a tradition would be repeated in one or more of these collections with various different chains of transmission;
> - that the tradition would be included in the works of an authority of legal consensus.

Al-Muḥaqqiq al-Dāmād said in the 29th part of his *Rawāshih*, after mentioning the four hundred source collections, 'And let it be known that taking *ḥadīth* from the reliable authentic *uṣūl* is one of the pillars used to authenticate transmission.'

According to the classical scholars, the mere existence of a tradition in a reliable *aṣl* (source collection) was ground enough to confirm its authenticity.

As for the rest of the available *ḥadīth* books, they would confirm the authenticity of their content only after having dispelled all the other possibilities that failed to fulfil the soundness of its origin, and they were not satisfied by the mere existence of the tradition in them, nor by the excellent faith of their authors.

These fundamental *uṣūl* excelled all other books, because of the strong certainty of their pure origin and the fact that they were closest to the authoritative sources and most likely to be correct.

This excellence filtered out into the *uṣūl* collections by virtue of a special quality possessed by their authors. This was due to their perseverance and diligence in compiling these works and preserving what others had failed to preserve; and as a result, they were much praised by the Imams (A).

Therefore, when a reporter is described, in the biographical dictionaries, as having written an *aṣl* (source collection), this is considered as a commendation of him, because it shows that he possesses certain characteristics and qualities such as accuracy, memory, avoidance of forgetfulness, distortion, mistakes and

[17] Vol. II, pp. 126–32.

heedlessness, and preparedness to receive traditions in the same form as that in which they originated from their sources. Such was the practice of the authors of these *uṣūl*.

Al-Shaikh al-Bahā'ī said in his *Mashriq al-Shamsayn*, 'We have been informed by our shaikhs – may Allah sanctify them – that one of the habits of the authors of *uṣūl* works was that, as soon as they heard a tradition from one of the Imams (A), they would hasten to write it down in their collections, so that they would not forget any of it as the days went by.'

Similarly, al-Muḥaqqiq al-Dāmād said in the 29th part of his *Rawāshiḥ*, 'It is said that the habit of the authors of *uṣūl* works was that, as soon as they heard a tradition from one of the Imams (A), they would hasten to record it in their collections without delay.'

The qualities present in these *uṣūl* and in their authors have led scholars to immerse themselves completely in reading, transmitting, memorizing and revising them, and treating them with extreme meticulousness, favouring them above all other collections. What leads us to conclude this is the fact that they have distinguished these *uṣūl* by compiling a special index to them and by assigning independent biographical sections to their authors in the biographical dictionaries, as al-Shaikh Abū al-Ḥusayn Aḥmad ibn al-Ḥusayn ibn ʿUbaydallāh ibn al-Ghaḍā'irī has done in his work *Al-Muʿāṣir li al-Shaikh al-Ṭūsī*.

Al-Shaikh al-Ṭihrānī has listed about 130 of these *uṣūl* collections in his book *al-Dharīʿah*.[18] Some of them are mentioned below:

- Sourcebook of the reliable authority Ādam ibn al-Ḥusayn al-Nakhās al-Kūfī
- Sourcebook of the reliable authority Ādam ibn al-Mutawakkil al-Kūfī, the pearl merchant
- Sourcebook of the reliable authority Abān ibn Taghlib al-Kūfī
- Sourcebook of the reliable authority Abān ibn ʿUthmān al-Aḥmar al-Bajalī
- Sourcebook of the reliable authority Abān ibn Muḥammad al-Bajalī
- Sourcebook of the reliable authority Ibrāhīm ibn ʿUthman Abī Ayyūb al-Khazzāz al-Kūfī

[18] Vol. II, pp. 125–67.

- Sourcebook of the reliable authority Ibrāhīm ibn Muslim al-Ḍarīr al-Kūfī
- Sourcebook of the reliable authority Ibrāhīm ibn Muhzim al-Asadī al-Kūfī
- Sourcebook of the reliable authority Aḥmad ibn al-Ḥusayn al-Ṣayqal al-Kūfī
- Sourcebook of the reliable authority Isḥāq ibn ʿAmmār al-Sābiṭī.

The Phase of Large *Ḥadīth* Collections

This is the phase of drafting and compiling large *ḥadīth* collections by putting together the *ḥadīth* literature from the previous phase. These larger collections differ from the collections of the previous phase in that there are additional reporters in the chain from the time of the *uṣūl* authors up to the time of the authors of these comprehensive collections, and also in that the chapters are arranged according to jurisprudence topics or specific subjects, to which a whole collection may be devoted.

These larger collections have come to be known among *Ḥadīth* scholars as early collections and later collections.

7. Other *Ḥadīth* Works

These are works (other than the four hundred source collections) that were also compiled during the lifetimes of the Imams (A). However, their authors did not necessarily adhere to transmitting traditions directly from the Imam, nor from one who narrated the traditions on the direct authority of the Imam, as the authors of the *uṣūl* undertook to do. Therefore, they may at times narrate directly from the Imam or directly from the author of an *aṣl* or from both of them with one or more intermediary narrator.

The following titles are cited from al-Shaikh al-Ṭihrānī 's *al-Dharīʿah* (vol. VI, pp. 303–):

- *Ḥadīth* Book of Abī Yaḥyā Ibrāhīm ibn Abī al-Bilād
- *Ḥadīth* Book of Ibrāhīm ibn Abī al-Kirām al-Jaʿfarī
- *Ḥadīth* Book of Ibrāhīm ibn Khālid al-ʿAṭṭār al-ʿAbadī
- *Ḥadīth* Book of Ibrāhīm ibn Ṣāliḥ al-Anmāṭī al-Asadī
- *Ḥadīth* Book of Ibrāhīm ibn ʿAbd al-Ḥamīd al-Asadī
- *Ḥadīth* Book of Ibrāhīm ibn Muhzim al-Asadī

- *Ḥadīth* Book of Ibrāhīm ibn Naṣr al-Juʿfī
- *Ḥadīth* Book of Ibrāhīm ibn Nuʿaym al-ʿAbdi
- *Ḥadīth* Book of Ibrāhīm ibn Yūsuf al-Kindī
- *Ḥadīth* Book of Abī Shuʿayb al-Muḥāmilī al-Kūfī.

8. The First Four Books

These are the books otherwise known as 'The Four Books' or 'The Four Fundamental Books':

a. *al-Kāfī*
b. *Man Lā Yaḥḍuruhū al-Faqīh*
c. *al-Tahdhīb*
d. *al-Istibṣār*

a. *al-Kāfī*

al-Kāfī (*The Sufficient*) by Abū Jaʿfar Muḥammad ibn Yaʿqūb al-Kulaynī al-Rāzī (d. 338 AH), who compiled it as 34 books and 326 chapters, containing 16,199 traditions. He divided it into two parts: the *Uṣūl* (sources of jurisprudence) and the *Furūʿ* (applied religious practices). The *Uṣūl* part contains traditions to do with faith and belief, whereas the *Furūʿ* part contains traditions to do with applied jurisprudence. He compiled it over a period of twenty years.

The *Uṣūl* part was first published on a lithograph in Iran in the year 1281 AH, compiled by Muḥammad Shāfiʿī al-Tabrīzī; and the *Furūʿ* part in the year 1315 AH. It was subsequently republished many times, both lithographically as well as in print.

The contents of his book are as follows:

- Book of Reason and Ignorance
- Book on the Excellence of Knowledge
- Book of Divine Unity
- Book of Divine Proof
- Book of Belief and Disbelief
- Book of Supplication
- Book on the Excellence of the Qurʾān
- Book of Social Interactions
- Book of Cleanliness
- Book of Menstruation

- Book of Funeral Rites
- Book of *Ṣalāt* (Prayer)
- Book of *Zakāt* (Alms)
- Book of Fasting
- Book of *Ḥajj* (Pilgrimage)
- Book of *Jihād* (Sacred War)
- Book of Trade and Livelihood
- Book of Marriage
- Book of Childrearing
- Book of Divorce
- Book on Manumission of Slaves
- Book of Hunting
- Book of Ritual Slaughter of Animals
- Book on Issues Relating to Eating
- Book on Issues Relating to Drinking
- Book on Issues Related to Clothes, Ornaments and Courteousness
- Book on Issues Related to Pets and Domesticated Animals
- Book of Bequests and Wills
- Book of Inheritance
- Book of Prescribed Punishments
- Book of Prescribed Compensations
- Book of Issues Relating to Legal Testimony
- Book on Principles of Governance and Implementation of Laws
- Book of Oaths, Vows and Atonements

b. *Kitāb Man lā Yaḥḍuruhū al-Faqīh*

Kitāb Man lā Yaḥḍuruhū al-Faqīh (*Every Man His Own Lawyer*), by Abū Jaʿfar Muḥammad ibn ʿAlī ibn al-Ḥusayn ibn Mūsā ibn Bābawayh al-Qummī (d. 381 AH), who divided it into four sections containing 5,998 traditions. The enumerations of al-Shaikh al-Bahāʾī can be seen in Table 1 (on page 70).

Kitāb Man lā Yaḥḍuruhū al-Faqīh was first published lithographically in Iran in the year 1325 AH, then many times subsequently, both lithographically and in print. The topics of the book have been listed in the following shaded columns.

Cleanliness
Ṣalāt (Prayer)
Zakāt (Alms)
Khums (Tax)
Fasting
Ḥajj (Pilgrimage)
Visitation (of Holy Shrines)
Judgements and Legal Rulings
Mediation
Advocacy
Judgement by Ballot
Bail
Assignment
Manumission of Slaves
Trade and Livelihood
Debt
Commerce
Selling
Silent Partnership
Cultivation of Virgin and Barren Lands
Sharecropping Contracts and Granting Asylum
Guarantee
Loans and Prepayments
Monopoly and Rates
Some Legal Rulings on Etiquettes of Selling
Usury
Barter
Lost and Found
Borrowing
Deposited Trusts
Pawning
Hunting and Ritual Slaughtering
Gold and Silver Vessels
Oaths and Vows
Atonements
Marriage
Rulings Relating to Children
Divorce
Prescribed Punishments
Bequests and Wills
Endowments
Inheritance

Table 1: A tally pertaining to the contents of *Kitāb Man lā Yaḥḍuruhū al-Faqīh*. For an explanation of the terms *musnad* and *mursal* see pages 105 and 125, respectively.

Volume	Chapters	No. of Traditions	No. of *musnad** Traditions	No. of *mursal*** Traditions
1	87	1618	777	841
2	288	1667	1094	573
3	173	1810	1295	515
4	178	903	777	126

c. *Al-Tahdhīb – Tahdhīb al-Aḥkām*

Al-Tahdhīb – Tahdhīb al-Aḥkām (*Refinement of Laws*), by Abū Jaʿfar Muḥammad ibn al-Ḥasan al-Ṭūsī (d. 460 AH). It has 393 chapters, containing 1,359 traditions. It has been published in lithographic as well as in print form several times. Its table of contents is as follows:

- Cleanliness
- *Ṣalāt* (Prayer)
- *Zakāt* (Alms)
- Fasting
- *Ḥajj* (Pilgrimage)
- Visitation (of Holy Shrines)
- *Jihād* (Sacred War)
- Judgements and Legal Rulings
- Profits
- Commerce
- Marriage
- Divorce
- Manumission of Slaves (according to various methods)
- Oaths, Vows and Expiations
- Hunting and Ritual Slaughtering
- Endowments and Recommended Alms
- Bequests and Wills
- Distributive Shares in Estates and Inheritance
- Prescribed Punishments
- Prescribed Compensations

d. *Al-Istibṣār fī mā Ikhtalafa min al-Akhbār*

Al-Istibṣār fī mā Ikhtalafa min al-Akhbār (*Insight into Disparities Between Reports*) also by Abū Jaʿfar al-Ṭūsī.

> It is in three parts; two of which are on ritual acts of worship and the third on other topics of jurisprudence, from contracts, treaties, and judgements to punishments and compensations. Although it contains many of the same chapters as *Tahdhīb al-Aḥkām*, it is confined to mentioning what is incongruous in the various reports and reconciling them, whereas *al-Tahdhīb* combines both the congruous and incongruous.[1]

It contains 5,511 traditions, and has been published many times in both lithographic and print form.

[1] *Al-Dharīʿah*, vol. II, p. 14.

9. The Later Collections

These are large collections that brought together the contents of the First Four collections or revised them or both. They are as follows:

a. *Al-Wāfī*

Al-Wāfī (*The Abundantly Sufficient*), by al-Shaikh Muḥammad ibn Murtaḍā, known as Muḥsin al-Kāshānī, nicknamed al-Fayḍ (d. 1091 AH). This is a compilation of the traditions of the First Four Books with important traditions from other sources, along with some commentary and explanations.

He said in his introduction, 'I have tried my best to ensure that no tradition or chain of transmission contained in the Four Books be omitted from this work, and I have briefly explained whatever may need clarification, as well as mentioning important traditions from other *ḥadīth* books and *uṣūl* collections by way of commentary.'

It contains 14 books and 50,000 traditions. The table of contents of its books is as follows:

- Book of Reason, Knowledge and Divine Unity
- Book of Divine Proof
- Book of Belief and Disbelief
- Book of Cleanliness
- Book of Ṣalāt
- Book of Zakāt
- Book of Fasting
- Book of Ḥajj
- Book of Jihād
- Book of Profit
- Book of Eating and Drinking
- Book of Marriage
- Book of Bequests and Wills
- Anthology of Admonitions, Rulings and Speeches

It has been published lithographically in Iran.

b. *Al-Wasā'il*

Al-Wasā'il – Wasā'il al-Shī'ah – Tafṣīl Wasā'il al-Shī'ah Ilā Taḥṣīl

Masāʾil al-Sharīʿah (*Detailed Exposition of the Instruments of the Shīʿa for Acquiring Legal Knowledge*), by Muḥammad ibn al-Ḥasan al-Ḥurr al-ʿĀmilī (d. 1104 AH).

He gathered in it all the traditions found in the first Four Books, and most of the traditions to do with legal rulings from Shīʿa books. This work consists of some seventy volumes that the great *Ḥadīth* scholars have in their possession. He categorized its contents into an index, explained its significance, and listed useful information on the science of reporters, not to be found anywhere else, at the end of the book.

He started off with traditions relating to acts of worship, and arranged the traditions pertaining to legal rulings in the form of a jurisprudence book with chapters ranging from Cleanliness to Compensations.

On the whole, it is the most comprehensive book of traditions relating to legal rulings, and its arrangement is even better than of *al-Wāfī* and *al-Bihār*, because *al-Wāfī* was limited to collecting specific subjects from the Four Books, even though its arrangement of them was straightforward, and *al-Bihār* was limited to traditions that were not to be found in the Four Books, and most of them were unrelated to legal rulings.

The relation of this work to the other later *ḥadīth* collections is as the relation of *al-Kāfī* to the rest of the first Four Books. And, like *al-Kāfī*, it also took 20 years to compile.'[2] It contains 35,850 traditions.

c. *Al-Biḥār*

Al-Biḥār – Biḥār al-Anwār al-Jāmiʿah li-Durar Akhbār al-Aʾimmah al-Aṭhār (*The Seas of Light Encompassing the Pearls of the Purified Imams' Reports*), by Muḥammad Bāqir ibn Muḥammad Taqī al-Majlisī (d. 1110 AH).

Al-Shaikh al-Ṭihrānī said:

> It is a comprehensive work unlike any other work written before or since, as not only does it comprise a collection of reports, but also detailed editing, annotations and explanations of them,

[2] *Al-Dharīʿah*, vol. IV, pp. 352–53.

which are usually not to be found in other books.[3]

Its table of contents, as listed by the author in his introduction, is as follows:

- Book of Reason, Knowledge and Ignorance
- Book of Divine Unity
- Book of Divine Justice and Resurrection
- Book Relating to Proofs, Debates and Encyclopedias
- Book on Stories of the Prophets
- Book on the Life and Times of Our Prophet (S)
- Book of Divine Leadership (*Imāmah*), including Lives of our Imams (A)
- Book of Trials
- Book on the Life of ʿAlī the Commander of the Faithful (A), his Virtues and Characteristics
- Book on the Lives of Faṭima, al-Ḥasan and al-Ḥusayn (A)
- Book on the Lives of ʿAlī ibn al-Ḥusayn, Muḥammad ibn ʿAlī al-Bāqir, Jaʿfar ibn Muḥammad al-Ṣādiq and Mūsā ibn Jaʿfar al-Kāẓim (A)
- Book on the Lives of ʿAlī ibn Mūsā al-Riḍā, Muḥammad ibn ʿAlī al-Jawād, ʿAlī ibn Muḥammad al-Hādī and al-Ḥasan ibn ʿAlī al-ʿAskarī (A)
- Book on the Occultation of al-Ḥujjah al-Qāʾim (A) and Matters Relating to Him
- Book on the Sky and the World
- Book of Belief, Disbelief and Noble Moral Traits
- Book of Etiquettes and Practices
- Book on Anthology of Admonitions, Rulings and Speeches
- Book of Cleanliness and *Ṣalāt*
- Book of Qurʾān and Supplication
- Book of *Zakāt* and Fasting
- Book of *Ḥajj*
- Book of Holy Shrines
- Book of Contracts and Treaties
- Book of Legal Rulings
- Book of Licenses

[3] Ibid., vol. III, p. 16.

It was published by lithography in Iran between 1303 and 1315 AH in 25 volumes according to the author's own divisions. It was subsequently published in print in 110 volumes, where the last three volumes were specifically devoted to the detailed index titled *Hidāyah al-Akhyār Ilā Fihris Biḥār al-Anwār* (*The Best People's Guide to the Index of* Bihār al-Anwār), written by al-Sayyid Hidāyatallāh al-Mustarhamī al-Isbahānī.

d. *Al-Mustadrak*

Al-Mustadrak – Mustadrak al-Wasā'il wa Mustanbiṭ al-Dalā'il (*Amendment of* al-Wasa'il *and Derivation of the Proofs*), by Mirza Ḥusayn al-Nūrī (b. 1320 AH).

It contains around 23,000 traditions, which are the author's amendment of *Wasā'il al-Shī'ah* by al-Ḥurr al-'Āmilī, and he has also arranged it accordingly.

It was published lithographically in Iran and in print in Lebanon.

CHAPTER FIVE

COMPONENTS OF THE TRADITION

The tradition comprises of two fundamental components, namely, the chain and the content. When we look into these two parts of the tradition we find that each part is a field of study and research in its own right. I have included them here because of their importance and the importance of the benefit derived by the student thereof. The contents of this chapter have been summarised in the figures on page 78.

1. Chain of Transmission[1]

A tradition can justifiably be ascribed to the one who uttered it, who is thus its first authority if it can be traced back to him and attributed to him. This is based on the dependence and reliance of the scholars on the chain for deducing whether the ascription of the tradition to a *maʿṣūm* is genuine or not.

The chain, therefore, is the path of transmission by way of which the tradition reaches the transmitter from the original narrator. It contains individual elements that make up the whole chain. These individual elements are its reporters, and they in turn, make up the compound, i.e. the transmission.

- The reporters: are the men who transmit it.
- The transmission: is the chain that links the reporters together.

We have previously mentioned that biographical studies investigates the reporters in the chain and the science of *Ḥadīth* investigates the transmission of the chain.

2. Content[2]

By this we mean the text of the tradition, which is the original

[1] Termed in Arabic *sanad* or *isnād*.
[2] The Arabic word for this is *matn*.

articulation of the speech uttered by the original narrator of the tradition.

The text itself is divided into two further components: the wording and the meaning.

i. The text is made up of words ordered in a structural grammatical arrangement. It can also be said that the textual wording consists of two components:

- the individual words
- the phrases formed with these individual words.

ii. The meaning or significance. Individual words have three types of meanings:

- The lexical meaning: which is deduced from the root of the word.
- The morphological meaning: which is deduced from the structure of the word.
- The grammatical meaning: which is deduced from the function and position of the word with respect to the whole speech.

These three meanings thus result in a general significance or a general meaning: which is deduced from the whole context.

All these meanings are defined by referring to a lexicon and by applying morphological, grammatical and rhetorical principles of language.

Neither of these two, neither the chain nor the content, can be elevated to the level of usage as proof for legal deduction, or as an authority for argumentation, unless the chain of transmission has first been elevated to the level of validity, and the text has been elevated to the level of lucidity.

Each of these two levels, in turn, can be defined by the science of the principles of jurisprudence only, as mentioned previously.

Example:
Al-Kāfī, Book of Belief and Disbelief: Chapter on loving for the sake of Allah and hating for the sake of Allah:

> On the authority of Ibn Maḥbūb, on the authority of Mālik ibn ʿAṭiyyah, on the authority of Saʿīd al-Aʿraj, on the authority of Abū ʿAbdallah (A). [chain]

He said: One who is firm in his belief loves for the sake of Allah and hates for the sake of Allah, [and] gives for the sake of Allah and withholds for the sake of Allah. [text]

Figure 1: First Synopsis.

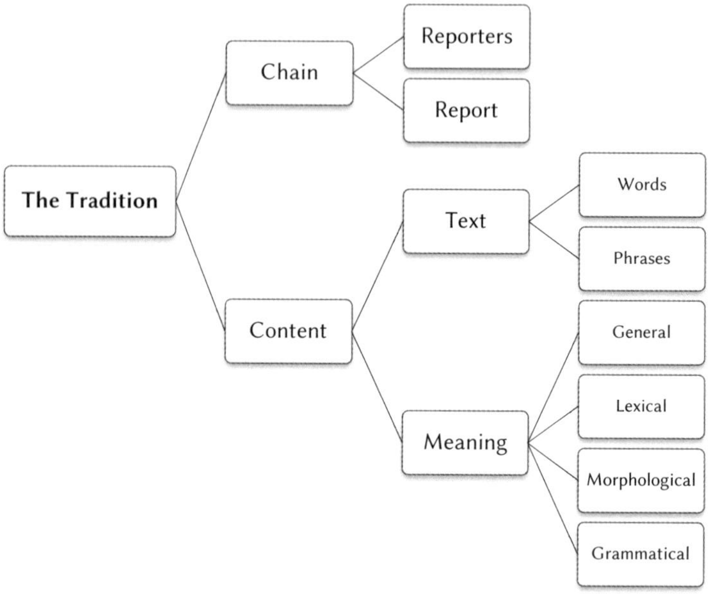

Figure 2: Second Synopsis.

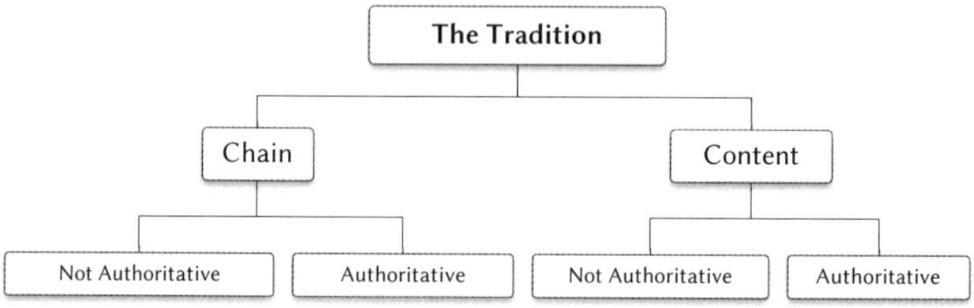

CHAPTER SIX

THE *MUTAWĀTIR* REPORT

Traditions are divided into two basic categories: *mutawātir*[1] (multiple successive) and *āḥād*[2] (solitary). In this chapter, the *mutawātir* report will be discussed.

1. Definition

The Arabic word for this is read both as *mutawātir* – the active form of the word – denoting that the report itself follows on in an uninterrupted continuous sequence, and *mutawātar* – the passive form of the word – denoting that the report is narrated in an uninterrupted and successive manner.

The root of this word comes originally from the verb *wātara*, which means 'to follow something in quick succession', both with and without a significant time difference in the succession. It appears that, lexically, this verb is used more often to mean 'following in succession with a time difference', although scholars of *Ḥadīth*, when they adopted it as a technical term for the report that we are about to define, had in mind the lesser meaning, which is 'absolute succession'; and it is up to the user of the term to invest it with meaning according to the demands of his science.

This is the lexical significance.

If we refer back to the books of *ḥadīth* studies in order to discover the technical meaning of the word '*mutawātir*', we see that the Shīʿa

[1] *Mutawātir*: a tradition from the Prophet (S) or an infallible Imām, repeatedly and widely narrated in an uninterrupted sequence, through successive reliable narrators. In the absence of a single English word to express this very specific meaning, I will continue to refer to this type of multiple successive tradition as *mutawātir*.

[2] *Āḥād* or *khabar al-wāḥid*: Although termed 'solitary report', this refers to any report that is not *mutawātir*. We will hereafter refer to this as a 'solitary report'.

books on the subject of *Ḥadīth* confine it to two textual definitions:

- The *mutawātir* tradition is one that has been narrated by such a great number of reporters that it would be impossible for them all to have agreed to fabricate it. This is similar to the way in which al-Shahīd al-Thānī has defined it in his *Dirāyah*,[3] namely, 'It is that [report] whose narrators reach such a great number that it is conventionally impossible for them to have colluded upon its fabrication'. Both al-Shaikh al-Māmaqānī in his *Miqbās*[4] and al-Sayyid Maʿrūf in his *Dirāsāt fil al-Ḥadīth wa al-Muḥaddithīn*[5] have adopted this definition.
- The *mutawātir* tradition is 'the report of a group of people such that it denotes certitude, by virtue of itself, decisively proving its authenticity'. This is the text of al-Shaikh al-Bahāʾī's definition of it in his *Wajīzah*.[6]

Al-Mīrzā al-Qummī has quoted both definitions together in his *Qawānīn*.[7]

If we analyse both definitions, we find that they are congruous in meaning, as both of them textually stipulate that it is the multitude of reporters that serves to verify the authenticity of the tradition.

The difference between them is that:

The first definition specifies that the method of verifying the authenticity of the report is through the multitude of its reporters such that it would be conventionally impossible for them all to have agreed to fabricate it.

The second definition does not mention the impossibility that a multitude of reporters would agree upon fabrication, but instead identifies the report as serving to verify its authenticity by virtue of itself, i.e. without relying on external evidence, as is the case when classifying the 'linked solitary report'.

Therefore, the tradition may generate certitude that it originated from a *maʿṣūm*, and it may also generate speculation about this.

That which generates certitude of its origin is further divided into:

[3] P. 12.
[4] Vol. I, p. 89.
[5] P. 33.
[6] P. 2.
[7] Vol. I, pp. 420–21.

- that which generates this by virtue of itself, which is the *mutawātir* report; and
- that which generates this with the aid of associated proof, which is the linked solitary report.

From a methodological viewpoint, if we wanted to divide something into two parts and define one of them by reference to an attribute that distinguishes it from the other, we would seek to expose that attribute, as was the case in the second definition.

Al-Shaikh al-Subḥānī observed of the first definition that:

> In this definition, multitude is highlighted, in that the number of reporters must be so large that their collusion in a lie is impossible. Ascertaining the impossibility of their collusion in a lie, or ascertaining the lack of agreement therein, is not evidence of the report's authenticity or of the absence of the reporters' intentional fabrication, for fabrication has causes and motives, other than what can be mutually agreed upon. Love and hate in individuals may give rise to rumours and lack of mutual agreement between individuals, especially if they are dissenters and propagandists.
>
> There are always major global powers whose hands scheme unscrupulously in the international media, so large numbers of people may utter the same thing in different places, at a single signal from the authorities, without one of them ever knowing the other. Therefore the mere fact that there is an absence of mutual agreement does not suffice to remove the very possibility of intentional fabrication. It is more adequate to add the following to the definition: 'and it is safeguarded from their intentional fabrication.'
>
> It is, therefore, strengthened by the large number of reporters as well as their reliability or by the fact that the subject matter is devoid of motives for fabrication, etc.[8]

This is a valid and good point.

In light of this, we should first adopt the second definition and then the first definition, after having qualified it with the above specification.

[8] Uṣūl al-Ḥadīth wa Aḥkāmuhu, pp. 23–24.

2. Conditions

The scholars of *Ḥadīth* have cited certain conditions to certify the authenticity of the *mutawātir* tradition. Unless these conditions are fulfilled, the *mutawātir* report cannot be certainly verified as originating from a *maʿṣūm*. These conditions can be divided into two types: those that pertain to the reporters and those that pertain to the listener.

a. Conditions that pertain to the reporters

Number of reporters

There is a difference of opinion as to the basis of the numerical condition, i.e. whether a specific number of reporters is required to provide certitude, such that if there were fewer than that number, this would not serve as sufficient evidence.

Shīʿa scholars hold the view that there is no specific number of reporters stipulated, believing merely that the number of reporters should reach such a level as to ensure that the report is safeguarded from intentional fabrication. The reason for this is that fabrication cannot logically be confined to a specific number of people. Furthermore, investigating the *mutawātir* reports within their social milieu shows us the inadmissibility of a specific number, for there are reports that denote certitude of their authenticity with a small number of reporters and others that denote certitude only with a large number. This is an obvious point.

Al-Shahīd al-Thānī says:

> This [i.e. the number of reporters needed to denote certitude] is not limited to an exact number. To be precise, it is the number that fulfils the specifications of the definition (which is that it be conventionally impossible for them all to have agreed upon fabricating it), and in some reports ten reporters or less may fulfil the specification, whereas in others it may only be fulfilled with a hundred, depending on their closeness to the definition of authenticity or the lack thereof.

In spite of this, our scholars have referred to the exact numbers stipulated by other scholars, some of which are:

- that the number of reporters should be no fewer than five, because the report of four veracious people cannot denote certitude, as is the case with witnesses for adultery. This statement has been ascribed to al-Qāḍī al-Bāqillānī.

- that the number of reporters should be no fewer than ten, as it is the first plural of multitude. This statement has been attributed to al-Iṣṭakhrī.
- that the number of reporters should be no fewer than twelve, for it is the number of the chieftains as mentioned in the Qur'ān: 'And we raised up among them twelve chieftains'.
- that they should be no fewer than twenty, because of the Qur'ānic verse 'If there are twenty among you persevering, they will vanquish two hundred'.
- that they should be no fewer than forty, because of the Qur'ānic verse 'O Prophet! Sufficient for you is Allah, and for those who follow you amongst the believers', who were forty in number.
- that they should be no fewer than seventy, because this was the number of people with Moses, as mentioned in the Qur'ān: 'And Moses chose seventy of his people'.
- that they should be no fewer than three hundred and thirteen, as this was the number of fighters in the battle of Badr, or because it was the number of the people of Ṭalūt.

All these statements, it will be seen, are no more than personal preferences that justify themselves with arguments that have nothing to do with the nature of the subject. As we have noted above, in order for the report to denote certitude, an exact number does not have to be established. Therefore, we need not take the trouble to refute these viewpoints at length or to list the discussions surrounding them found in other exhaustive books.

Al-Shaikh al-Mamaqānī said,

> All these statements are invalid, as each of these numbers is such that the required specification of certitude may be attained with it, or may fall short of it, so the number cannot be a standard for it. Al-Shahīd al-Thānī was absolutely right when he wrote the following statement in his *Bidāyah*: 'It is obvious that these differing statements arise from haphazard guesses and from any link this number may have with what is intended and with whatever it is that distinguishes any number from other numbers mentioned in the Qur'ān.' The true cause, buried in the verbose discussions of this subject, centres on ascertaining evidence and

invalidating the stipulation of an exact number.[9]

Al-ʿAllāmah al-Ḥillī said, 'What I am referring to here is the attainment of certainty or the lack of it; if it is attained, then it is *mutawātir*; and if not, then it is not.'[10]

The reporters' knowledge of the content of the report

There are three different opinions concerning the extent of this knowledge:

i. It is incumbent on each and every reporter to know the content of what he is narrating. Not every reporter of an event or incident, however, will necessarily know about this incident...and if this is the case, it is not good enough for the reporter to be speculating about it or one to report it knowingly and another to do so speculatively. This is a well-known opinion.
ii. It is allowed for reporters to report on the basis of speculation...the justification for this is that the speculations of all the reporters will cumulatively add up, thereby affording a degree of certainty and thus rendering the reports admissible as authentic evidence.
iii. It suffices for the reports of some of the reporters to stem from certain knowledge of the incident, even though the rest of them may be speculating on the content of the report. Al-Muḥaqqiq al-Qummī was of this opinion, accepting that the certitude derived from multiple successive transmission is attained by virtue of the accumulation of reports.

Let us pause here for a moment and differentiate between reports about social incidents or occurrences that are not legislative and those that are, because in this science we are investigating the transmission of *ḥadīth* by means of multiple successive transmission, and not just the concept of multiple successive transmission itself, be it in legislative or other matters.

Hence, reporters may be relating reports about incidents, such as an action of the *maʿṣūm* or the *maʿṣūm*'s tacit approval of another's action or statements.

In the first case, the reporter must have certitude about the

[9] Miqbās al-Hidāyah, vol. I, p. 114.
[10] Mabādi' al-Wūṣūl, p. 202.

incident and must transmit it with certitude rather than speculation. For example, if the narrator were to see somebody drinking a liquid in the presence of the Prophet or Imam, he must ascertain the nature of the liquid and whether the Prophet or Imam disapproved or approved of it. It would not suffice for him merely to speculate that the drink was water or that it was an intoxicant.

As regards a statement of the *maʿṣūm*, it is not that the reporter must have certitude about the significance of the content of his report, but rather that he be certain that what he is reporting is the actual speech of the *maʿṣūm*, whether word for word or in meaning. The requirement that the reporter be certain and report from personal perception confirms this, because the accumulation of reporters' speculations, even if the listener were to accept them as denoting certitude of the reports' authenticity, does not alter anything about the incident if the report was about a *maʿṣūm*'s action or approval, as has been said. Furthermore, the required condition here is the reporters' certitude, not the listener's certitude, because speculation added to speculation only amounts to speculation in the reporter, even though it may denote certitude for the listener. Consequently, the listener's certitude (or any action based on it) attained from the accumulation of speculative reports does not mean that the report is *mutawātir* with a multiple successive transmission explicitly verifying that it originated from a *maʿṣūm*, as would be the case if the reporters all possessed certitude about the report.

Therefore, it is essential that the reporters have certitude that the wording of the report originated from a *maʿṣūm*, if it be a statement, and that they know the content of it, if it be an action or a tacit approval.

The reporters' basing their knowledge of the wording or content of the report on personal perception

This means that the nature of the reported matter must be perceivable by sight, hearing or any of the other five senses. Basing knowledge on reason – as, for example, in contemplating the theory of the existence of the world – cannot bring certitude because of the frequency of misgivings and mistakes that occur in relation to scientific theories.

The fulfilment of all the above conditions in each level of reporters

This means that the above conditions (namely, of multitude of reporters, their knowledge of the content of the report and their basing their knowledge on sensory perception) must be fulfilled in the first generation of reporters, then in the second, and so forth. Only then can a report attain the status of having been transmitted through a multiple successive transmission, hence *mutawātir.*

b. Conditions pertaining to the listener

That the listener be previously unaware of the report's content

The reason for this is that if he already knew the content of the report, then what he is being informed of is either the 'source of the knowledge that he himself had witnessed or something else. The first instance is tautological and thus inconceivable; and the second consists of the coming together of two similar things, which is also inconceivable.'[11]

> That no element of suspicion about or blind imitation of the mutawātir report be present in the listener's mind previously, such that it causes him reject the report and its significance.[12]

These two prerequisites are clearly not conditions that contribute towards achieving a multiple successive transmission, for which the conditions have already been cited. They are, however, obstructions that prevent the listener from apprehending the certitude of the multiple successive transmission, either because of his prior knowledge of it or because of some suspicion in his mind preventing him from believing it.

It is more appropriate, therefore, to say that these are conditions for ensuring the efficacy of the multiple successive transmission for the listener, as the certain authenticity of a *mutawātir* report, even in the absence of these two conditions, would still be safeguarded by virtue of its multiple successive transmission.

Here we must point out one more thing to clarify the difference of opinion existing among researchers – that is, the nature of the knowledge attained by the listener from the *mutawātir* report, whether it is a necessary type of knowledge or a theoretical type. This issue is essentially based on an absolutist view of the *mutawātir* report as a reliable transmission of information about social incidents.

[11] Miqbās al-Hidāyah, vol. I, p. 105.
[12] Ibid., vol. I, p. 106.

We students of *Ḥadīth*, however, investigate the certitude of a report's authenticity and the soundness of the contention that its origin was a *maʿṣūm*, not its significance and purport, because delving into significances and purports of things, even if they are self-evident things (such as that the whole is greater than the parts) requires at least some cultural background knowledge.

We investigate whether such-and-such a reporter is truthful in his narration of the report from the *maʿṣūm* and whether the report has originated from the *maʿṣūm*. These are facts the appraisal of which does not need any cultural background because they are not scientific concepts but social concepts that engage all humans, even though scientific points may spring from them, especially in the field of semantics.

In light of this, therefore, we can say that the knowledge that the listener attains from the *mutawātir* report is of the necessary (self-evident, spontaneous) type of knowledge, not of the theoretical (acquired, learned) type.

3. Types of *Mutawātir* Report

The *mutawātir* report can be divided into two types, the *mutawātir* by wording and the *mutawātir* by meaning.

a. The *mutawātir* by wording

This is the report that all the reporters on every level of the chain transmit with the same literal wording with which it originally issued from the one who uttered it. An example of this is the noble tradition of the Prophet (S): 'Whoever intentionally speaks falsely on my authority has taken his place in the fire.' Al-Shahīd al-Thānī said,

> We can safely assert that the tradition 'whoever intentionally speaks falsely on my authority has taken his place in the fire' has come down with a multiple successive transmission for it has been reported by such a multitude of people that the number of Companions who narrated it is said to have been forty, while some even say seventy or more, and this number is still on the increase.[13]

[13] *Al-Dirāyah*, p. 15. (Page numbers for *al-Dirāyah* refer to the Arabic edition).

b. The *mutawātir* by meaning

This refers to the meaning that is arrived at from frequent repetition and reference to it in traditions of differing wordings, which are so many in number that they cannot have been fabricated, such as the traditions about the coming of the Mahdī. In spite of their different wordings, therefore, they are all based on a single common denominator or a certain decree.

From examination and study of *ḥadīth* source material, we can see that the traditions that are *mutawātir* in their wording are very few indeed, and most of the traditions that are described as being *mutawātir* are *mutawātir* in meaning. Al-Shahīd al-Thānī said, 'Multiple successive transmission is achieved in fundamental legal rulings, such as the obligatory nature of the daily prayers, the number of units in them, *zakāt* (alms tax) and *ḥajj* (pilgrimage).'[14] The multiple successive nature of their transmission is determined by their meaning rather than their wording, inasmuch as the reports indicating a single meaning resemble each other.

The attainment of a multiple successive transmission in traditions reported exactly word for word is scarce, owing to the incongruence between the two ends and the middle of the transmission. Their meaning, however, has come down with a multiple successive transmission, such as reports testifying to Imam ʿAlī (A)'s bravery or Ḥātim's generosity or other such personal reports. Each individual tradition reporting that ʿAlī (A) killed so-and-so or achieved such-and-such is not *mutawātir*, nor is a report indicating that Ḥātim gave away so many horses and camels and spears. However, the common significance (of Imam ʿAlī's bravery or Ḥātim's generosity) behind these reports is *mutawātir* and is achieved through the unanimity of all the individual solitary (*āḥād*) reports.

The reports laid down by al-Shaikh al-Murtaḍā al-Anṣārī and his followers as being *mutawātir*, whether they are literally worded or not, have also come down in this manner; as there is no doubt that each of those reports is *āḥāḍ*. He has indicated this in *Masāʾil al-Tabāyunāt.*

No report that has allegedly attained multiple successive transmission has been proven to be so until now; indeed, Ibn al-Ṣalāḥ

[14] Ibid., pp. 14–15.

said that if someone was asked to give an example of it, his futile quest for it would exhaust him, in spite of the multitude of the narrators of the report, both old and modern, and in spite of their spreading to all the regions of the earth. Al-Shahīd al-Thānī said that the tradition '*Actions are to be done with intentions*' is not *mutawātir*, even though the number of people who have transmitted it exceeds the amount required for it to be considered *mutawātir* by several times and all the scholars in the world are narrating it today. The reason for this is that there are now additional reporters interposed in the chain to those present in the beginning, where originally it had been narrated by a set number of people only, together with those who acknowledged the fact that it was a solitary (*āḥād*) report.

Most of the reports claimed as *mutawātir* are of this type, where the one who asserts them as such looks only at the attainment of the multiple successive transmission during his time period or the one preceding his, without investigating all time periods. Were he to take a balanced look throughout the ages, he would find not only that the report was non-existent in most of them but also that a fabricated tradition had probably become *mutawātir* through successive repetition, even though the conditions for the attainment of multiple successive transmission were missing at its outset.

4. Legitimacy of the *Mutawītir* Report

What is meant by this title is whether the *mutawātir* tradition can be considered valid legal evidence, admissible as a source and a reliable basis in the field of legal reasoning, and from which legal ruling can be deduced.

The legitimacy of the multiple successive transmission has not been researched within the science of the principles of jurisprudence specifically for its use as certitude, as it has been incorporated within the study of 'legitimacy of certitude'.

What is meant by certitude here is certain knowledge, as in al-ʿAllāmah al-Ḥillī's description of it, as mentioned above; or definiteness and decisiveness as expressed by the legal historians.

Knowledge or certitude of this class – being the highest possible class – in its true essence means the exposition of truth for the legally responsible person.[15] And when this person uses the means of independent jurisprudential investigation (*ijtihād*) and legal reasoning, he does so in order to adopt thereby a way to the truth, to expose it so that he may come to know the required legal ruling; such that when the truth is exposed in front of him, he does not need to use any other means to aid him in uncovering the truth.

This means that when the multiple successive transmission denotes certitude that the report originated from the *maʿṣūm*, it becomes itself a tenet for the authenticity of the report and the soundness of its origin's being a *maʿṣūm*, which in turn means that there is no need to furnish further evidence to prove this.

This is where the legitimacy of the multiple successive transmission and its significance as a legal source comes in, which scholars have expressed by their use of the phrase '*tawātur* (multiple successive transmission) is an authority', by which they unanimously understand and intend what we have just explained above.

[15] Termed in Arabic *mukallaf*: one who has reached the Islamic legal age of maturity and thus has become responsible for performing Islamic duties.

CHAPTER SEVEN

THE ĀḤĀD REPORT

Traditions are divided into two basic categories: *mutawātir*[1] (multiple successive) and *āḥād*[2] (solitary). In this chapter, the *āḥād* report will be discussed.

1. Definition

We can categorize the various definitions given for the solitary report as follows:

> Definitions stating that the solitary report is any report in which multiple successive transmission has not been attained, whether it has one reporter in its chain or more than one.

The scholars who have defined it as such are al-Shahīd al-Thānī in his Dirāyah,[3] al-Shaikh al-Māmaqānī in Miqbās,[4] al-Shaikh al-Muẓaffar in Uṣūl al-Fiqh,[5] al-Sayyid Maʿrūf in al-Dirāsāt,[6] and others.

> That the solitary report is any report that cannot denote certitude by virtue of itself. Al-Shaikh al-Subḥānī has given this definition in his *Uṣūl al-Ḥadīth wa Aḥkāmuhu.*[7]

[1] *Mutawātir*: a tradition from the Prophet (S) or an infallible Imām, repeatedly and widely narrated in an uninterrupted sequence, through successive reliable narrators. In the absence of a single English word to express this very specific meaning, I will continue to refer to this type of multiple successive tradition as *mutawātir.*

[2] *Āḥād* or *khabar al-wāḥid*: Although termed 'solitary report', this refers to any report that is not *mutawātir*. We will hereafter refer to this as a 'solitary report'.

[3] P. 15.

[4] Vol. I, p. 125.

[5] Vol. II, p. 69.

[6] P. 40.

[7] P. 34.

> The definition combining the first two, that the solitary report is a report that has not attained multiple successive transmission, whether its reporters are many or few in number, and that cannot denote certitude by virtue of itself. This is al-Shaikh al-ʿĀmilī's definition of it in *Maʿālim al-Dīn.*[8]

> That the solitary report is a report that denotes speculation, even though its reporters are many. This is al-ʿAllāmah al-Ḥillī's definition in *Mabādiʾ al-Uṣūl.*[9]

If we try to compare all these definitions, we find that the first category is the result of using 'not' and is a logical negation of a proposition, whereby when we give a definition, we are at the same time giving the definition of its opposite simply by adding 'not' to the first. By defining the *mutawātir* report, we have no need to define the solitary report further than saying that it is 'not *mutawātir*', or 'it is that to which the definition of *mutawātir* does not apply'. Therefore, it is the report transmitted by one reporter or more, such that the possibility of the reporters' forging it is *not* conventionally impossible.

The second category is based on negating the main quality that the *mutawātir* report has, which is that it denotes certitude of its own authenticity by virtue of itself. Therefore, the solitary report – being 'not *mutawātir*'- is that which cannot denote certitude by itself.

The category combining the two definitions takes the best of both definitions to differentiate between the two types of report.

For the fourth category, which is al-ʿAllāmah al-Ḥillī's definition, we may need to add a stipulation so that the definition incorporates the two different types of solitary report that exist, namely the unlinked solitary report, which denotes speculation, and the solitary report linked to associated proof of its authenticity, thereby denoting certitude itself. The necessary stipulation for defining these is: 'it can denote valid speculation or certitude with the aid of associated proof'. With this added stipulation, we can adopt any of these definitions, as they can all be applied to the meaning of the solitary report.

2. Types of Solitary Report

There are two main types of solitary report. They are the linked and

[8] P. 342.
[9] P. 203.

the unlinked, or as some people call them, the supported and unsupported, or the furnished and the unfurnished with associated proofs (*qarāʾin*).[10]

a. The linked solitary report

The solitary report was defined previously as one that does not denote certitude of its authenticity by virtue of itself, and can only denote such when it is linked to associated proof that helps to confirm its authenticity and the soundness of its origination from a *maʿṣūm*. Al-Shaikh al-Mufīd has defined it in *Uṣūl al-Fiqh*[11] as follows: 'The decisive solitary report is that to which some kind of proof is linked informing the observer that the reporter is of sound repute'. Al-Shaikh al-Ṭūsī has defined it in the introduction to *al-Istibṣār* as follows: 'That which is not *mutawātir* is divided into two types: the first is a report that denotes certitude by being linked to associated evidence proving its authenticity.'

There are numerous associated proofs that may aid in confirming the authenticity of a solitary report and the soundness of its origin:

i. Those cited by al-Shaikh al-Mufīd in accordance with his definition. This evidence could be

- a logical proof
- a testimony of customary practice
- or a unanimous consensus.

ii. Those cited by al-Shaikh al-Ṭūsī in accordance with his definition. They may:

- be logical proofs
- correspond with the text of the Qurʾān
- correspond with definitive Sunnah
- correspond with what the Muslims unanimously agree on
- correspond with the unanimous agreement of a truthful party of people.

[10] *Qarāʾin* (sing. *qarīnah*): external evidence linked to a report that proves the soundness of its origin.

[11] P. 41.

iii. Those cited by al-Ḥurr al-ʿĀmilī in the conclusion of *al-Wasāʾil*, entitled 'Eighth Supplement: Exposition of Proofs Associated with the Report'. He begins this supplement by citing the renowned scholars' definition of an associated proof, namely some proof that is separate from the actual report, but is admitted to confirm its authenticity.

He divides such proofs into three types: a) Something that proves that the origin of the report is a *maʿṣūm*, b) something that proves the authenticity of the content of the report, and c) something that proves the preponderance of the report above a report contradicting it.

He goes on to enumerate them in general, listing the same proofs mentioned by al-Shaikh al-Ṭūsī with a few additions, the most important of which are:

- that the reporter is of honest repute, such that it is certain that he would not normally lie; this would serve to ascertain the authenticity of the report and the soundness of its origin
- the existence of the report in a unanimous book of *ḥadīth* or in a book by a reliable authority
- the existence of the report in one of the four canonical *ḥadīth* collections
- the existence of the report in a book by an authority in legal consensus
- frequent repetition of the report in numerous authorized books
- the absence of any report contradicting it.

All of these are logical proofs, some of which are to do with verifying the content of the report, such as correspondence with the Qurʾān or definitive Sunnah; while others are to do with verifying the chain of transmission, such as the report's existence in a book by an authority of reliable repute or legal consensus.

For this reason, they are established as a result of independent jurisprudential investigation, which a jurist may decide upon according to his individual legal judgement. Hence, a report may denote certitude to some and not to others, owing to differences in their individual legal investigations and the outcomes resulting thereof. This is probably why some scholars are of the opinion that the solitary report cannot, under any circumstances, denote certitude, whether it is linked to associated proofs or not.

Al-ʿAmilī said,

> The solitary report is that which does not attain the level of multiple successive transmission, whether its reporters are many or few in number; and it does not denote certitude by itself. It may, however do so with the aid of combined proofs supporting it; although some people claim that, even then, it cannot denote certitude. The first opinion is more correct.[12]

The most accepted and most widespread opinion is that the solitary report can be associated with proofs that ascertain its authenticity and the soundness of its origin. This issue relates to societal aspects of life, which is clearly the determining factor of this widespread opinion.

Al-Shaikh al-Subḥānī says,

> There is much debate surrounding its use to denote certitude, which is to no avail, for it is as if the disputers are detached from the social circumstances that face us every day, and many a report is supported by associated proofs, as a result of which it becomes a substantiated report that no one doubts.[13]

Legitimacy of the linked solitary report

Whatever we have said with regard to the legitimacy of using the *mutawātir* report to ascertain its origin as a valid source of legislation applies here equally, and for the same reason, namely that the linked solitary report also denotes certitude, and certitude is inherently authoritative.

Al-Shaikh al-Mufīd says in his *Uṣūl al-Fiqh*,

> Authoritative proof in traditions is what is denoted by the certitude attained from analysing the validity of the reporter, by removing any doubt and suspicion about him. Any report that does not attain validity about the genuineness of its reporter does not have any authority in religion and cannot obligate any action. The reports that denote certitude through analysis are of two types. The first is the *mutawātir* report, whose fabrication without collusion or agreement thereon is impossible, and the second is the solitary report linked to proofs on which the *mutawātir* is based, for establishing the genuineness of its own reporters and eliminating any falsehood or

[12] Maʿālim al-Dīn, p. 342.
[13] Uṣūl al-Ḥadīth wa Aḥkāmuhu, p. 35.

suspicion about them.[14]

Al-Shaikh al-Ṭūsī, in the introduction to *al-Istibṣār*, says, 'That which functions in this manner, therefore, obligates action too, just like the first type [the *mutawātir*]'.

Al-Shaikh al-Muẓaffar in his *Uṣūl al-Fiqh*,[15] says,

> There is no doubt that such a report is an authority. There is no need then to investigate it further, for when it can denote certitude it has attained the highest degree of demonstrative power, as there is no further level to be attained beyond certitude, and the demonstrative power of every authority leads up to that.

b. The unlinked solitary report

Definition

The definition of the unlinked solitary report becomes clear from the definitions of the *mutawātir* report and the linked solitary report. An unlinked solitary report is a report that neither attains the level of multiple successive transmission, nor is it linked to associated proofs that aid it in ascertaining the soundness of its origin. The most that this report can be used for, if the respective conditions of authenticity are fulfilled in its chain, is speculation that its origin is a *maʿṣūm*.

Legitimacy

The scholars of the principles of jurisprudence have raised the question of its authority and the legitimacy of action following such a report, because acting and relying upon speculation is legally prohibited unless proof of its legitimacy has been furnished.

Al-Shaikh al-Ṭūsī says in *ʿUddat al-Uṣūl*,[16]

> If one were to act upon a solitary report, he would do so if there were a proof indicating the obligation to act upon it, either from the Qurʾān or from the Sunnah or from legal consensus, for then he would not be acting without certitude.[17]

[14] P. 40.
[15] Vol. II, p. 69.
[16] Vol. I, p. 44.
[17] Al-Muẓaffar, *Uṣūl al-Fiqh*, vol. II, p. 69.

This issue is the subject of great controversy, with many differing opinions and ever-expanding investigation into it.

The first point of controversy we come across is the position of reason in relation to acting on the basis of the report. Ibn Qibbah (Muḥammad ibn ʿAbd al-Raḥmān al-Rāzī) was of the opinion that acting in accordance with it is logically unacceptable – in other words, that reason rejects acting in accordance with it.

Others, however, have allowed acting according to such a report. Al-Sharīf al-Murtaḍā said,

> Reason does not reject acting in accordance with *qiyās* (analogical reasoning), nor acting in accordance with a solitary report. If one were to worship Allah in accordance with such a report, it would be permissible and admissible as sound, because worshipping Him as a result of that constitutes certitude, which obligates acting according to it.[18]

After having considered the logical acceptability of worshipping in accordance with it, dispute arises about the legal permissibility of worshipping in accordance with it. Al-Shaikh al-Mufīd, al-Sayyid Murtaḍā, Abū al-Makārim ibn Zuhrah, al-Qāḍī ibn al-Barāj, al-Ṭabarsī and Ibn Idrīs all held the opinion that it is not authoritative and that it is not legally permissible to act in accordance with it. Al-Shaikh al-Mufīd said, 'When a solitary report is devoid of any decisive proof establishing its authenticity, it is not authoritative, and it cannot impose knowledge or action under any circumstance.'[19]

Al-Sharīf al-Murtaḍā said,

> It is essential that there be a means of arriving at certitude in legal rulings...For this reason, action in accordance with solitary reports is invalid in Islamic law, because they cannot impose knowledge or action; and action has to be carried out in accordance with certitude. Even if a solitary report is adequate, the most it can constitute is speculation about its own authenticity, and a reporter whose honesty is the subject of mere speculation could well be a liar.[20]

Other scholars, who form a large majority, believe that worshipping

[18] Ibid., p. 70.
[19] Uṣūl al-Fiqh, p. 41.
[20] Ibid., p. 70.

in accordance with it is legally permissible because of existing evidence supporting this, the most important of which is:

i. Allah's statement in the Qur'ān: 'If a corrupt person comes to you with any news, ascertain the truth lest you harm people unwittingly and afterwards come to regret what you have done.'

> It tells us, in other words, that the nature of news is such that, when they are informed of it, it is appropriate and natural for people to believe in it and act upon it, and it is also in their nature to do so. If this were not the case, then taking news from a corrupt person would not have been condemned specifically on the grounds of his corruptness. Here Allah urges believers to take heed not to trust every report that comes to them from any source, and if a corrupt person brings it, not to accept it without careful consideration. It is essential that they ascertain the truth lest they harm people unwittingly, i.e. because of any foolishness or lack of wisdom it may contain.
>
> The key point here is that the corrupt person is expected to be dishonest in his report, which, therefore, must not be believed and acted upon. According to this concept, the verse insinuates that the report of a reliable person is expected to be true, and there is no need for ascertainment or caution against harming people unwittingly. Therefore, this inevitably renders it authoritative.[21]

ii. The report of ʿAbd al-ʿAzīz ibn al-Muhtadī on the authority of al-Imām al-Riḍā (A), saying:

> I said: 'I am hardly ever able to come to you to ask you everything I need to know about religious practices. So is Yūnus ibn ʿAbd al-Raḥmān a reliable person from whom I can accept information about religious practices?' He (A) said, 'Yes'.[22]

Al-Shaikh al-Anṣārī said,

> We can clearly see from the report that accepting the statement of a reliable person was an established matter and was taken for granted by the narrator, as he was asking about the reliability of

[21] Ibid., p. 73.
[22] Al-Wasāʾil: Characteristics of the Judge.

> Yūnus in order to determine that he could accept his sayings.[23]

The great number of traditions of this type has reached the level of multiple successive transmission in their meaning; i.e. to the extent that the report of a reliable person can be accepted.

Common sense

Al-Shaikh al-Muẓaffar says,

> It is a decisive fact – which doubt cannot cloud over – that it is in the nature of all sensible people to see their practical conduct, regardless of their individual inclinations and experiences, in accordance with the report of one whose statement they trust and of whose honesty they are convinced and who they are certain would not lie; and even for conveying their own aims, they depend upon reliable persons.
>
> The practical conduct of Muslims, like everybody else, functions in the same way, namely, that they have sought to utilize legal rulings from history, because they are together on the same path with the rest of humankind, and in matters other than legal rulings, they behave as sensible people.
>
> If the conduct of sensible people, including Muslims, in accepting the solitary report of a reliable person has been established, then the venerable lawgiver also treads that path with them, being not only one of them but at the very head of them. Therefore, we inevitably know that he has also adopted this logical, sensible path like everybody else, so long as we are not aware of any other invented means of his own that he uses for deducing rulings apart from the logical means; for if he did have some special means that he had invented other than that, he would have informed people of it, it would have become evident and the Muslim way of conduct would be different from that of the rest of humankind.

This is definitive proof that doubt cannot pervade, because it is made up of two decisive premises:

- The fact that the nature of sensible people causes them to rely upon and accept the report of a reliable person.
- The fact that the lawgiver also conforms to this same nature and

[23] Al-Muẓaffar, *Uṣūl al-Fiqh*, vol. II, p. 83.

> behaves in the same way as sensible people, leading the same way of life as they do.[24]

Al-Shaikh al-Nāʾīnī is quoted in the accounts of his student al-Kāẓimī to have said,

> The method used by sensible people is the pillar of proofs, because even if there is room for argument in other proofs, there is definitely no room for it in their debates when it comes to the logical, sensible method furnished here, as evidence for relying upon and trusting the report of a reliable person.[25]

Al-Shaikh al-Khāqānī said,

> In any case, the validity of the report that comes from a reliable source has been established in every age and generation, through the furnishing of proofs from the *mutawātir* reports, to ascertain its authoritativeness for acts of worship and conventional customary practices of people.[26]

From this controversy about the authority of unlinked solitary reports stems a second point of difference from the legal perspective, to do with the solitary reports of reliable persons mentioned in the books of our esteemed scholars. Some people hold that they are not authoritative unless they are linked solitary reports, where they then denote certitude; and action in accordance with them is allowed and has been carried out, as we can clearly see from the scholars' various legal deductions from them in their books and studies. Others, however, hold that these reports are authoritative in their appropriateness for deducing legal rulings, if the conditions stipulated for proving their conjectured origination from a *maʿṣūm* are fulfilled.

A third point of controversy stems from this, namely, that some people consider the aforementioned reports to be linked solitary reports. Given that a valid tradition is one that denotes certitude, the only valid traditions according to these people are *mutawātir* reports and linked solitary reports. They refer to these as 'authentic'. Similarly, they consider the traditions that denote certitude of their origination from a *maʿṣūm* – whether they denote speculation or less

[24] Ibid., vol. II, pp. 91–92.
[25] Vol. III, p. 69.
[26] *Anwār al-Wasāʾil*, vol. I, pp. 5–6.

than that – to be 'invalid' traditions, which they also term 'weak'. This is summarised in Figure 3 and Figure 4.

Others, however, are of the opinion that these reports constitute both traditions that denote certitude as well as those that do not, as demonstrated in Figure 5 and Figure 6.

Figure 3: A summary of traditions as they relate to certitude.

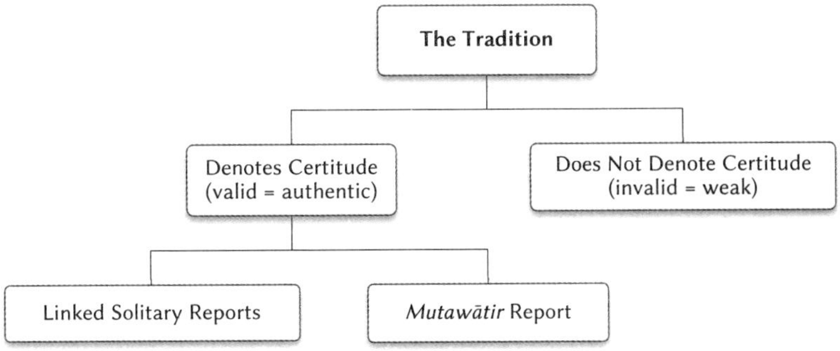

Figure 4: Another way of summarising Figure 3.

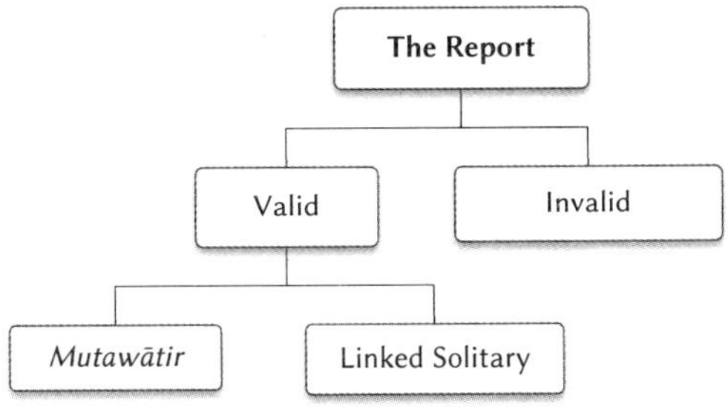

Figure 5: A different summary of traditions as they relate to certitude.

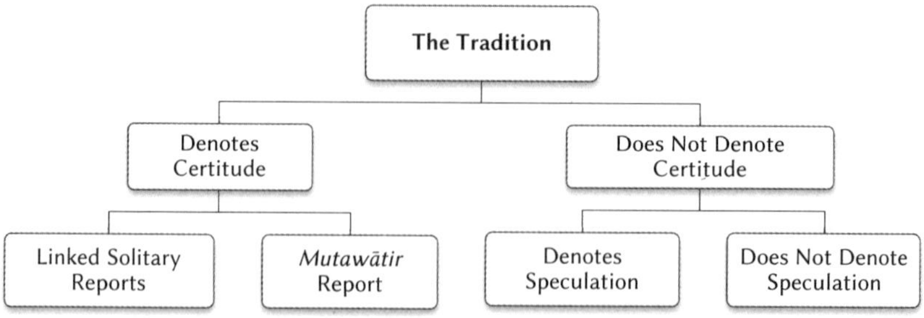

Figure 6: Another way of summarising Figure 5.

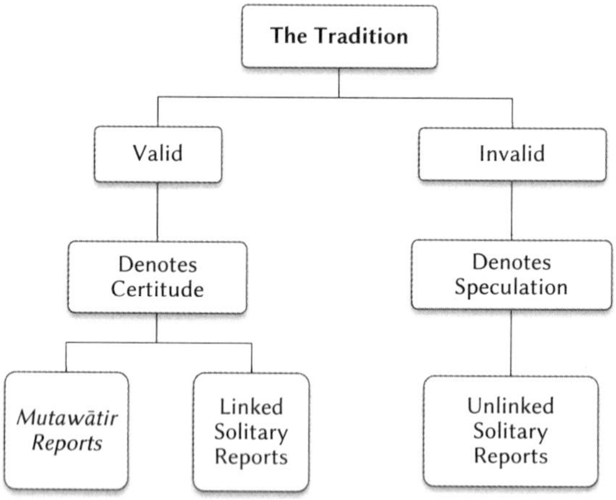

Al-Shaikh al-Ṭūsī was one of the first people who, by virtue of his study of reports in his book entitled *'Uddat al-Uṣūl*, made it possible to deduce this categorization of reports. He was also one of the first people to legally permit carrying out acts of worship in accordance with the unlinked solitary report, saying in his book,

> I am of the opinion that the solitary report does not denote certitude, even though it is allowed to worship in accordance with it as a result of logical implementation. It is permissible to act upon the report legally, provided that it is founded on a specific method of transmission, in which the narrator adheres to

> the true school of thought, is competent in his narration, and possesses the necessary attributes of reliability and honesty to render his report credible.[27]

This stance conflicts with the opinions of his two teachers, al-Mufīd and al-Murtaḍā. But, thanks to the proofs he cited his book, which he used to support his opinion concisely and in detail, his opinion triumphed over his teachers' opinions, became renowned amongst the scholars and gained predominance in the Shīʿa intellectual milieu.

In the seventh century, when the Islamic seminary at al-Ḥillah was established and began to contribute actively towards the publications of works in the various fields of Islamic learning taught in the Shīʿa seminaries, such as biographical studies – of which the jurists were in great need for exercising their independent legal reasoning – al-Sayyid Jamāl al-Dīn Aḥmad ibn Ṭāwūs al-Ḥillī composed his work *Ḥall al-Ishkāl fī Maʿrifat al-Rijāl* (*Resolving Ambiguity in Biographical Studies*).

The insight he gained into the circumstances of reporters from his investigations in this book allowed him to condense and categorize these circumstances in such a way that the chains of transmission could subsequently be classified according to the circumstances of their narrators. Reporters were classified as follows:

i. veracious *imāmī*
ii. commendable *imāmī*
iii. non-*imāmī* but dependable
iv. of weak bearing or unknown.

He gathered that the possible circumstances of reporters were limited to these, and thus came to the conclusion that a chain of transmission could be such that:

i. all its reporters are veracious *imāmīs*
ii. all its reporters are *imāmīs*, but some are veracious and the rest commendable
iii. among its reporters are veracious and commendable *imāmīs* as well as dependable non-*imāmīs*
iv. it includes weak or unknown persons.

[27] Vol. I, p. 290.

Based on this, he set about classifying chains of transmission into four categories, which he termed authentic (*ṣaḥīḥ*), good (*ḥasan*), dependable (*muwaththaq*) and weak (*ḍaʿīf*). This classification is convenient, from a practical point of view, permitting easy assessment of the reporters in the chain and subsequent evaluation of the chain. This was probably al-Sayyid ibn Ṭāwūs's goal and what his student al-ʿAllāmah al-Ḥillī also thought important.

All the scholars of the Uṣūlī school of jurisprudence who came after these two continued to use this method; whereas the scholars of the Akhbārī school continued with the two-part classification of reports as illustrated above. This legal state of affairs continued until the Akhbārī studies stopped altogether because of Uṣūlī domination in the Shīʿa centres of knowledge and in the intellectual discussions resulting therefrom. The old school advocating the two-part classification of reports became merely a circumstance to be remembered in the study of history, allowing the development of biographical and *Ḥadīth* sciences.

Types

If we look back at the history of Islamic law to find out when *Ḥadīth* studies were laid down as a science in Sunni scholarship, and when they were laid down in Shīʿa scholarship –this is usually indicated by the first book written on the subject – we find that the first book of the Ahl al-Sunnah to be written on *ḥadīth* terminology, as they refer to it, was *al-Muḥaddith al-Fāṣil Bayna al-Rāwī wa al-Wāʿī* by al-Qāḍī Abī Muḥammad Ḥasan ibn ʿAbd al-Raḥmān ibn Khallād al-Rāmahurmuzī (d. 360 AH). We mentioned previously that the oldest Shīʿa book to be written in this field was *Sharḥ Uṣūl Dirāyat al-Ḥadīth* by al-Sayyid ʿAlī ibn ʿAbd al-Karīm ibn ʿAbd al-Ḥamīd al-Najafī al-Nīlī, an eighth-century scholar.

This means that the Ahl al-Sunnah were chronologically the first to write about *Ḥadīth* studies. The reason for this is that they rely primarily on traditions transmitted by the Companions, the last of whom lived until the end of the first century; and the Followers and those who came after them, who lived up until the end of the third century. Upon the death of these generations, the associated proofs on which scholars relied to determine the authenticity of the *ḥadīth* were found to be greatly deficient, and they needed more than ever to lay down principles and regulations to ensure the authenticity of the *ḥadīth*. They set about this task at the beginning of the fourth century.

Because the Shīʿa's contact with the Imams did not come to an end until the last part of the fourth century, they relied upon books of *ḥadīth* that had been written in the lifetime of the Imams. These sourcebooks continued to exist alongside the associated proofs for determining the authenticity of *ḥadīth* until the time of al-Muḥaqqiq al-Ḥillī (d. 676 AH) when they were lost. Again there was a lack of associated proofs and an urgent need arose in Shīʿa scholarship to lay down the principles of *Ḥadīth* studies.

It is a historical fact that the latter always makes use of the experiences of the former, both methodologically and technically; and this is true of al-Shahīd al-Thānī's book *al-Dirāyah*, which is the oldest extant book on the science of *Ḥadīth* and which was influenced methodologically and technically by *ḥadīth* works of Sunni scholars. This influence led him to include categories of *ḥadīth* that have no basis in our *ḥadīth*, like some categories of 'weak' reports. Even though he retained these Sunni influences, his contribution to the field was remarkable for he included other categories present in ours which they do not have, such as the *qawī* ('strong') and the *muḍmar* ('ambiguous'). All those who came after him followed in his footsteps.

In Figure 7, I have presented only what exists in our *ḥadīth* and has been cited in books of deductive jurisprudence.

3. The *Musnad* (Supported) Tradition

a. Definition

The *musnad* ('supported') tradition contains all the names of its reporters in its chain. In other words, it has a complete and consecutive chain of transmission.

An example of this is a tradition quoted by al-Shaikh Ibn Idrīs in his book *Mustaṭrafāt al-Sarā'ir*,[28] extracted from the book of Abān ibn Taghlib al-Kūfī who records:

[28] P. 39.

> al-Qāsim ibn ʿUrwah al-Baghdādī related to me on the authority of ʿUbayd ibn Zurārah, who said, ʿI asked Abū ʿAbdallah (A): What is your opinion on killing small ants?' He (ʿUbayd) said: ʿHe (A) replied: You can kill them, whether they harm you or not.'

Most of the traditions in our books are 'supported' traditions, especially those found in older books.

Figure 7: The solitary report. The terms in this diagram will be explained in this chapter.

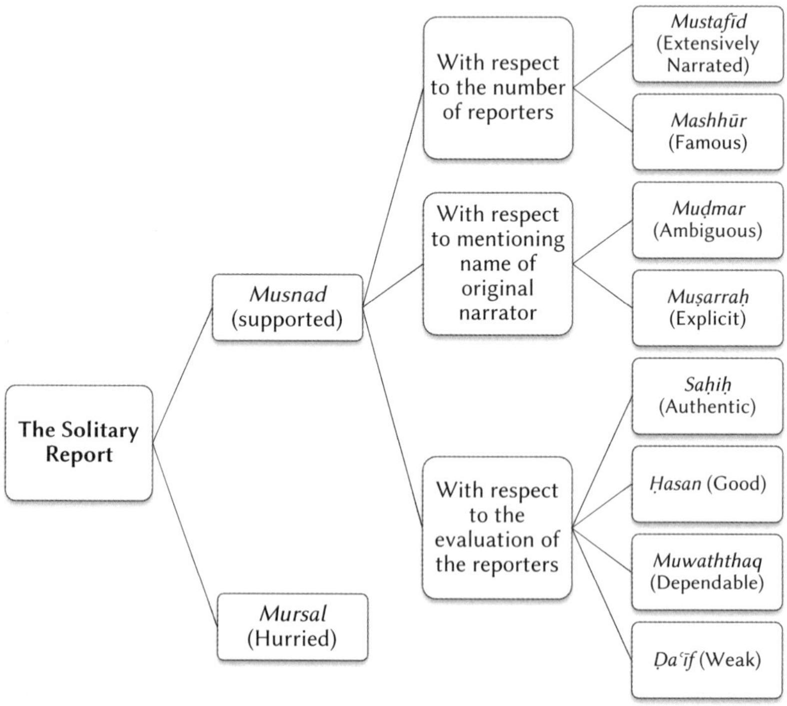

b. The *Muʿallaq* (Suspended) Tradition

A sub-category of the 'supported' tradition is a tradition termed *muʿallaq* ('suspended'), in which the names of one or more of the reporters in its chain have been omitted. This is the case with most of the chains of transmission quoted by al-Shaikh al-Ṣadūq in his book *Man Lā Yaḥḍuruhu al-Faqīh* and al-Shaikh al-Ṭūsī in his two books *al-*

Tahdhīb and *al-Istibṣār*. Both scholars intentionally omitted the first few reporters in the chain, referring back to their reliable sources whom they listed and mentioned at the end of the book. They both did this in order to avoid repetition and achieve conciseness.

Al-Shaikh al-Māmaqānī says in this regard,

> Most of the traditions in *Man Lā Yaḥḍuruhu al-Faqīh*, *al-Tahdhīb* and *al-Istibṣār* are such that the authors of these books (i.e. al-Ṣadūq and al-Ṭūsī) have omitted a sentence from the beginning of the chain of authorities. Both of them have explained and listed the names of the omitted reporters saying, 'That which I narrate from x, I am actually narrating from z, on the authority of y, on the authority of x.'[29]

They did this because the omitted (suspended) part of the chain was established and known as referring to reliable authorities, which were duly mentioned. Hence, the 'suspended' narration is included under the 'supported' narration.

An example of this is the following tradition quoted by al-Shaikh al-Ṣadūq in *Man Lā Yaḥḍuruhu al-Faqīh*:[30]

> ʿAmmār ibn Mūsā al-Sābāṭī asked Abū ʿAbdallah al-Ṣādiq (A) about the permissibility of performing dry ablution in the place of ritual ablution (*wuḍūʾ*) and obligatory purification (*ghusl*) after sexual intercourse and during menstruation. He (A) said, 'Yes'.

When we refer back to the list of reliable authorities at the end of the fourth volume of *Man Lā Yaḥḍuruhu al-Faqīh*, we find the following on the first page:

The author of this book, Muḥammad ibn ʿAlī ibn al-Ḥusayn ibn Mūsā ibn Bābawayh al-Qummī says:

> All that I narrate as being from ʿAmmār ibn Mūsā al-Sābāṭī I have actually narrated from my father and Muḥammad ibn al-Ḥasan ibn Aḥmad ibn al-Walīd, on the authority of Saʿd ibn ʿAbdallah, on the authority of Aḥmad ibn al-Ḥasan ibn ʿAlī ibn Faḍāl, on the authority of ʿAmr ibn Saʿīd al-Madāʾinī, on the authority of Muṣaddiq ibn Ṣadaqah, on the authority of ʿAmmār ibn Mūsā al-Sābāṭī.

[29] *Al-Miqbās*, vol. I, p. 215.
[30] Al-Aʿlamī's edition, vol. I, p. 72, no. 216.

If we repeated the whole chain of reliable authorities that he has just mentioned and added it to the beginning of the tradition quoted above, the chain would be as follows:

> On the authority of my father and Muḥammad ibn al-Ḥasan ibn Aḥmad ibn al-Walīd, on the authority of Saʿd ibn ʿAbdallah, on the authority of Aḥmad ibn al-Ḥasan ibn ʿAlī ibn Faḍāl, on the authority of ʿAmr ibn Saʿīd al-Madāʾinī, on the authority of Muṣaddiq ibn Ṣadaqah, on the authority of ʿAmmār ibn Mūsā al-Sābāṭī, who asked Abū ʿAbdallah al-Ṣādiq (A)...

c. Categories of 'Supported' Tradition

The 'supported' tradition is divided into three categories, with respect to the various components of the chain that are taken into consideration, as shown in the chart above.

The First Category

This is divided, with respect to the number of reporters in the chain, into two types of report: the *mustafīḍ* and the *mashhūr*.

— *The mustafīḍ (extensively narrated) report*

Mustafīḍ literally means 'abundant' or 'exhaustive', although there are two different opinions regarding its technical meaning:

- Most people hold that it is a report that has more than three reporters on each level and that has not attained multiple successive transmission.
- Some people hold that it is a report that has more than two narrators on each level and that has not attained multiple successive transmission.

— *The mashhūr (famous) report*

Again, although the literal meaning of *mashhūr* is 'famous' or 'well-known', there are two different opinions with regard to its technical meaning:

Some people say that there is no difference between this and the *mustafīḍ*, as everything that holds true as being *mustafīḍ* also holds true as being *mashhūr*.

Others say that the difference between *mashhūr* and *mustafīḍ* is that, in the *mashhūr*, it is not stipulated that the required number of reporters be attained on all its levels.

An example of this is the famous tradition 'Actions are to be done with intentions', which, in the beginning levels of the chain, is reported by too small a number of reporters to render it *mustafīḍ*, i.e. they do not make up the number required for a tradition to be *mustafīḍ*.

Al-Shahīd al-Thānī says,

> It is possible to differentiate between them – i.e. the *mustafīḍ* and the *mashhūr* – in that *mustafīḍ* can be said of whatever fulfils the requirements of the *mustafīḍ* at its beginning and end, and *mashhūr* is more flexible and broader than that.[31] The tradition 'Actions are to be done with intentions' is, therefore, *mashhūr* ['famous'] and not *mustafīḍ* ['extensive'], because it did not achieve fame until the middle generations of reporters.[32]

— *Legitimacy of the mustafīḍ and mashhūr*

Because the *mustafīḍ* and the *mashhūr* do not attain multiple successive transmission whereby they can denote certitude of their authenticity, they are not taken as authoritative unless they fulfil the conditions for authenticity (which will be explained in the section dealing with the four types of traditions).

The Second Category

The 'supported' tradition is further divided with respect to the presence or absence of the mention of the *maʿṣūm*'s name, respectively the *muṣarraḥ* ('explicit') and the *muḍmar* ('ambiguous').

— *The muṣarraḥ ('explicit')*

A report in which the name of the *maʿṣūm* on whose authority the tradition is narrated is explicitly stated. The vast majority of our traditions are of this type. It has been termed 'explicit' in contrast to its opposite, the *muḍmar*, where a personal pronoun is used instead of an omitted explicit word. (This is termed a 'metonymy'[33] by Kufan

[31] *Al-Dirāyah*, p. 16.

[32] Translator's Note: The word *mustafīḍ* implies extensiveness and abundance on all the levels, whereas *mashhūr* implies general fame and prevalence, not necessarily attained on all the levels.

[33] A metonymy is the substitution by the name of an attribute of a thing for

grammarians, its opposite being explicitness.)

— *The muḍmar ('ambiguous')*
A report in which a personal pronoun is substituted for the name of the *maʿṣūm*, such that the reporter would say, 'I asked him' or 'I heard from him' or 'on his authority' or 'he said'. An example of this is a tradition quoted in *al-Wasāʾil*.[34]

> On the authority of Samāʿah, who said, 'I asked him about the man who has a wound such that he can neither bandage it nor wash away the blood. He said, "He should pray, washing his clothing only once a day, for it would be impossible for him to wash it every hour."'

Another tradition from *al-Wasāʾil*[35] also illustrates this. 'On the authority of Samāʿah, who said, "He said, 'If a person has a doubt in the first two units of a *ẓuhr* or *ʿaṣr* prayer as to whether he has prayed one or two units, he must start his prayer again'."'

Al-Sayyid al-Gharīfī says in *Qawāʿid al-Ḥadīth*:[36] 'They [the *muḍmar* reports] constitute a large number of traditions confirmed by the classical *ḥadīth* scholars in their books.'

The most famous of these are the *muḍmar* reports of Samāʿah ibn Mahrān,[37] 'which amount to 390 reports', the *muḍmar* reports of Zurārah ibn Aʿyan, 'which amount to 78 reports',[38] the *muḍmar* reports of Muḥammad ibn Muslim al-Thaqafī and the *muḍmar* reports of ʿAlī ibn Jaʿfar.

The *muṣarraḥ* ('explicit') is also referred to as *mawṣūl* ('connected') and the *muḍmar* ('ambiguous') as *maqṭūʿ* ('disconnected').

When the large *ḥadīth* collections were being compiled, their authors embarked on a subject classification of the various traditions of a book or the paragraphs within a long tradition into chapters of jurisprudence and legal matters. They refrained from substituting the

---

the name of the thing itself, e.g: 'the crown' may be used to refer to monarch; here a personal pronoun is used to refer to the *maʿṣūm*.

[34] Vol. II, ch. 22 on Impurities.

[35] Vol. V, ch. 1 on Disturbances in the Prayer.

[36] P. 215.

[37] *Muʿjam Rijāl al-Ḥadīth*, vol. VIII, p. 294.

[38] Ibid., vol. VII, p. 247.

name of the Imam with the personal pronoun lest that be considered unlawful alteration of *ḥadīth* on their part.

Reasons for the concealed identity of the *maʿṣūm*

The scholars have given various reasons for the phenomenon of the concealed identity of the maʿṣūm in *muḍmar* reports, which they have gathered from analysing the development of traditions narrated and recorded in the ḥadīth collections, and which are as follows.

*Dissimulation (*taqiyyah*)*

Some reporters could not explicitly mention the name of the Imam because of the harsh political circumstances in which they were living under the dominance of Umayyad or Abbasid suppression and terrorism, so they used personal pronouns when referring to the Imams. This is a well-known historical fact that does not need justification or example.

Disconnection of the reports from their sources

This would occur in two instances:

1. When traditions on the authority of a specific Imam are quoted by the author in a single book, where he would mention the Imam's name at the beginning of the book. Thereafter, he would refer to him only by the personal pronoun, which, by avoiding the unnecessary repetition of the name, would allow him to be more concise and observe the rules of composition.
2. When the reporter is narrating a long tradition consisting of a large number of questions and their answers, where he would mention the name of the Imam at the beginning of the tradition, then continue by saying, 'and I asked him about...' or 'so he said...', etc.

This is explained in *al-Wasāʾil* as follows: 'Many of the classical reporters of traditions and authors of *ḥadīth* books used to transmit traditions on the authority of the Imams (A) orally, and they would quote the sum of their narrations in their books as a whole, even though the traditions consisted of different rulings. The author, at the beginning of his book, would say, 'I asked x', naming the Imam from whom he was narrating; thereafter, it would suffice for him to refer to the Imam using the personal pronoun, e.g. 'and I asked him...', until he came to the end of the reports he was quoting. There is no doubt that observing the rules of composition requires one to do that, because repetition of the name in all these places would be completely inconsistent with the text. When these traditions were subsequently quoted in other books, the name was omitted altogether and there was no reference left for the personal pronoun.'

Al-Shaikh al-Māmaqānī says in *al-Miqbās*:[39]

> The reason for the concealed identity is either dissimulation, or the disconnection of reports from their sources...as narrators used to write in the middle of their questions, 'I asked x about...then I asked him about...so he said...', etc. Then after they were disconnected from their original sources and compiled into books, they began to be doubted.

In the margin of *al-Rawḍah al-Bahiyyah*[40] is an explanatory remark about al-Shahīd al-Thānī's statement regarding the *muḍmar* tradition of Muḥammad ibn al-Muslim, the text of which is:

> His statement that 'the person questioned in the report is unknown' is not a criticism of the report, because it was customary for the Companions of the Imams (A) to mention the name of the Imam being questioned at the beginning of the narration, then to continue with 'then I asked him about...', inserting the personal pronoun instead of the name. When the *ḥadīth* scholars compiled these reports and classified them according to subject matter, they quoted them exactly as they found them in the sourcebooks, and they subsequently became disconnected.

The reporter would rely upon evidence accompanying the tradition that proved that the personal pronoun in it referred to the Imam. Then, owing to unforeseen circumstances, the evidence would be lost.

Al-Sayyid al-Gharīfī pointed out this factor in his book *Qawāʿid al-Ḥadīth*.[41]

Authoritativeness of the *muḍmar* ('ambiguous')

There are three different opinions regarding the authoritativeness of the *muḍmar* tradition and the legitimacy of referring to it as a valid source.

Opinion 1

The first opinion differentiates between the *muḍmar* report of a narrator

[39] Vol. I, p. 334.

[40] Lithographic print, vol. I, p. 141.

[41] P. 222.

who is one of the great reliable scholars, in which case his *muḍmar* report would be authoritative; and any other narrator whose report would not be authoritative. This is what the majority of people believe.

In the commentary on *al-Rawḍat al-Bahiyyah* entitled *Ḥadīqat al-Rawḍah,* there is an explanatory remark about the author's statement:

> The *disconnected* (*maqṭūʿ*) tradition of Muḥammad ibn Muslim: The *disconnected* tradition is one in which it is unknown whether its original narrator was a *maʿṣūm* or not, such as in the statement, 'I asked him'. This is also known as a *muḍmar* ('ambiguous') report. If the person who transmits it is one of the great and prominent scholars, such as Zurārah and Muḥammad ibn Muslim, then for most people this means it is authoritative, because it is a well-known fact that such people put questions to a *maʿṣūm* only; and if not, then it is not, i.e. if the reporter is not from among the great and prominent scholars then his *disconnected* report is not authoritative.

> Among those who hold this view is al-Shaikh al-Khurāsānī who, in his book *Kifāyat al-Uṣūl,*[42] comments on the *muḍmar* report of Zurārah, which he uses for legal deduction of a ruling. In it Zurārah said, 'I said to him that the man is sleeping...' He comments, 'Even though this is a *muḍmar* report, its ambiguity does not affect its validity when its reporter is someone like Zurārah, who almost never questioned anyone other than the Imam (A), especially with this degree of importance attained from repetition of the question.'

Opinion 2

The opinion that it is absolutely authoritative – whether the reporter is a great prominent scholar or whether he is simply a reliable authority; on condition that the report fulfils all the other prerequisites of authenticity.

This is the opinion of al-Shaikh al-Hasan al-ʿĀmilī, author of *Maʿālim al-Dīn,* whom al-Shaikh al-Baḥrānī quotes in his *al-Ḥadāʾiq*[43] in the course of demonstrating the legal deduction of a ruling exempting blood in the prayer. 'The second of the two [methods] constitutes the aforementioned *ḥasan* 'good' report from Muḥammad ibn Muslim used by the Shaikh, and the report of Ismāʿīl al-Juʿfī.' He goes on to refute this in *al-Mukhtalif,*

[42] Annotated by al-Sayyid al-Ḥakīm, vol. II, pp. 400–401.
[43] Vol. V, pp. 311–12.

saying that Muḥammad ibn Muslim did not ascribe this report to the Imam (A), even though he was reputed to solicit reports from the Imams only, and that the report that he himself mentioned, i.e. the tradition of Ibn Abī Yaʿfūr, has no cause for suspicion in it.

Al-Shaikh Ḥasan is to be congratulated for refuting this so excellently in *al-Maʿālim*, saying,

> The counter-attack on the second method is under consideration, as experience in the field shows that the reason for concealing the identity of the Imam in reports was that traditions were interconnected in early books narrating on the Imams' authority; and it was common for several traditions on different legal rulings to be found transmitted together from a single Imam without any breaks between them necessitating the repetition of the Imam's name. So the scholars, in order to be concise, referred to them by personal pronouns. Then when these reports were detached from their sourcebooks and transferred to larger compilations, they became open to doubt. This may be attributed to the compiler's negligence; if that is not the reason, however, it is even more pertinent that modern scholars consider these carefully, as they are unacquainted with the contents of the sourcebooks. Ease of expression is perhaps a palatable explanation, though in fact after detachment from their sourcebooks the traditions were scattered far and wide. Upon investigation and further thought, it is clear that no person with the slightest bit of sense would transmit a tradition on a legal ruling on the authority of an anonymous person, to whom he then goes on to refer with a personal pronoun corresponding to a specific person. So what about the great scholars and companions of the Imams (A) such as Muḥammad ibn Muslim and Zurārah?

The ʿAllāmah (al-Ḥillī) would have had more reason to counter the use of this tradition for the ruling with the superior authenticity of the tradition from Ibn Abī Yaʿfūr, for that tradition surpasses Ibn Muslim's tradition in validity, so he could have used the argument that the other tradition is *ṣaḥīḥ* ('authentic') whereas Ibn Muslim's is *ḥasan* ('good').

Opinion 3

The opinion that it is absolutely not authoritative, whether the reporter of the *muḍmar* is a great and prominent scholar like Zurārah or simply another reliable reporter, because of the possibility that the personal pronoun might refer to a non-*maʿṣūm*, which is enough to render it inauthoritative.

Al-Shaikh al-Ḥasan ibn al-Shahīd al-Thānī attributed this opinion to a group of Companions. Both al-Shaikh al-Ḥasan and al-Shahīd al-Thānī preferred this. Al-Shahīd al-Thānī criticized the *muḍmar* report of Muḥammad ibn Muslim ('I asked him about a man who does not know whether he has prayed two or four units. He said, "He must start his prayer again."') as having 'an unknown original narrator', to which al-Shaikh al-Ḥasan added, 'who might well be a non-*imāmī*'.

Similarly, al-Shaikh Muḥammad Ḥasan was also of this opinion, for in his *Jawāhir* he criticizes the *ṣaḥīḥ* ('authentic') report of Muḥammad ibn Ismāʿīl ibn Bazīʿ ('A man asked him about someone who dies and leaves two brothers behind...'), saying that it is quoted as a *muḍmar* report in both *al-Kāfī* and *al-Tahdhīb* and so is not worth refuting.

The Third Category

The *musnad* ('supported') tradition is further divided with respect to the standard of the reliability or unreliability of the reporters. In other words, it is divided based on evaluating the chain of transmission in terms of its validity or invalidity into four categories: *ṣaḥīḥ* ('authentic'), *ḥasan* ('good'), *muwaththaq* ('dependable') and *ḍaʿīf* ('weak').

— *The ṣaḥīḥ ('authentic') tradition*

The word *ṣaḥīḥ* in Arabic can denote either an active or a passive meaning. It can be used to mean 'authentic' in an active sense, in which the thing described as 'authentic' itself fulfils the conditions of authenticity. And it can also be used to mean 'authenticated' in a passive sense, where the thing being described as 'authentic' has been authenticated by the scholars, according to the precepts of authenticity. Scholars often use the word 'authenticated' (*muṣaḥḥaḥ*) in the passive voice, referring, for example, to 'the *muṣaḥḥaḥ* ('authenticated tradition') of Zurārah', meaning 'the *ṣaḥīḥ* ('authentic tradition') of Zurārah'.

The lexical meaning of *ṣaḥīḥ* is true, real, actual, veritable.

Al-Shahīd al-Thānī and his son al-Shaikh al-Ḥasan, the author of *Maʿālim*, have defined the technical meaning of a *ṣaḥīḥ* tradition as 'a tradition whose chain of transmission is consecutively linked to the *maʿṣūm* through an accurate and reliable transmission on all the levels'.[44]

Therefore, the 'authentic' tradition is the 'supported' tradition that is consecutively linked from its last reporter all the way back to the *maʿṣūm* from whom the tradition originated, provided that every single reporter in every generation of the transmission is *imāmī*, veracious and accurate in his memorization and transmission of the tradition.

— The ḥasan ('good') tradition

Al-Shahīd al-Thānī, in his *Dirāyah*, has defined the *ḥasan* report as a report whose chain of transmission is consecutively linked to the *maʿṣūm* by commendable *imāmīs* whose reliability has not been affirmed, provided that this is the case on all the levels, or that some of them are commendable *imāmīs* while the rest are veracious *imāmis*.

The condition that some or all of the reporters in the chain be commendable *imāmīs* is probably what gave this category its designation *ḥasan* in the first place, as the word *ḥasan* ('good') has been given three lexical meanings by scholars: a) naturally harmonious, b) an attribute of perfection, c) praiseworthy or commendable, which is the meaning adduced here.

— The muwaththaq ('dependable') tradition

Al-Shaikh al-ʿĀmilī in his *Maʿālim*[45] has defined it as follows: 'The *muwaththaq* ("dependable") tradition is a report transmitted by someone who is not an *imāmī*, though his trustworthiness has been established by scholars'... 'It has also been termed *qawī* ("strong").'

One may differentiate between the *muwaththaq* ('dependable') and the *qawī* ('strong'), in that *muwaththaq* is specifically used to describe the type of report defined above, whereas *qawī* is the term given to a tradition transmitted by an *imāmī* who has been neither commended nor criticized in the biographical dictionaries.

Al-Shahīd al-Thānī says in his *Dirāyah*, 'The term qawī ('strong') can be given to that which is narrated by an imāmī who has been

[44] *Al-Dirāyah*, p. 19, and *al-Maʿālim*, p. 367.
[45] P. 367.

neither commended nor criticized'[46] such as Nūḥ ibn Darrāj, Nājiyah ibn ʿAmmārah al-Ṣaydāwī, Aḥmad ibn ʿAbdallah ibn Jaʿfar al-Ḥumayrī and others like them, of whom there are many.

Based on this, there are then five categories into which the traditions can be divided: authentic (*ṣaḥīḥ*), good (*ḥasan*), dependable (*muwaththaq*), strong (*qawī*) and weak (*ḍaʿīf*). The four-part categorization, however, is much more common.

This type of tradition has been termed *muwaththaq* from the word *wuthūq*, which signifies 'trust', thus the reporter is trusted in his transmission of the report. Hence, our scholars have stipulated that the dependable non-*imāmī* reporter be dependable and trusted in his transmission of the tradition, by our scholars' standards rather than just within his own school of jurisprudence.

— *The* ḍaʿīf *('weak') tradition*

This has been defined as the tradition that does not fulfil the requirements of any of the above three categories, in that its chain of transmission contains a weak or unknown reporter.

5. Authoritativeness of the Categories of Traditions

The *Ḥadīth* scholars usually investigate the authoritativeness of each of the four categories of *ḥadīth*, and express their opinions accordingly. Because these categories are the 'principles of *Ḥadīth*' – as explained previously – they are the clearest corroboration we have, for substantiating the *unlinked solitary report*, thus their authoritativeness reflects its authoritativeness. The methodology of this investigation requires the scholar to ascertain the substantive capacity of each category, by examining whether the conditions for the authoritativeness of the unlinked solitary report are fulfilled in it, and whether the proof of its authoritativeness is inclusive.

The scholars in the principles of jurisprudence have listed more than one proof for investigating the legitimacy of the unlinked solitary report. The proofs that we are concerned with here are as

[46] Pp. 23–24.

follows:

The Holy Qur'ān, especially in *ayah al-naba'* (the aforementioned verse about hearing news), whose literal wording instructs us to verify the information when hearing it from a corrupt person. From the implied meaning of this verse we can gather that there is then no need to verify the report of a veracious person.

Common sense, because of the Islamic lawgiver's confirmation and establishment of it as a reliable source; for it dictates the permissibility of relying upon the report of a trustworthy person, as well as the permissibility of believing and having confidence in its true origin.

Therefore, the object of our investigation – the authoritativeness of the four categories – can be dealt with as follows:

If we take the Qur'ānic verse as proof of the authoritativeness of the unlinked solitary report, then we are restricted to acting in accordance with the *ṣaḥīḥ* ('authentic') reports only. Such a report would be considered valid and authoritative, because it becomes the touchstone for corroborating solitary reports, in keeping with the prerequisite of veracity implied in the verse, (since a *ṣaḥīḥ* report is the only one narrated by a veracious person).

Some of the scholars who use the verse as their proof have expanded its sphere of authority to include the second category, which is the *ḥasan* ('good'), based on the idea that the very function of praise and commendation is to exclude the possibility of the reporter's being unreliable; thus the necessary conditions implied in the verse are fulfilled.

If we take common sense as proof for the authoritativeness of the report, which dictates that the dependability of the reporter and confidence in the pure origin of the report suffice for us to consider it authoritative, then the sphere of authority is further expanded to include the *muwaththaq* ('dependable') report.

If we take into account al-Shaikh al-Ṭūsī's opinion, that the veracity required of a reporter differs from the veracity of a judge, a *marja*ʿ *al-taqlīd*,[47] or a witness, because here it solely implies the meaning of 'reliability', then the sphere of authority includes all three

[47] *Marja*ʿ *al-taqlīd*: grand jurisconsult who is the most learned in the field of jurisprudence and extrapolation of legal rulings, and has the legal capacity to pronounce juristic verdicts (*fatwa*).

categories: the *ṣaḥīḥ*, the *ḥasan* and the *muwaththaq*, whether the proof one relies upon is the verse or common sense.

As for the fourth category, there is unanimous consensus that the 'rejected' *ḍaʿīf* ('weak') report is invalid and inauthoritative. However, the area in which dispute does arise between the scholars is when considering the authoritativeness of the 'acceptable' weak report, which is known in juristic terminology as *al-ḍaʿīf al-munjabar* (the 'reinforced weak' report).

According to those who do consider this type of report, 'reinforcement' is achieved by one of two ways:

i. Renown through transmission: Al-Shahīd al-Thānī has explained this, saying that, 'this is when the report has been transmitted and quoted a numerous amount of times, be it word for word or in meaning'.[48]
ii. Renown through a legal ruling: This is when jurists have relied upon the report for deducing legal rulings, have furnished it as a proof in legislation and have formed legal rulings according to its content, provided that it is renowned both in the books of deductive jurisprudence and on the lips of jurists in their research and extrapolation.

Al-Shahīd al-Thānī said, 'Most people are of the opinion that it is absolutely forbidden to act in accordance with the weak report, though others have deemed it permissible if it is backed up by its own renown in transmission and legislation.'[49]

It must be noted here that scholarly opinion and discussion restrict the renown of the report to legislation, and term it 'implementing the content of the report'. They justify this by saying that the very fact that the report has achieved renown through widespread action in accordance with it is proof that its origin was a *maʿṣūm*. Or, as al-Shahīd al-Thānī expressed it, 'The report's renown, attained through implementation of it, strengthens the speculation about the reporter, "even though the path of transmission may be weak, for a report may well be established because of the renown of its content, in spite of its weak chain of transmission."'[50]

[48] *Al-Dirāyah*, p. 27.
[49] Ibid.
[50] Ibid.

Most people are of the opinion that renown does reinforce the report, and consider the reinforced weak tradition as an authority that can be used in legislation in accordance with its content.

This is the import of al-Muḥaqqiq al-Ḥillī's statement in *al-Mu'tabar*: 'What scholars accept or what the evidence proves to be authentic can be acted upon; and what scholars reject or what lacks sufficient evidence must be discarded.'

Al-Muḥaqqiq al-Hamadānī's statement about this in *Miṣbāḥ al-Faqīh*[51] is very clear:

> There are almost no traditions to be found for which we would be able to ascertain the veracity of their reporters through accurate means, if it were not for resorting to a certain degree of leniency with respect to their path of transmission, and implementing them with unconfirmed speculations. The central pivot must be to ascertain the dependability of the reporter and the confidence in the origin of the report, even if it be by means of external evidence, i.e. that it be found in one of the Four Books, or that it be quoted from one of the *uṣūl* source collections, provided always that the scholars have a regard for it and have not rejected it... Because of all this, I personally do not investigate the circumstances of reporters, contenting myself with the fact that the report has been described as authentic by our classical scholars, who thoroughly investigated the circumstances of its reporters.[52]

Al-Shaikh al-Khāqānī's lucid statement in *Anwār al-Wasā'il* is similar: 'The essential prerequisite in authenticating and validating a chain is whatever generates confidence in its origin, even if this be the scholars' reinforcement of a weak report.'[53]

Others, however, are of the opinion that a tradition reinforced by the scholars because of their legislation in accordance with its content is inauthoritative.

Al-Shahīd al-Thānī is one of the proponents of this view, saying:

> We reject any such renown that they claim as having a reinforcing effect on the weak report, for this would hold true only if this renown was achieved before the time of al-Shaikh (i.e.

[51] Chapter of the Prayer, p. 12.
[52] Qawā'id al-Ḥadīth, p. 110.
[53] Vol. I, p. 5.

> al-Shaikh al-Ṭūsī). But this is not the case at all, for the scholars who came before him either prohibited action in accordance with the solitary report altogether, or combined all sorts of traditions without any regard whatsoever to authenticating the sound reports or rejecting the invalid ones; and any investigation into legislation by anybody other than these two groups was very scarce, as those acquainted with their circumstances will confirm. Therefore, any such legislation implementing the content of a weak report with a view to reinforcing its weakness, before al-Shaikh's time, has not been substantiated. Al-Shaikh himself gave rulings according to the content of a weak report in his books of positive law and the majority of the scholars who came after him imitated him in this regard, apart from those who dissociated themselves from him, none of whom investigated traditions and inquired into their proofs independently in the first place. The exception was al-Shaikh al-Muḥaqqiq Ibn Idrīs, and he did not permit the implementation of the solitary report at all. So when the later scholars came, they found that al-Shaikh and his followers had legislated in accordance with the content of the weak report, the cause of which they could not perceive; and may Allah excuse them for it, for they supposed this legislation to be renowned and deemed this renown as serving to reinforce the weak report. If an impartial person pondered over this matter and if a scholar revised it, they would find that all this goes back to al-Shaikh, and that the renown of a weak report is not sufficient to reinforce it.[54]

Al-Shaikh al-Māmaqānī refuted this view in *al-Miqbās*, saying,

> As for those who reject any effect of this supposed renown on the weak report, I believe that this rejection holds no ground at all; for whoever can see that the proofs for these types of reports existed in abundance at the time immediately after the Imams (A), and yet are no longer available to us now, can be certain that the implementation of the weak report has achieved renown because of its sound origin. Similarly, the impartial person will find that confidence in the reliability of the report attained through its renown is no less significant than the confidence attained through the authentication of the reporters in its chain. As regards the idea that, because the report had not yet achieved renown at al-Shaikh's time, this automatically becomes the basis

[54] *Al-Dirāyah*, pp. 27–28.

> for rejecting it, we can say as follows: if we accept the fact that there was no need for it to be substantiated through renown in his time, and that it sufficed for it to be substantiated through his and his colleagues' rulings, as long as confidence and certainty about its sound origin were central to those rulings, and if this very certainty was achieved through renown of the report after al-Shaikh's time, then there is nothing wrong with putting it on the same level as the certainty attained by al-Shaikh and those who succeeded him.[55]

Another proponent of this view (that it is inauthoritative) is al-Sayyid al-Khūʾī, followed by a significant number of his students, including al-Shaikh al-Muḥsinī.[56]

To conclude, we can say as follows. If the essential criterion is the reliability of the reporter, if this can be established, or, if not, then absolute confidence in the sound origin of the report, which is what most modern scholars believe, then the renown of the weak report does serve to reinforce it.

We can go a step further and say that, in light of this, the four-part classification of traditions serves a useful purpose in the field of preponderance among the chains of contradictory reports; whereas in the field of legal deduction and extrapolation of legal rulings based on reports, there is no difference between these classifications.

This controversy about the reinforcement of the weak report applies equally to the abandonment of the *ṣaḥīḥ* (authentic) report, which has been rejected by the scholars. So, whoever accepts the reinforced weak report must similarly abandon the *authentic* report that has been rejected by the scholars for legislation, and vice versa.

Accepting the Rejected Weak Report

The scholars all agree upon the inauthoritativeness of the rejected weak report because it does not even denote legally valid speculation about the soundness of its origin. As a result of this, they hold that it is not permissible to refer to such reports to derive legal rulings about *ḥalāl* and *ḥarām*. In other words, they hold that it is not permissible to use such reports as proofs in the deduction of legal rulings

[55] Vol. I, pp. 193–94.
[56] See *Fawāʾid Rijāliyyah*, margin of p. 110.

pertaining to *wājibāt* (obligatory acts) and *muḥarramāt* (forbidden acts).

Their opinions do, however, differ when it comes to using them for deriving rulings pertaining to *mustaḥabāt* (legally recommended acts) and *makrūhāt* (undesirable acts). Thus, if we were to come across a weak tradition that recommended the performance of an act or discouraged committing an act, in order to gain reward from Allah, then is it or is it not permissible for us to use the tradition as legal proof in support of or avoidance of that act? There are two opinions about this:

i. that it is permissible

The main justification given by the proponents of this opinion is other traditions.

Al-Ḥurr al-ʿĀmilī quotes nine such traditions in *al-Wasāʾil* (Chapter 18, under the title 'Recommendation of performing every legal act to which they (A) have accorded merits'). These traditions exceed the number required for them to be considered *mustafīḍ* ('extensively narrated'), and are *mutawātir* in meaning.

Al-Shaikh al-Anṣārī, in his treatise *On the Proofs of Leniency When Dealing with Recommended and Undesirable Acts*, when listing the proofs for the permissibility of using weak traditions towards this end, says, 'Third: The *mustafīḍ* ["extensively narrated"] reports that are likely to be *mutawātir* in meaning.'

Among such reports are some very clear 'authentic' and 'good' traditions, like:

- the authentic report of Hishām ibn Sālim, quoted by Muḥammad ibn Yaʿqūb with his chain going back to the Imams (A), that 'whoever hears about [the merits of] a good action and performs it accordingly will have the reward of whatever he has heard, even though the matter may not actually be as he has been told.'[57]
- the good report of Hishām ibn Sālim, quoted by Muḥammad ibn Yaʿqūb on the authority of ʿAlī ibn Ibrāhīm, on the authority of his father, on the authority of Ibn Abī ʿUmayr, on the authority of Hishām ibn Sālim, on the authority of Abū ʿAbdallāh (A) who said, 'Whoever hears about a meritorious thing and performs it

[57] ʿUddat al-Dāʿī, p. 12.

will have his reward, even if the matter is not actually as he has heard'.[58]

- from the Ahl al-Sunnah: that which has been transmitted by ʿAbd al-Raḥmān al-Ḥilwānī as having been narrated by Jābir ibn ʿAbdallāh al-Anṣārī, who said, 'The Prophet (S) said, "Whoever hears of an excellent quality of Allah's, and he adopts it and acts upon it according to his belief in Allah and hope for his reward, Allah grants him that reward, even if the matter is not such."'[59]

Based on these traditions, the scholars have said that there is a certain degree of leniency in reports pertaining to recommended acts, where only the weak traditions that have not been fabricated are accepted, for recommended acts and undesirable acts.

Al-Shahīd al-Thānī said,

> Most people have allowed action in accordance with the weak report for things such as stories, warnings and the merits of certain acts, but not for subjects such as the attributes of Allah or legal rulings about *ḥalāl* and *ḥarām*. This is deemed acceptable by the scholars who allow a degree of leniency in proofs pertaining to recommended acts, as long as the weakness in the report has not reached the extent of fabrication or forgery.[60]

ii. that it is not permissible

The proponents of this view have basically justified their opinion by saying that *istiḥbāb* or recommendation of an act is as much a legal command as obligation of it is; and just as we need to establish obligation through an authoritative and valid legal proof, so too we need to establish recommendation through authoritative and valid legal proof, 'for there is no cause to differentiate between them nor to content ourselves with reports from weak or unknown people. The same goes for the abomination of an act and the prohibition of an act'.

This has been countered as follows: 'Legally recommending something that pertains to a weak report does not really rely on that weak report as a basis for doing so, but rather uses the traditions

[58] Ibid., p. 13.
[59] Ibid.
[60] *Al-Dirāyah*, p. 29.

quoted in support of this.'[61]

Al-Shaikh al-Ṭarīḥī, in his book *Jāmiʿ al-Maqāl*, after quoting the traditions in favour of this, says, 'Actions, in reality, depend on what the sum of these traditions says, not what the weak report contains'.

However, the general opinion is that the legal validity of the action prescribed by the weak report must be substantiated through authentic means, by first combining these reports with the conditions of veracity in the reporter, by means of which the reward of the action can be determined, even if it is not true. Hence, legal rulings cannot be deduced absolutely and solely from this type of report.

As for those people who neither prohibit implementation of such a report nor stipulate veracity in the reporter, they base their legislation on speculation and so obviously do not consider whether the report is dubious in any way.

6. The *Mursal* ('Hurried') Report

a. Definition

Irsāl ('forwarding') lexically means 'to dispatch, release freely, hurry on'. Therefore, when it is said, 'he dispatched [*arsala*] the bird from his hand', it means that he released it so that it can fly. And when it is said, 'he hurried [*arsala*] his speech', it means that he spoke without any restraint. This is why the Arabs call prose that is free from the constraint of rhyme '*al-nathr al-mursal*', or free prose.

The tradition to which we refer here has been termed *mursal* ('hurried') because the reporter has forwarded it on freely without the constraints of a chain of transmission. Technically, the *mursal* tradition is a report in which the chain of transmission is incomplete, because either *all* or *some* of the intermediary reporters between the present narrator and the *maʿṣūm* from whom the report originated have been omitted. It is so termed provided that the name of the omitted reporter is actually unknown, since a reporter who was known and then later omitted would render the report *musnad* ('supported') and *muʿallaq* ('suspended'), not *mursal*.

Al-Shaikh al-Ṣadūq and al-Shaikh al-Ṭūsī have omitted the names

[61] *ʿUddat al-Dāʿī*, p. 13, margin.

of some or all reporters in many of the chains, in their books *al-Faqīh* and *al-Tahdhīb* respectively, in order to be concise and to avoid repetition; they have mentioned all these omitted names at the end of their books. This omission on their part does not render the traditions quoted as *mursal*, because the reporters in the chain are knowingly omitted and their names can be looked up under *Mashyakhah* at the back of the books. (These traditions are termed *muʿallaq*, as mentioned previously.)

Some examples of *mursal* ('hurried') traditions are:

- where *all* the intermediary reporters in the chain have been omitted, such as the narration of al-Qāḍī al-Nuʿmān al-Maghribī, who said, 'On the authority of Jaʿfar ibn Muḥammad (A): that upon mentioning the circumambulation between the mountains of al-Ṣafā and al-Marwah, he said, "One should come out of the gate of al-Ṣafā and climb al-Ṣafā, then descend from it and climb al-Marwah, then repeat this seven times, starting out at al-Ṣafā and ending up at al-Marwah."'[62]
- where *some* of the intermediary reporters in the chain have been omitted, such as:
- the report quoted by al-Ḥurr al-ʿĀmilī on the authority of al-Shaikh al-Ṭūsī, 'Muḥammad ibn al-Ḥasan, with his chain of transmission from Muḥammad ibn Aḥmad ibn Yaḥyā, on the authority of Yaʿqūb ibn Yazīd, on the authority of Ibn Abī ʿUmayr, on the authority of some of our associates, on the authority of Abū ʿAbdallāh (A), who said, "*Kurr* water is that which cannot be made impure and is 1200 *raṭal*".'[63]

The omission from the above chain of transmission is those to whom Ibn Abī ʿUmayr has referred as 'some of our associates'. This is why this tradition would be called the *mursal* ('hurried') tradition of Ibn Abī ʿUmayr because he is the one who has hurried it and dispatched it without its chain of transmission between the Imam and himself.

b. Legitimacy

[62] Daʿāʾim al-Islām, vol. I, p. 316.

[63] *Al-Wasāʾil*: Chapter 11, from the chapters on pure water.

The jurists and *Ḥadīth* scholars have all investigated the legitimacy of the *mursal* tradition and have held differing opinions with regard to it.

i. ***Authoritativeness of the* mursal *tradition of a reliable person***
This means that if the reporter who has hurried the report on is reliable, his *mursal* tradition is accepted and considered a reliable authority.

This opinion has been attributed to Abū Jaʿfar Aḥmad ibn Muḥammad ibn Khālid al-Barqī, the author of *Kitāb al-Maḥāsin*, and to his father Muḥammad ibn Khālid al-Barqī, who were companions of Imam al-Riḍā and Imam al-Jawād (A).

The justification for this opinion is that the report of a reliable person is in itself a certification of whoever narrated it to him, 'because if this veracious person had been narrating from an unreliable person and wished to hide the fact, this would be fraudulent on his part, and incompatible with his veracity'.[64]

We counter this by saying that 'this would be the case only if the question of veracity were confined to his narration from a veracious or reliable person, and this is clearly not the case'.[65]

ii. ***Absolute inauthoritativeness of the* mursal *tradition***
The argument here is that, whether the reporter of the *mursal* is reliable or not, and whether he merely 'forwarded' traditions on the authority of reliable persons or not, it is inauthoritative.

Al-ʿAllāmah al-Ḥillī was of this opinion, and justified it in his book *Tahdhīb al-Uṣūl*,[66] saying that, 'the prerequisite for accepting a report is the knowledge that the initial reporter is veracious, and this has not been established, because the report of a veracious narrator does not necessarily prove this',[67] as the veracity is more general.

iii. ***Authoritativeness of the* mursal *tradition if the reporter is known to forward traditions on the authority of reliable people only***
This has been said about Muḥammad ibn Abī ʿUmayr.

Al-Mīrzā al-Qummī is of this opinion, and justifies it in *al-Qawānīn*, saying,

[64] Uṣūl al-Ḥadīth wa Aḥkāmuhu, p. 96.
[65] Ibid.
[66] Ibid.
[67] *Al-Miqbās*, vol. I, p. 347.

> When a reporter is known to forward reports on the authority of reliable persons only, this shows that he relies upon reliable means and has confidence in his report. There is no doubt that this is speculation about the soundness of the report, and that it is no less than the speculation about the soundness of the corrupt person's report after confirmation of it.[68]

Al-Shaikh al-Subḥānī made a note of this, saying that

> it is based on his fundamental viewpoint [i.e. al-Mīrzā al-Qummī's] about the authoritativeness of mere speculation, and this goes against the actual state of affairs. Therefore, regarding it, speculation [about the soundness of a corrupt person's report after confirmation of it] is not authoritative proof either, and does not attain the level of lucidity and normal certainty.[69]

These are the most important opinions with regard to the legitimacy of the *mursal* tradition, though a fourth opinion can be added to them.

The accepted *mursal* tradition

This means that if a *mursal* tradition is inauthoritative – in the opinion of those who hold this – then it falls to the level of the weak report, and is treated within the divisions of weak reports, and the various rulings pertaining to it are applied according to the acceptance or rejection of it, as in the weak report.

When we find that the scholars have accepted a *mursal* tradition, and have legislated in accordance with its content, then it is on the same level as the accepted weak report.

We already mentioned that the scholars' acceptance of and reliance upon a weak report in legislation may reinforce its weakness, such that it becomes admissible within the sphere of validity because of its renown; equally, it may not reinforce the weakness, in which case it would then remain invalid, as most people believe.

Therefore, whatever has been said with respect to the accepted weak report applies equally to the accepted *mursal* report, as acceptance here may be considered as a reinforcement of the weakness it attains in spite of its hurriedness, in which case it would

[68] Uṣūl al-Ḥadīth wa Aḥkāmuhu, p. 96.
[69] Ibid., pp. 96–97.

become authoritative; on the other hand it may not be validated as such and would remain inauthoritative.

7. The *Marfūʿ* ('Traced') Report[70]

In the technical terminology of jurists and *Ḥadīth* scholars, the term *marfūʿ* ('traced') may be applied to the *mursal* ('hurried') tradition, because the narrator of the tradition traces it back to the *maʿṣūm*, or to the one who narrated it to him on the authority of the *maʿṣūm*, omitting some reporters between them in the process. An example of this is:

The *marfūʿ* ('traced') report of Zurārah, which al-Shaikh Abī Jumhūr al-Iḥsāʾī quoted in his book *Ghawālī al-Laʾālī*, on the authority of al-ʿAllāmah al-Ḥillī, traced back to Zurārah, who said, 'I said to Abū Jaʿfar (A), "May I be your sacrifice, if I hear two contradictory traditions from you, which of them do I take?..."'

8. The *Shādh* ('Unusual') Report

This is a type of unlinked solitary report, and has been termed *shādh* 'unusual'. The term itself has been coined from various traditions from the Imams (A) themselves, such as:

The accepted tradition of ʿUmar ibn Ḥanẓalah: 'The two contradictory traditions that they both report on our authority and legislate with should be examined, and the one that is agreed upon by the scholars should be accepted, and the unusual (*shādh*) one that is not well-known by scholars should be discarded.'

The *marfūʿ* ('traced') tradition of Zurārah: 'O Zurārah, take whatever is well known among your associates and discard what is unusual (*shādh*) and rare.'

It seems that the word *shādh* has been used technically to signify the same as its lexical meaning, which is 'something rare, exceptional, and unusual'. When we say that something is 'unusual' we mean that there is a group or a collectivity from which this thing is separate and different.

[70] *Marfūʿ* ('traced'): in technical terminology, it may be applied to any tradition that is traced back to a *maʿṣūm*, regardless of the continuity in its chain of transmission.

In light of all this, we can define the *shādh* tradition technically as one that is rare and unusual, in contrast to another more famous one, known to the majority of scholars.

An example of a *shādh* 'unusual' tradition is:

> The tradition of Ḥudhayfah ibn Manṣūr, on the authority of Maʿādh ibn Kathīr, who said, 'I said to Abū ʿAbdallāh (A), "Verily people are saying that the Prophet (S) fasted for 29 days, more often than that he fasted 30 days." So he replied, "They are lying. The Prophet (S) did not fast even a single day less than 30 days from the time Allah appointed him until his death, and the month of Ramaḍān has never been less than 30 days and a night, since Allah created the heavens."'

Al-Shaikh al-Ṭūsī has quoted this in his book *al-Tahdhīb*,[71] and has commented on it, saying,

> Action in accordance with this tradition is incorrect from various aspects: first, that the text of this tradition cannot be found in any of the source compilations, but is to be found among rare traditions only; and second, that the book of Ḥudhayfah ibn Manṣūr – may Allah have mercy on him – in spite of being famous and well known, does not contain it.[72]

[71] Vol. IV, p. 167, no. 477.
[72] Vol. IV, p. 169.

CHAPTER EIGHT

EVALUATING NARRATORS

We will now explain the key concepts behind the categories of *ṣaḥīḥ*, *ḥasan*, *muwaththaq*, and *ḍaʿīf*. These concepts are:

i veracity
ii commendation
iii dependability
iv weakness

Veracity (*ʿadālah*)

There are two different opinions with regard to the concept of veracity.

Opinion 1

The first opinion on veracity is:

> that veracity is integrity in one's comportment by adherence to obligatory religious duties and avoidance of prohibited acts. Or, as it generally known, 'a stable mental disposition which leads one to be of righteous conduct, to stop committing major sins and keep away from minor sins; in addition to avoiding committing acts that are contrary to honourable morality and that imply a lack of regard for religion, such that one would not be trusted to keep away from sins'.[1]

This is the legal definition of 'veracity' used in jurisprudence matters such as acceptance of testimony and *taqlīd*.[2] Having established its authority thus far, the above meaning of veracity holds true for the veracity of the reporter; and this is the opinion of the majority of

[1] Miqbās al-Hidāyah, vol. II, pp. 33–34.
[2] *Taqlīd*: following a veracious legal authority in matters of jurisprudence.

Ḥadīth scholars, in accord with the scholars of jurisprudence.

Opinion 2

The second opinion on veracity is that veracity is reliability in the transmission of *ḥadīth*. Al-Shaikh al-Ṭūsī is of the opinion that it is a specific term that he derived from the procedure carried out by *Ḥadīth* scholars in determining whether to accept or reject reports and whether to prove or disprove the reporter's integrity. He said,

> Regarding one who commits certain wrongdoings or physical sins or is corrupt, yet who is at the same time reliable and conscientious in his narration, there is no need to reject his report, and action in accordance with such as report is permissible, as the veracity required in transmission has been achieved. Committing physical acts of wrongdoing does, however, prevent his legal testimony from being accepted while it does not hinder the acceptance of his report. On account of this, the community accepts reports from such people.[3]

Al-Muḥaqqiq al-Ḥillī denied the existence of any such procedure carried out by *Ḥadīth* scholars as alluded to by al-Shaikh al-Ṭūsī and from which he construed this meaning of veracity in the reporter. He said,

> The second issue: the veracity of the reporter is a prerequisite for acting in accordance with [i.e. accepting] his report. Al-Shaikh [i.e. al-Ṭūsī] said that it suffices that he should be reliable and guard against lying in his report, even though he commits physical wrongdoings; and he has claimed that the community acts in accordance with the reports of such people. We reject this claim and demand proof of it. If we were to accept it, we would be limited to acting in accordance with certain reports and prevented from extending beyond them. The allegation that one can guard against lying while outwardly committing sins is a far-fetched notion, as one who outwardly commits sins cannot be trusted in his outward display of guarding against lying.[4]

Al-Shaikh Ḥasan al-ʿĀmilī commented in turn on al-Muḥaqqiq al-Ḥillī's criticism of al-Shaikh al-Ṭūsī's opinion, saying, 'This is an

[3] *Al-ʿUddah*, vol. I, p. 382.
[4] *Al-Maʿārij*, p. 149.

excellent statement. I am also of the opinion that veracity is a necessary requirement...'[5] [i.e. veracity in its broadest sense and as generally understood].

Al-Shaikh al-Subḥānī discussed al-Muḥaqqiq al-Ḥillī's objection, saying, 'His objection is out of context, because denying that the community acts in accordance with the reports of non-veracious people does not hold true in reality, and this is obvious to one who practises in the field of jurisprudence, and this denial is extremely uncharacteristic of al-Muḥaqqiq',[6] as he is an expert in this field and has explored its depths and profundities, so it is surprising and odd that he should fail to see the clarity in this evident matter.

It appears to me that the controversy in this matter is due to the fact that al-Shaikh al-Ṭūsī relied on investigation (i.e. considering the way in which the community deals with the reporters as evidence for his opinion); and that the community relies on the Qur'ānic verse 'O you who believe! If a corrupt person comes to you with any news, ascertain the truth'. This explicitly states the necessity of ascertaining the truth when accepting the report of a corrupt person and equally that it is not necessary to ascertain the truth when it comes to the report of a veracious person, given that corruptness or wrongdoing here mean the opposite of veracity, which is what scholars take it to be.

If we look for the meaning of 'corrupt or wrongdoing person' in its Qur'ānic usage (*fāsiq* in Arabic), we find that the word was never used in the Arabic language to describe humans before the revelation of the Qur'ān. Al-Rāghib al-Iṣfahānī in *al-Mufradāt*, under the root word *fasaqa*, quotes the reliable authority Ibn al-ʿArābī, a linguist, as saying, 'The word *fāsiq* ('corrupt') was never used by the Arabs to describe humans, for they would use it to say, "the ripe date has *separated* from its peel"'.

In *Muʿjam Alfāẓ al-Qur'ān al-Karīm*,[7] under the entry *fasaqa*, it says, 'The ripe date *separated* from its peel; Mr x *travelled* far and wide in the world; Mr x *squandered* all his wealth.' From this we can deduce the meaning of the word *fāsiq* in its usage adopted in Islam, since it had never been heard of in pre-Islamic poetry or prose. In

[5] *Al-Maʿālim*, p. 353.
[6] Uṣūl al-Ḥadīth wa Aḥkāmuhu, p. 118.
[7] Dictionary of Qur'ānic Vocabulary.

Islamic law, it means committing indecencies in disobedience of Allah, as the word happens to be one of the many words that have changed in meaning owing to various additions, legal rulings and conditions, resulting in the linguistic development in meanings of words. The Islamic meaning of the word *fasaqa*, therefore, has come to be used in opposition to belief as:

> 'disbelief': 'And none disbelieve in them except the *fāsiqūn* [corrupt people].'
>
> 'hypocrisy': 'Indeed the hypocrites are the *fāsiqūn* [corrupt people].'
>
> 'deviation': 'Among them are the guided, and many of them are *fāsiqūn* [corrupt].'
>
> and as various types of 'disobedience'.

Therefore, corruptness or wrongdoing encompasses more than disbelief.

This means that it is not this Qur'ānic meaning of the word that has been coined for its usage in Islamic law, to mean the opposite of 'veracious', which has been deduced from such reports as the authentic report of ʿAbdallah ibn Abī Yaʿfūr, who said,

> I asked Abū ʿAbdallah (A), 'How can a man's veracity among fellow Muslims be ascertained so that his testimony for or against them be accepted?' So he (A) replied, 'That they know him to be of good reputation, to be virtuous and to restrain his stomach (from eating unlawfully), his private parts, his hands, and his tongue. And he is known to avoid all major sins for which Allah has threatened to punish men in the fire, such as drinking alcohol, adultery, usury, disobeying parents, running away from the battlefield and other such sins. And the clue leading to all this is that he should conceal all his flaws, for it is forbidden for Muslims to inquire about any flaws or faults he may have beneath the surface.'[8]

The word *fāsiq*, then, was coined as a specific term meaning the opposite of 'veracious', after reports such as Ibn Abī Yaʿfūr's authentic report came out, and scholars of jurisprudence used it to fix the meaning of 'veracity'. Therefore, we cannot ascribe the Qur'ānic

[8] *Al-Wasā'il*, ch. 41: Testimonies, Tradition 1.

usage of the word *fāsiq* to its meaning as the opposite of 'veracious'.

It is essential, therefore, that we look for some other proof of this other than the Qur'ānic verse, and this can only be arrived by the application of common sense and logical reasoning, and from seeing how sensible people behave when they receive reports from one another. Based on this, we have to first ascertain where the prerequisite for a tradition to be acceptable is:

i. the veracity of the reporter?
ii. the reliability of the reporter?
iii. or the certainty that the report originates from a *maʿṣūm*?

Because we are dealing with the report here as Sunnah (prophetic practice) or as relating to Sunnah, the requirement is to ascertain that the origin of the report is a *maʿṣūm*. The veracity or reliability of the reporter is only a means to achieving certainty of the report's origin. The fact that the solitary report linked to associated evidence, denoting its certain origin from a *maʿṣūm*, does not require a veracious or reliable reporter supports this. This is because such a requirement of veracity is only a precursor to attaining certitude of the report's origin, and if this certitude is attained without it, we do not need it.

Hence we can say,

> Just as logical common sense proves the authoritativeness of a reliable person's word, so it proves the authoritativeness of every report whose origin from a *maʿṣūm* has been ascertained, whether the reliability of the reporter has been established or not, for that is only a precursor to attaining certitude about the origin of the report.[9]

The veracity of the reporter can be ascertained through evaluative statements mentioned in the biographical dictionaries, which we will consider soon.

Commendation

This means that the statements that biographers use to commend a reporter when evaluating him, in addition to his being an *imāmī*, should demonstrate reliability in his transmission. This applies to

[9] Uṣūl al-Ḥadīth wa Aḥkāmuhu, p. 53.

both the *hasan* ('good') and the *muwaththaq* ('dependable') reporter; they differ only in their school of jurisprudence, in that the reporters of the *good* tradition all have to be *imāmīs*, whereas in the *dependable* tradition, some or all can be non-*imāmīs*. In both of these categories, their reliability must be ascertained, either through commendation or through affirmation of their dependability.

Dependability

This again means that the reporter must be reliable and dependable in his transmission, although dependability must be ascertained by our scholars' standards and not merely in his own school of jurisprudence.

Weakness

What this means is that the reporter has attained the level neither of veracity nor of reliability, because he is unknown or because of his circumstances or because he is known not to be veracious or reliable, and this has been textually noted by the biographers.

Expressions denoting veracity and reliability

There are specific words that biographers use to demonstrate that a reporter is *imāmī* and veracious or non-*imāmī* but reliable. Through this we can find out the worth of the reporter when evaluating the narrators in the chain of transmission. Al-Shahīd al-Thānī mentioned some of these words in his *Dirāyah*:[10]

- equitable (*'adl*)
- reliable (*thiqah*)
- competent authority (*ḥujjah*)
- narrates authentic traditions (*ṣaḥīḥ al-ḥadīth*)

These evaluations have been recorded so that we can gather the veracity of the reporter from such characteristic descriptions mentioned in biographical dictionaries. It is worth noting here that

[10] P. 75.

some words such as *ʿadl* and *ḥujjah* do not feature in the biographical dictionaries of al-Najāshī and al-Ṭūsī, who invariably use the word *thiqah*, which encompasses the meanings of both these words. It is often repeated or linked to other words denoting further qualities, which, when describing a non-*imāmī*, indicate that his report is *muwaththaq* ('dependable') and, when referring to an *imāmī*, indicate that his report is *ṣaḥīḥ* ('authentic') or *ḥasan* ('good'), depending on the words used.

In order to study this methodically, it is necessary to refer to these source biographical dictionaries and examine the use of these various words of commendation. The following shaded list of phrases has been extracted from the biographical dictionaries of al-Najāshī and al-Ṭūsī, to illustrate this:

There is a clear disparity between the concept of veracity among the various scholars of *Ḥadīth*: al-Shaikh al-Ṭūsī does not differentiate between veracity and reliability, whereas the mainstream majority of scholars do differentiate between them, saying that reliability is specific to honesty in statements and can apply to both the *imāmī* and the non-*imāmī* whereas veracity applies to all facets of voluntary human behaviour and is exclusive to the *imāmī*. Based on this, al-Shaikh al-Ṭūsī does not differentiate between a reliable *imāmī* and a *reliable* non-*imāmī* and in his eyes all these phrases are suitable for describing the reliability of either of them.

The mainstream majority of scholars however, divide these phrases into those that indicate veracity and those that indicate reliability. The statements that specify the reliability of a reporter in terms of his narration would render his report to be classified as *muwaththaq* ('dependable'), whereas the general statements that are not limited to narration but also qualify the character of the reporter would render the reporter to be termed veracious. This means that the statements indicating the narrative reliability of an *imāmī* reporter – according to mainstream opinion – can render his report classifiable only as *ḥasan* ('good'). The reporter of a *ḥasan* report is described as 'commendable' by virtue of the fact that his veracity has not been proven, but this does not mean that his reliability has not in fact been proven, for reliability in *ḥasan* reports is paramount, whether it is gathered from commendation of the reporter or affirmation of his reliability.

most reliable and credible of people in his narration

most reliable of people in his narration

most reliable among his contemporaries according to *Ḥadīth* scholars

the extent of his reliability cannot be put into words

reliable, he is unequalled in his esteem, his religiosity and his piety

reliable, credible, eminent personality

reliable, esteemed, is lucid in his transmission, of good conduct

reliable, distinguished, no objection or doubt with regard to him

reliable, distinguished, accurate

reliable, distinguished, trustworthy

reliable, distinguished

reliable, credible

reliable, authentic

reliable, authentic in his narration

reliable in his narration

reliable, believable in his narration

reliable, reliable in his narration, his transmission is trusted, incontrovertible, of good conduct

reliable in his narration, his transmission is trusted

reliable in traditions, authentic in his transmission, credible, believable in his narration

reliable in traditions, credible, believable

reliable, excellent in traditions, of immaculate transmission, believable

reliable in his narration, well-versed in his narration

reliable in his narration, upright in his religious practices

reliable in his narration, honest

reliable in his narration, steadfast

reliable in his narration, flawless

reliable in his narration

reliable in traditions

reliable, sound in his narration

reliable in his transmission

reliable in his transmission, reliable, believable

reliable, his *aṣl* ('primary collection') is dependable

reliable, distinguished, narrates authentic traditions

reliable, distinguished, of immaculate narration

reliable, distinguished, lucid in his narration

reliable, distinguished in his narration

reliable, distinguished, of good conduct

reliable, distinguished, of sound conviction

reliable, distinguished, honest

reliable, distinguished

reliable, honest

reliable, famous, narrates authentic traditions

reliable, narrates authentic traditions

reliable, of sound reception

reliable, narrates authentic traditions, clear in his transmission

reliable, trusted, untarnished reputation

reliable, esteemed, of exalted position amongst the scholars

reliable, esteemed, of high social standing

reliable, esteemed, of untarnished reputation

reliable, esteemed

reliable, of untarnished reputation

reliable, eminent personality

reliable, tenacious

reliable, leading personality

reliable, of good conduct

reliable, virtuous

reliable, righteous

reliable, of sound mental disposition

reliable, flawless

reliable, from a sound school of thought

reliable, unobjectionable

one of our reliable associates

dependable

reliable

Phrases specifically denoting veracity

These phrases are used to denote veracity and are used specifically to describe veracious *imāmīs* (to render a report *ṣaḥīḥ*, or 'authentic')

- of esteemed ranking, exalted position with regard to the Imams (A)
- esteemed among our scholars, exalted in ranking and position
- esteemed among our scholars, exalted in position
- esteemed among our scholars, exalted in ranking
- of esteemed ranking among the elite companions of the Imam
- is esteemed in worldly and religious affairs
- one of the esteemed personalities and great jurists of the Shīʿa
- a leading personality and most respected among our scholars, exalted in position
- an eminent personality among our scholars, *Ḥadīth* scholars and jurists
- an eminent personality among our scholars, a leading personality, exalted in position
- a leading personality, exalted in position
- exalted in rank, of noble position, of sound conviction

Phrases specifically denoting commendation

These are phrases in commendation of the reporter, which denote reliability and render a report *ḥasan* ('good') or *muwaththaq* ('dependable'):

- one of the most esteemed scholars of *Ḥadīth*
- narrates authentic traditions, sound
- narrates authentic traditions, from a sound school of thought
- narrates authentic traditions
- immaculate in narration
- has a good knowledge and understanding of traditions
- memorizes traditions
- distinguished, trusted in his transmission
- trusted in his transmission
- good at memorization, narrates authentically
- memorizes, good at memorization
- of sound conviction, narrates authentically
- devout, of sound conviction
- from a sound school of thought, of sound conviction
- *imāmī*, of righteous conduct
- of righteous conduct, virtuous
- renowned
- accurate in his tradition
- religious, learned
- unobjectionable
- eminent among our scholars
- one of our scholars
- one of our respected scholars
- well-known among our scholars
- specifically narrates our traditions
- an elite companion of the Imam
- distinguished companion of the Imam

Phrases specifically denoting weakness

These are phrases in condemnation of the reporter, which denote weakness and render a report *ḍaʿīf* ('weak'):

liar

liar, extremist, there is nothing good about him, he cannot be believed in his transmission

weak

narrates weak traditions, exaggerates in his speech

very weak, his school of thought is known to exaggerate

narrates weak traditions, cannot be believed

narrates weak traditions

narrates weak traditions, dubious in terms of religiosity

narrates weak traditions, follows a corrupt school of thought, estranged in his transmission

weak, his transmission is defective

weak, careless in his transmission

weak, follows a corrupt school of thought

weak, extremist

very weak

very weak, cannot be taken into consideration

very weak, follows a corrupt school of thought

very weak, corrupt in his belief, cannot be believed in anything

very weak, cannot be trusted and whatever he alone narrates cannot be taken into consideration

our scholars have declared him to be weak

a group of our scholars have proved him to be weak

our scholars proved him to be weak

extreme in his school of thought

extremist, follows a corrupt school of thought

extremist, dubious in terms of religiosity

extremist, liar, follows corrupt school of thought and his transmission is defective

he exaggerates and is arrogant

he has been accused of weakness and extremism

he has been accused of extremism, he has been criticized, very weak

confused

confused circumstances

his narration is confused

his narration is confused as is his school of thought

his transmission is confused, he follows a corrupt school of thought, cannot be taken seriously

some of his traditions are acceptable and some are unacceptable

some of his traditions are acceptable and some are unacceptable or half-way between the two

his transmission is somewhat acceptable and unacceptable

what he says in not found in other traditions, some of his traditions are acceptable and some are unacceptable

his circumstances are dubious, some of his traditions are acceptable and some are unacceptable

careless about the circumstances of his traditions, some of his traditions are acceptable and some are unacceptable

careless

careless circumstances

careless about the circumstances of his traditions

his narration is not immaculate

his narration is not that immaculate

what he narrates does not exist in *Ḥadīth* or in our school of thought and is weak in itself

follows a corrupt school of thought, and his transmission is defective

of blameworthy character

unsatisfactory

has been inconsistent

is inconsistent

his narration cannot be taken into consideration

fabricates traditions

These are the expressions found in the biographical dictionaries of al-Najāshī and al-Ṭūsī. Because some of the terms are quite ambiguous, we shall go on to clarify what they mean.

Terminology

1. Extremism

This is a dogmatic term, extracted from the Qur'ānic verse, 'O People of the Book, do not exceed the limits in your religion'. It addresses the People of the Book, of whom the Jews could be regarded as extreme in downgrading Jesus, the viceregent (*walī*), from his divine position and the Christians were extreme in elevating his status beyond his prophetic position. Al-Zamakhsharī says, 'The Jews went to excess in downgrading Jesus from his position and even declaring him to be of illegitimate birth, and the Christians went to excess in elevating him beyond his position and declaring him to be a god.'[1]

Al-Ṭabarsī reported on the authority of al-Ḥasan al-Baṣrī, who said,

> The Christians went to extremes with respect to Jesus, and said, 'He is the son of God,' while others even said, 'He is God,' and yet others said, 'He is the third of three: the Father, the Son, and the Holy Ghost.' The Jews went to extremes with respect to him too saying, 'He was born illegitimately.' Extremism is therefore inherent in both parties.[2]

Extremism can thus consist in deviation from the true creed either towards excess or towards neglect. There are also groups of Shīʿa who exaggerate with respect to the Ahl al-Bayt (A), elevating them above their status as designated by Allah, and these are called *ghulāt* (extremists). When a reporter is described as an extremist it means that he is one of these types of people.

2. Exaggeration in speech or school of thought

What this means is that the reporter believes or utters things that exaggerate the attributes of the Imam to the point of extremism. It

[1] *Al-Kashshāf*, vol. I, p. 584.
[2] *Majmaʿ al-Bayān*, vol. I, part 5, p. 300.

has been called exaggeration because it relates to the excessive aspect of extremism.

3. Carelessness

As a technical *ḥadīth* term it means laxity in transmitting traditions. This could apply to a case in which the reporter does not memorize the tradition exactly or transmit it word for word as he heard it. He does not care on whose authority he transmits, nor whose traditions he accepts, and he combines both the insignificant and the significant, the worthless and the precious.[3]

4. Acceptable and unacceptable

This expression has more than one meaning. Al-Shaikh al-Māmaqānī, in the fifth point in the introduction to his book *Tanqīḥ al-Maqāl*, says, 'Biographers, especially Ibn al-Ghaḍā'irī, often repeat the expression "His traditions are both acceptable and unacceptable" or "sometimes acceptable and sometimes unacceptable" when referring to reporters of *ḥadīth*.' Although the significance of this phrase has been explained in *al-Miqbās*, we shall explain it here too because of the frequency with which it occurs in the statements of scholars. There are various opinions with regard to its significance:

i. that in the phrase 'some of his traditions are acceptable and some are unacceptable', 'unacceptable' means that the content of the report does not contain anything that corresponds with the Qur'ān and the Sunnah, and 'acceptable' means that it does contain such associated evidence.
ii. that some of his traditions are 'unacceptable' in that their content contradicts the sources, and some are 'acceptable' in that they are in accordance with the sources. This is quite similar to the first opinion.
iii. that 'unacceptable' refers to extraordinary things found in the report, such as what al-Shaikh said about Jaʿfar ibn Muḥammad ibn Mālik in his biography;[4] and 'acceptable' is the opposite of that.

[3] Miqbās al-Hidāyah, vol. II, p. 303.
[4] Al-Shaikh, in his biographical dictionary said, 'He narrated some unheard-of

iv. that it literally means that it is sometimes 'accepted' and sometimes not.
v. that 'acceptable' means that the meaning of the tradition is known, and 'unacceptable' means that it is a report whose text is confused. Some people have chosen this explanation, saying, 'What al-Ghaḍā'irī refers to when he says "acceptable and unacceptable" is confusion in the text of traditions.'
vi. that the phrase 'acceptable and unacceptable' is an extension of the statement 'careless', meaning that the reporter does not memorize the tradition accurately.

5. Differences in school of thought

One of the factors that lead to the inadmissibility of a reporter's narration is a disparity in school of thought, which means that he has not been approved as dependable by our scholars. Expressions such as 'follows a corrupt school of thought' or 'corrupt in his belief' feature among phrases denoting weakness, as a result of the reporter's being a non-*imāmī*. This, in turn, has led many a scholar of *Ḥadīth* to mention or list the various Islamic sects in their books. Another reason for doing so is that many biographers, when describing a reporter, would also mention his association with a particular school of thought.

The sects that have been mentioned in both the indexes[5] are: the Zaydiyyah, the Jārūdiyyah, the Faṭḥiyyah, the Wāqifah, the ʿĀmmah (lit. 'general majority'), the Nāwūsiyyah, the Extremists, the Kaysāniyyah, the Muʿtazilah and the Khaṭṭābiyyah.

What is meant by ʿĀmmah ('general majority') is the Ahl al-Sunnah; in contrast to them are the Khāṣṣah ('elite minority'), meaning the Shīʿa Ithnā ʿAsharī.

Most of these groups that have been called sects or schools of thought are actually just followers of either one individual who formed his opinion, tried to proliferate it and defended it; or of a group of people who adopted the opinion of a certain individual, proliferated it and defended it. This is why they have now become

---

things about the birth of the Mahdī' (p. 458).

[5] Of al-Najāshī and al-Ṭūsī.

extinct and faded away as mere historical oddities. However, because they crop up so often in the biographical dictionaries, in works on different creeds and sects, and in heresiographies that *Ḥadīth* scholars perpetuate their mention in their own works, which is why I myself have decided to list them briefly here, quoting from heresiographical works, and especially al-Shaikh al-Subḥānī's book *Buḥūth fī al-Milal wa al-Niḥal* (*Investigations into Sects and Creeds*).

The Principal Sects

The principal sects in Islam are the Shīʿa and the Ahl al-Sunnah, after which the Khārijite sect came about in the aftermath of the famous *taḥkīm* incident in the Battle of Siffīn.[6] This was the first separation in Islam, and is considered by heresiographers to be a third principal sect. The divisions of theses three principal sects have been listed in Figure 8, Figure 9, and Figure 10.

Degrees of Strength or Weakness in Reports

A report can attain three different degrees of strength: authentic (*ṣaḥīḥ*), good (*ḥasan*) and dependable (*muwaththaq*). Similarly, the weak (*ḍaʿīf*) report also has varying degrees of weakness.

Al-Shahīd al-Thānī says,

> Its [the weak report's] degrees of strength vary according to how far it is from fulfilling the conditions of authenticity; the further the reporters are from being authentic, the weaker the report is, and similarly the more weak reporters there are in the chain, the weaker it is.[7]

In the same way, the degrees of *authentic*, *good*, and *dependable* also vary according to prevailing attributes. So, the report narrated by a reliable, pious, and accurate *imāmī* jurist such as Ibn Abī ʿUmayr is

[6] *Taḥkīm*: refers to the slogan of the group of people from among Imam Ali's supporters in the battle of Siffīn who broke away from him because they were opposed to arbitration, saying, 'There is no judgement except with Allah' (*Lā ḥukma illā lillāh*). *Taḥkīm* means the repetition of this phrase, which was the early Khārijites' basic creed.

[7] *Al-Dirāyah*, pp. 24–25.

more authentic than the report of one who lacks some of these qualities, and so on till the lowest degree of authenticity.

Similarly, the narration of a reporter who has been commended very highly, such as Ibrāhīm ibn Hāshim, is better (more 'good') than the report of someone who hasn't been commended so highly.

The same goes for the dependable report, for reports whose chains of narration include reporters such as ʿAlī ibn Faḍāl and Abān ibn ʿUthmān are stronger than other dependable reports, etc.'

This classification is of use in dealing with contradictory reports.

Figure 8: The different Shīʿa groups.

Ismāʿīliyyah (Ismailis) Imāmiyyah (Shīʿā Ithnā ʿAsharī) Zaydiyyah (Zaydis) Extremists Faṭḥiyyah Kaysāniyyah Wāqifah	*...of which the Zaydiyyah are further divided into:* Batariyyah Jārūdiyyah Sulaymāniyyah Ṣāliḥiyyah	*...and the Extremists are further divided into:* Khaṭṭabiyyah Muḥammadiyyah Mughīriyyah Mufawwiḍah Nāwūsiyyah Nuṣayriyyah

Ashāʿirah (Ashʿarīs) Jabarīyyah Salafiyyah (Salafīs or 'People of Ḥadīth', as they call themselves) Māturīdiyyah Murjiʿah Muʿtazilah (Muʿtazalīs)	*of which the Jabariyyah are further divided into:* Jahmiyyah Ḍarāriyyah Najāriyyah	*...and the Muʿtazilah are further divided into:* Bishriyyah Bahshamiyyah Thamāmiyyah Jāḥiẓiyyah Jubbā'iyyah Khābiṭiyyah Khayyāṭiyyah Murdādiyyah Maʿmariyyah Niẓāmiyyah Hudhayliyyah Hishāmiyyah Wāṣiliyyah

Figure 9: The different groups of the Ahl al-Sunnah.

Figure 10: The different groups of the Khārijites.

Ibāḍiyyah	Ḥafṣiyyah	ʿAjāridah
Azāriqah	Ḥamziyyah	Ghasāniyyah
Aṭrāfiyyah	Rashīdiyyah	Muḥakkimah
Bayhasiyyah	Shaybāniyyah	Mukarramiyyah
Thaʿālibah	Ṣāliḥiyyah	Maymūniyyah
Thawbāʾiyyah	Ṣufriyyah	Najadāt
Ḥārithiyyah	Ṣalatiyyah	Yazīdiyyah
Ḥāzimiyyah	ʿUbaydiyyah	Yūnisiyyah

Types of weak report

The weak tradition can be divided into two types: the accepted and the rejected.

The accepted: This refers to the weak tradition that jurists have accepted and implemented. In other words, the jurists use it as evidence when deducing legal rulings and form legal opinions according to it.

An example of this is the accepted report of ʿUmar ibn Ḥanẓalah al-ʿAjalī al-Kūfī, about the prohibition of taking a legal case before official judges appointed by an Abbasid ruler, and the prescription of taking them instead to *imāmī* jurists. It has been quoted by al-Ḥurr al-ʿĀmilī[8] with the following chain of transmission:

> On the authority of Muḥammad ibn Yaʿqūb, on the authority of Muḥammad ibn Yaḥyā, on the authority of Muḥammad ibn al-Ḥusayn, on the authority of Muḥammad ibn ʿĪsā, on the authority of Ṣafwān ibn Yaḥyā, on the authority of Dāwūd ibn al-Ḥaṣīn, on the authority of ʿUmar ibn al-Ḥanẓalah, who said, 'I asked Abū ʿAbdallāh (A) about two Companions of ours who had a dispute about some debt or inheritance, so they took the case to the Sultan and the judges. Is this allowed?...'

This report is weak because Muḥammad ibn ʿĪsā and Dāwūd ibn al-Ḥaṣīn are in its chain, whom al-Shahīd al-Thānī considered weak: 'They have termed it [the tradition of Ibn Ḥanẓalah] acceptable,

[8] *Al-Wasāʾil*, vol. XVIII, p. 75, Chapter 9 on the Qualities of a Judge.

because Muḥammad ibn ʿĪsā and Dāwūd ibn al-Ḥaṣīn are in the chain of transmission, and they are weak reporters.'[9]

In addition to this, ʿUmar ibn Ḥanẓalah has been established as neither veracious nor flawed by the scholars, but because the jurists have accepted the report and implemented its content in the topic of litigation, and in the field of preponderance between contradictory reports, it has been termed 'acceptable' and has been admitted among the valid traditions.

Al-Shahīd al-Thānī says,

> In spite of what you perceive in its [the accepted weak report's] chain of transmission, the scholars have accepted its content, implemented it, used it as a basis in jurisprudence, derived various rulings from it and termed it 'acceptable'; and there are many such reports among the traditions of jurisprudence.[10]

The Rejected: This is the weak report that the scholars have rejected. They have forbidden reference to it, as well as action in accordance with it, owing to the absence of any evidence that may redress its weakness. The archetype of this is the fabricated (*mawḍūʿ*) tradition, which will be discussed in the next chapter.

[9] *Al-Dirāyah*, p. 44.
[10] Ibid.

CHAPTER NINE

THE FABRICATED (*MAWḌŪ*ʿ) TRADITION

1. Definition

The fabricated tradition is the false, invented, and made-up tradition.

The documented tradition that al-Kulaynī reported, on the authority of Imam ʿAlī (A), and which we quoted in Chapter 2, explicitly states that fabrication of traditions used to occur as early as the time of the Prophet (S). It seems that it was a difficult phenomenon, which moved the Prophet (S) to combat it with all his might, as dangers to belief, legislation and society can all result from the fabrication of traditions.

This is what Imam ʿAlī (A) said about this problem:

> Even in the lifetime of the Holy Prophet, people attributed false statements to him to such an extent that he himself stood up and addressed the people: 'O people, those who attribute false statements to me are in great numbers. Whoever intentionally attributes any false statement to me has taken his seat in Hell.'[1]

Yet the people continued attributing false statements to him after his death.

2. Motives for Fabrication

The various motivations for fabrication can be summarized as follows:

a) Political
b) Religious [Anti-Islamic]
c) Sectarian

[1] *Al-Kāfī*: Chapter on Disparate Traditions, vol. I, no. 191. Also see page 41.

d) Islamic propagation
e) Social
f) Economic
g) Personal

a) The political motivation

This is clearly illustrated through Muʿāwiyah ibn Abī Sufyān's actions geared towards consolidating the foundations of his rule, among which was the distortion of traditions.

When Muʿāwiyah embraced Islam on the day of the Conquest of Makkah, he did not do so of his own accord, but rather because Islam had become the accomplished fact to which the whole Umayyad family had to surrender. The only way they could regain their pre-Islamic control and power, of which this new phenomenon of Islam had stripped them, was to go along with it until they could fulfil their aim through other means.

Their prime opportunity to take the reins of power came first at the time of Abū Bakr's caliphate when he appointed Yazīd ibn Abī Sufyān as the commander of one of his armies sent to conquer Damascus; and subsequently when ʿUmar ibn al-Khaṭṭāb appointed him as ruler of Damascus and his brother Muʿāwiyah to govern Palestine. Furthermore, when Yazīd ibn Abī Sufyān died, ʿUmar included Damascus under Muʿāwiyah's governorship, which was further extended to include the whole of Syria when ʿUthmān ibn ʿAffān became caliph. After ʿUthmān's death, Muʿāwiyah seized the caliphate, disobeying the rightful caliph, ʿAlī ibn Abī Ṭālib (A) , in the process and sowed discord among the community of Muslims through the civil strife he brought about between the people of Iraq and the people of Syria. When he had established his authority after the murder of Imam ʿAlī (A) 'the caliphate was transformed into a throne, whose ruler ascended it by force of the sword, shrewd policies and conspiracies'.[2]

Muʿāwiyah knew very well that he had no legal capacity or right to the caliphate as he was one of the *ṭulaqā'*,[3] of which fact many

[2] Ḥasan Ibrāhīm Ḥasan, *Tārīkh al-Islām*, vol. I, p. 447.

[3] *Ṭulaqā'* (sing. *ṭalīq*): lit. 'freed'. This was the name given to those Makkans who remained heathens until the Conquest of Makkah, when they were

Companions and Followers reminded him, illustrating their low opinion of him and their general attitude towards him.

Al-Masʿūdī narrates in *Murūj al-Dhahab*:[4]

> Manṣūr ibn Waḥshī narrated on the authority of Abī al-Fayāḍ ʿAbdallāh ibn Muḥammad al-Hāshimī, on the authority of al-Walīd ibn al-Bakhtarī al-ʿAbasī, on the authority of Ḥārith ibn Masmār al-Baḥrānī, saying, 'Muʿāwiyah imprisoned Ṣaʿṣah ibn Ṣawṣān al-ʿAbadī, ʿAbdallāh ibn al-Kawāʾ al-Yashkurī and other men from among the Companions of Imam ʿAlī and from among the Quraysh. He came to them one day, saying, 'I beseech you by Allah to say, in all honesty and truth, which of the caliphs you see me resembling the most?!' So Ṣaʿṣah spoke out, saying, 'O son of Abū Sufyān, you revolted and achieved this as a result, and you accomplished what you wanted, though the matter is not how you consider it to be, for how can a caliph become a ruler over people by force and subjugate them brashly and seize power through lies and trickery?! By Allah, on the day of Badr, you had neither weapon nor tent and you were completely helpless and paralysed. Both you and your father were among the *ʿīr* and the *nafīr*[5] in instigating attacks on the Prophet (S). You are nothing but a *ṭalīq* and the son of a *ṭalīq*, whom the Prophet (S) freed, so how can a *ṭalīq* be fit for the caliphate?!' So Muʿāwiyah said, 'I would surely kill you were it not for Abū Ṭālib's statement *Some simple-minded people crossed my path, but desisting from beating them was nobler.*'

In Imam ʿAlī's letter to Muʿāwiyah, there is another reference to the fact that a *ṭalīq* is not allowed to accede to the caliphate. In this letter, Imam ʿAlī invites Muʿāwiyah to pay allegiance to him:

> The swearing of allegiance to me in Medina has made it imperative for you too, being in Syria, because those who swore allegiance to Abū Bakr, ʿUmar, and ʿUthmān have sworn allegiance to me on the same basis on which they swore allegiance to them. Hence, he who was present had no choice [to exercise], and he who was absent had no right to reject, as the advisory

---

captured, made Muslims and subsequently freed by the Prophet.

[4] Vol. III, pp. 40–41.

[5] *ʿĪr* is a technical term referring to the caravan of the Quraysh coming from Syria with Abū Sufyān, and *nafīr* refers to the troop led by ʿUtbah ibn Rabīʿah who rose from Makkah to defend it from the Muslims.

> council was restricted to Muhājirs and Anṣārs. If they agreed upon an individual, taking him as their leader, this denotes Allah's pleasure. If anyone were to desist from their decision by objection or innovation, they would make him return to that from which he desisted. And if he were to refuse, they would fight him for following a course contrary to the believers, and Allah would put him back from where he had run away, and would make him enter Hell, an evil destiny. Verily, Ṭalḥā and al-Zubayr swore allegiance to me, and then renounced it, which was paramount to rejecting it, so I fought them on that matter until the truth prevailed and Allah's decree was evident, which they despised. You have said a lot about killing ʿUthmān. First join what the people have joined [i.e. allegiance], then seek a verdict about the accused people from me, and I shall settle the matter between you and them according to the Book of Allah. As for what you are aiming at [the caliphate], it is like the artificial teat given to a child to wean him off his mother's milk. By my life, if you were to see with your reason rather than your passion, you would find me the most innocent of all in respect to ʿUthmān's blood. I know that you are one of the *ṭulaqā'* [freed by the Prophet] for whom the caliphate is not permitted, and who cannot be considered by the advisory council. I have sent Jarīr ibn ʿAbdallah to you, and to those before you [to secure allegiance], and he is a believer and a Muhājir, so swear allegiance, and there is no power except with Allah.[6]

The statement of ʿAbd al-Rahmān ibn Ghanam al-Ashʿarī to Abū Hurayrah and Abu al-Dardā', when Muʿāwiyah sent them to ʿAlī (A) is as follows:

> What right does Muʿāwiyah have to be considered in the advisory council? For he is one of the *ṭulaqā'* for whom the caliphate is not permissible, and both he and his father were chiefs of the armies against the Muslims, and how can the matter be settled in his favour when ʿUmar clearly said, 'This post is for those who took part in the Battle of Badr, if there are any of them left, then for those who fought at Uḥud, etc...' and a *ṭalīq* has no right to it, nor the son of a *ṭalīq*, nor one who embraced Islam as a result of the Conquest of Makkah.[7]

[6] Dr Naẓmī ʿAbd al-Badīʿ Muḥammad, al-Adab al-Siyāsī fī al-Nizāʿ bayna Alī wa Muʿāwiyah, p. 75.

[7] Aḥādīth Umm al-Mu'minīn ʿĀ'ishah, p. 392; Usd al-Ghābah, vol. IV, p. 387;

Al-Shuʿbah ibn Gharīḍ said to him,

> Your people were killed by the truth in pre-Islamic times and also in Islamic times, for in pre-Islamic times you fought the Prophet (S) and Divine Revelation, until Allah foiled your plots. In Islam, you have deprived the grandson of the Prophet (S) of the caliphate, while you do not even deserve it, for you are a *ṭalīq* and the son of a *ṭalīq*.[8]

Therefore, Muʿāwiyah had no other means but to resort to fabricating traditions supporting his sovereignty and rule, so he gathered sick-minded idlers and people who wished to conspire against Muslims and Islam, and who fabricated traditions for him towards this end.

Among the traditions to be fabricated is that the Prophet (S) supposedly said,

> After me, the good ruler will rule over you with his goodness, and the oppressor will rule over you with his tyranny, so listen to and obey everything that corresponds with the truth, for if they [the rulers] are good, then it is in your best interest as well as theirs, and if they are bad, then it is still in your best interest, even though it may not be in theirs.[9]

The hints of fabrication in this tradition are obvious, and it is evident that it was invented to invalidate the concept of justice, which is a legally required quality in the caliph and also to invalidate the fact that it is obligatory to stand up to an oppressive ruler until he becomes righteous and his social justice is regulated. In spite of this, Muʿāwiyah encountered many thorns in his path on the way to fulfilling his ambition of transforming the caliphate into an Umayyad monarchy, and these thorns came in the shape of the faith that the Muslims had in the rightful caliphate of Imam ʿAlī and his sons. So he set about surmounting these obstacles with all his might.

> Al-Madāʾinī narrates in *Kitāb al-Aḥdāth* that 'Muʿāwiyah wrote a circular to his governors, after the year called *ʿām al-jamāʿah* [lit. Year of the Union],[10] saying, 'Anyone who narrates a single thing

---

al-Ṭabaqāt, vol. III, p. 248.

[8] Ibid., p. 394.

[9] Ḥasan Ibrāhīm Ḥasan, *Tārīkh al-Islām*, vol. I, p. 447.

[10] *ʿĀm al-Jamāʿah*: The year 40 AH was termed 'Year of the Union' because the majority of the Muslim community came together in recognizing Muʿāwiyah as

on the virtues of Abū Turāb [the title of Imam ʿAlī] and his family should be held liable and punished.' After this, the people to be most severely maltreated were the people of Kufa.

Muʿāwiyah then wrote to his officials in all parts of the Arab lands, advising, 'Do not accept the testimony of anyone from among the followers of ʿAlī and his family. Choose your agents from among the followers and friends of ʿUthmān. Attend the meetings of those who speak of ʿUthmān's virtues, befriend them and accord them respect; communicate every single one of their narrations to me, along with all their names, the names of their fathers and their tribe.'

So they did this until a large number of fabricated narrations regarding ʿUthmān's virtues and feats were widespread, for Muʿāwiyah would send them large amounts of money, gifts of clothing and a good deal of property. This became common in every city, such that narrators would compete with one another in inventing his virtues to get greater rewards, and no sooner would anyone bring reports about ʿUthmān's virtues to Muʿāwiyah's governors than he would be noted, promoted, and honoured for it.

This state of affairs continued for some time until Muʿāwiyah wrote to his governors, saying, 'The traditions in praise of ʿUthmān are many and have spread in all the cities. When you receive this circular from me, give orders that people should speak about the virtues of the Prophet's Companions, and the first three caliphs. Ensure that, against every tradition quoted about the virtues of ʿAlī, a similar tradition is coined about the virtues of the Companions, because this is what I would love most and would make me happiest, while it would be most effective in rebutting ʿAlī's position and even more hateful to his followers than the spread of ʿUthmān's virtues.'

His circular was subsequently read out to the people, and in obedience to it they narrated multitudes of fabricated reports about virtues of the Companions, which contained no truth. People continued to do this, even going so far as to declaim praises from the pulpits, and schoolteachers would teach them to young children, to the point where the children would narrate and learn these traditions as they learnt the Qur'ān. They even

caliph, although the minority followers of Imām ʿAli (A) did not.

> taught them to their daughters, womenfolk, and servants. As a result of all this, there were a great number of fabricated traditions and lies in circulation, on which jurists, judges, and governors based their rulings.[11]

Ibn ʿArafah said,

> Most of the fabricated traditions spread in praise of the Companions were invented by people at the time of the Banū Umayyah, in order to gain their good favour and in defiance of the Banū Ḥāshim.[12]

Ibn Abī al-Ḥadīd says in his *Sharḥ Nahj al-Balāghah*[13] that al-Shaikh Abū al-Iskāfī said that Muʿāwiyah instructed a group of Companions and a group of Followers to narrate unpleasant things about ʿAlī, in order to tarnish his reputation and distance people from him, rewarding them for it with unique gifts. So they began inventing things to please him. Among the Companions who did so were Abū Hurayrah, ʿAmr ibn al-ʿĀṣ and Mughīrah ibn Shuʿbah and, from among the Followers, ʿUrwah ibn al-Zubayr and others.

Al-Zuhrī narrates that ʿUrwah ibn al-Zubayr reported to him, saying,

> ʿĀʾishah narrated to me, 'I was with the Prophet, when al-ʿAbbās and ʿAlī approached, so he said, 'O ʿĀʾishah, indeed these two will die upon a creed [or religion] other than mine.'

ʿAbd al-Razzāq narrated on the authority of Maʿmar,

> ʿUrwah had two traditions in his possession, on the authority of ʿĀʾishah about ʿAlī (A) , so one day I asked him about them, and he replied, 'Do not act in accordance with them, nor with their narrations. Allah best knows what they are like, and I am wary of them from among the Banū Hāshim.'

Abū Jaʿfar said,

> We quoted the first of these two traditions above. The second one is narrated on the authority of ʿUrwah, who claims that ʿĀʾishah narrated to him, "I was with the Prophet (S) when al-ʿAbbās and

[11] *Aḥādīth Umm al-Muʾminīn ʿĀʾishah*, pp. 395–96, quoted from *Sharḥ Nahj al-Balāghah* by Ibn Abī al-Ḥadīd, vol. III, pp. 15–16.

[12] Ibid.

[13] Vol. I, p. 358, Old Egyptian edition.

> ʿAlī approached, so he said, 'O ʿĀʾishah, if you would like to see two people who will go to Hell, then look at these two men approaching,' so I looked and they were al-ʿAbbās and ʿAlī ibn Abī Ṭālib.'

A tradition from ʿAmr ibn al-ʿĀṣ – which both Bukhārī and Muslim have quoted in their *ṣaḥīḥ*s and which is both 'supported' and 'consecutive' in its chain of transmission – says that he said,

> I heard the Prophet (S) say, 'The family of ʿAlī are not my friends, for indeed my friend is only Allah and the righteous one from among the believers.'

There is a tradition from Abū Hurayrah that Imam ʿAlī (A) proposed to Abū Jahl's daughter in the lifetime of the Prophet (S), so the Prophet became enraged at him and made a public address from the pulpit, saying,

> No, by Allah, the daughter of Allah's vicegerent and the daughter of Allah's enemy can never come together. Fāṭimah is a part of me, and whatever hurts her hurts me, so if ʿAlī wants the daughter of Abū Jahl, then he should separate from my daughter, and he can do whatever he wants.

This is a famous tradition quoted on the authority of al-Karābisī, which has also been quoted in *Ṣaḥīḥ al-Bukhārī* and *Ṣaḥīḥ Muslim*, on the authority of al-Musawwir ibn Mukhrimah al-Zuhrī. Al-Murtaḍā has also quoted it in his book *Tanzīh al-Anbiyāʾ wa al-Aʾimmah*, saying that it is a narration from Ḥusayn al-Karābisī who was well known for his detachment from the Ahl al-Bayt (A) and for his enmity and hostility towards them, so his traditions are not accepted.

In order to spread and propagate this report, Marwān ibn Abī Ḥafṣah mentions it in his poem in praise of al-Rashīd, in which he talks about the progeny of Fāṭimah and insults them and also insults Imam ʿAlī (A) extensively.

Abū Jaʿfar said,

> al-Aʿmash narrated, saying that when Abū Hurayrah arrived in Iraq with Muʿāwiyah in the Year of the Union, he came to the mosque of Kufa, and when he saw the number of people who had come to meet him, he dropped down to his knees and started beating his bald head, saying 'O people of Iraq, do you think that I would lie about Allah and his Prophet (S) and allow myself to burn in the fire of Hell, for I swear by Allah that I have heard the

> Prophet (S) say that "Every Prophet has a sanctuary and mine is in Madinah between ʿĪr and Thawr (two mountains), so whoever transgresses therein, may Allah's, the angels' and all peoples' curse be upon him, and I bear witness by Allah that ʿAlī has transgressed therein".'

Abū Jaʿfar said,

> According to our scholars, Abū Hurayrah is mentally deranged, and related unacceptable traditions. ʿUmar said to him, 'You narrate too many traditions and you are most probably lying about the Prophet (S)'.

Sufyān al-Thawrī narrated on the authority of Manṣūr, on the authority of Ibrāhīm al-Tamīmī, saying, 'We never used to accept anything from Abū Hurayrah, except reports about heaven and hell.'

Abū Usāmah narrated on the authority of al-Aʿmash,

> Ibrāhīm was authentic in his traditions, such that when I heard a tradition, I would go to him and verify it with him. So one day, I took some reports to him from the tradition of Abū Ṣāliḥ, on the authority of Abū Hurayrah, upon which he told me, 'Stop narrating Abū Hurayrah's traditions, for they [the previous scholars] used to discard a large amount of what he narrated.'

Imam ʿAlī (A) is reported to have said,

> Indeed, the person who lies the most (or 'the person from among the contemporaries of the Prophet (S) who lies the most') is Abū Hurayrah al-Dūsī.

Abū Yusuf reported,

> I said to Abū Ḥanīfah, 'How do you treat a report that comes down on the authority of the Prophet (S), which is inconsistent with analogical reasoning (*qiyās*)?' He said, 'If it has come down through reliable people, we act upon it and disregard personal opinion in the matter.' So I replied, 'How do you regard traditions on the authority of Abū Bakr and ʿUmar?' He replied, 'They're absolutely fine.' So I asked, 'What about ʿAlī and ʿUthmān?' So he said, 'They too'... and when he saw that I was considering the Companions, he said, 'Most of the Companions are veracious, except for a few,' among whom he mentioned Abū Hurayrah and Anas ibn Mālik.

Sufyān al-Thawrī reported on the authority of ʿAbd al-Raḥmān ibn al-Qāsim, on the authority of ʿUmar ibn ʿAbd al-Ghaffār:

> When Abū Hurayrah arrived in Kufa with Muʿāwiyah, he used to sit at Bāb Kindah in the evenings and people would sit with him. One day a young Kufan man came and sat with him, and said, 'O Abū Hurayrah, I beseech you by Allah that I have heard that the Prophet (S) used to say the following with reference to ʿAlī ibn Abī Ṭālib: "O Allah, befriend those who befriend him [ʿAlī] , and be an enemy of those who are his enemies". So he said, "By Allah, yes.' So he (the young man) said, 'Then I bear witness by Allah that you have befriended his enemy and made an enemy of his friend.' Then he got up and left him.

The only thing left for us to say about him is that he officially opened the door of fabrication – as we saw – and as a result, harmed theological thought, belief and religious practices in such a way that its consequences still resonate, burdening and impeding Muslims, for he polluted, distorted and spoiled traditions.

b) The [anti-Islamic] religious motivation

What I mean here is the factor that led people of other religions to fabricate traditions, in their bid to scheme against Muslims.

The most prominent example of this is what is technically known in the field of *Ḥadīth* as '*isrāʾīlīyyāt*' and '*ghulww*' – *isrāʾīlīyyāt* being reports that have been fabricated by Jews, and *ghuluww* reports being reports that have been fabricated by Christians. When the light of Islam radiated in Ḥijāz and settled in Madinah, which the Prophet adopted as the capital of the Muslim state, thed Muslims set about driving the Jews away from there, so some of them moved to Syria and others to Iraq. At that time, there were also a significant number of Jews living in Yemen, who decided to take revenge for their fellow Jews in Ḥijāz, so they moved from Yemen to Madinah, pretending to embrace Islam. The most prominent of such envoys from the Jews of Yemen were:

Kaʿb al-Aḥbār. He was one of the chief scholars of the Jews in Yemen. It is said that he embraced Islam during the reign of Abū Bakr and came to Madinah during the reign of ʿUmar.

Wahb ibn Munabbih. He was one of the chief scholars of the Jews, versed especially in legends of past peoples, especially those related to the Israelites (*Banī Isrāʾīl*). These Jews infiltrated in order to fulfil their goal of exploiting the very ideology of Muslims, by instilling the *isrāʾīlī* ideology into it, disguised in the form of various traditions. These *isrāʾīlī* traditions represent a larger bulk of traditions than even anthropomorphic traditions, which also emanated from Jewish thought and which clearly echo the contents of the distorted Torah. These traditions are rife in Sunni *ḥadīth* and have penetrated into their most sacred *ḥadīth* collections, 'the authentic (*ṣaḥīḥ*) canonical collections'.

Maḥmūd Abū Rayyah has quoted the following tradition under the title 'Examples of Traditions Narrated by Abū Hurayrah', in his book *Abū Hurayrah*:

> Muslim and Bukhārī have quoted on his authority, saying that the angel of death came to Moses, saying, 'Respond to your Lord's call'. Moses punched the angel of death in the eye and gouged it out; so the angel of death returned to Allah and said, 'You sent me to a servant who does not wish to die for he gouged my eye out', so Allah gave him his eye back, and said, 'Go back to my servant and tell him, "If you wish to live, then place your hand on the back of a calf, and however many of its hairs your hand covers is the number of years you will live".'

Al-Thaʿālibī has quoted this same tradition in his book *al-Muḍāf wa al-Mansūb*, in a section entitled 'The Punch of Moses', and says of it, 'This is a legend from folklore, and the angel of death featured therein is one-eyed... I bear no responsibility for this story'.

What is astonishing is that al-Thaʿālibī describes this tradition as folklore, whereas Bukhārī and Muslim relate it in their 'authentic' *ḥadīth* collections, which only goes to show that these two books were not considered as sacrosanct in the early centuries as they have been made out to be in subsequent times, for al-Thaʿālibī – as we know – died in the year 429 AH.

Bukhārī and Muslim narrated on his (Abū Hurayrah's) authority that the Prophet (S) said:

> Heaven and Hell were disputing with each other. Hell said, 'I have been exclusively assigned the arrogant people and tyrants'; so Heaven replied, 'Why do only weak people and miscarried foetuses enter me?' So Almighty Allah said to Heaven, 'You are my Mercy, with which I am Merciful towards whomsoever I wish from among my servants,' and to Hell He said, 'You are My Wrath, and I will afflict it on whomsoever I wish from among my

> servants; and each of these two have their own capacity – and Hell will not be satiated until He puts His leg inside it, whereupon it will say, 'Enough, enough!', for it will be full to the brim, and its contents will be spilling over each other.'

Bukhārī and Muslim have narrated on his authority, 'Our Lord descends to the sky of this world every night, when only the last third of the night remains, and says, "Who is there to call upon me so I can answer him?"'

Bukhārī and Muslim have also narrated on his authority, narrating in turn on the authority of the Prophet (S), that, 'Allah created Adam in his own image, his height being 60 cubits.'[14] Aḥmad ibn Ḥanbal added, on Abū Hurayrah's authority, that he measured 7 cubits in span.

This tradition is exactly the same as the 27th verse from the first scripture of the Book of Genesis (Old Testament), which reads as follows: 'so God created man in His own image, in the image of God He created him; male and female He created them'. If we take into account that Abū Hurayrah was one of Kaʿb al-Aḥbār's most prominent students, then we truly come to understand where these traditions really came from.

Abū Rayyah says,

> No sooner did Abū Hurayrah return to Madinah, dismissed from his governorship of Bahrayn, than the chief rabbi, Kaʿb al-Aḥbār, seized him and began to instruct him in his *isrāʾīlīyyāt* and craftily corrupt him with his legendary fables.

Muslims used to refer to him (Kaʿb) for things that they did not know about, especially after he told this outright lie to Qays ibn Kharashah: 'The Torah revealed to Moses contains information about every single inch of the earth, what is on its surface, and what comes from within it.'

This is why Abū Hurayrah hastened to him, to learn from him and study under him; and their narrations flowed in abundance, especially since they dominated the scene, after the death of ʿUmar and his aversion for Abū Hurayrah.[15]

The same kind of thing is done by certain classes of Shīʿa known

[14] A cubit is a unit of length, equivalent to about 0.6 to 0.8 metres.
[15] Ibid., pp. 89–90.

as the *ghulāt*, or 'extremists', who exaggerate the sanctity of the Ahl al-Bayt (A) and fabricate traditions by elevating them above their designated statuses. The most famous people to proliferate these extremist traditions among the Shīʿa, mentioned in Shīʿa *ḥadīth* books, are:

Al-Mughīrah ibn Saʿīd, a contemporary of Imam Muḥammad Bāqir (A).

Al-Kashshī reported on the authority of Muḥammad ibn ʿĪsā ibn ʿUbayd, on the authority of Yūnus, on the authority of Hishām ibn al-Ḥakam, who said that he heard Abū ʿAbdallāh (A) (i.e. Imam Jaʿfar al-Ṣādiq) saying,

> al-Mughīrah ibn Saʿīd used to lie intentionally about my father, and take his Companions' books. His own companions would pose as companions of my father, they would take his real Companions' books and turn them over to al-Mughīrah, who would tamper with them and corrupt them with blasphemous and atheistic ideas, attributing the sayings to my father. Then he would urge his companions to circulate these books among the Shīʿa. So all exaggerations contained in the books of my father's companions are machinations of al-Mughīrah ibn Saʿīd in these books.[16]

Muḥammad ibn Miqlāṣ al-Asadī al-Kūfī the Disfigured, also known as Muḥammad ibn Abī Zaynab, and more commonly as Abū al-Khaṭṭāb, who was a student of al-Mughīrah ibn Saʿīd.

He was a companion of al-Ṣādiq (A), who was at first upright in his affairs. ʿAlī ibn ʿUqbah said of him, 'Abū al-Khaṭṭāb, before he became corrupt, used to take questions on behalf of the Companions and bring back the answers (as mentioned in *al-Kāfī* under 'The Virtue of Trade'). Then he began to claim various ignominies, such as pretences of prophethood, etc., whereupon some unfortunate people joined him and he became a repulsive and accursed figure. When people came to know about his pretentious claims, they killed him and his followers.

The Khaṭṭābīyyah are attributed to him, may Allah's, the angels' and all people's curse be upon them.

It is written in *Ikmāl al-Dīn* in the very handwriting of the Master

[16] *Tanqīḥ al-Maqāl*, vol. III, p. 236.

of our time (the 12th Imam) – May Allah hasten his reappearance – that 'Abū al-Khaṭṭāb Muḥammad ibn Abī Zaynab al-Ajdaᶜ is cursed, as are his followers, so do not sit in the company of anyone who claims what they do, and desist from them, as I and my fathers (A) do.'[17]

Among their extravagant pretences were statements inflating the status of the Ahl al-Bayt (A), which portrayed them as gods or prophets or claimed that they inherently (by virtue of themselves) knew the secrets of the unseen or that they knew about everything in the universe.

They said that knowing the Imam exempts one from legal obligations.

And this – as we can see – is clearly an echo of Messianic thought present in the distorted testaments. This is especially relevant if we bear in mind that the people who spread these kinds of notions, such as al-Mughīrah ibn Saᶜīd and his student Abū al-Khaṭṭāb and their followers, were from Kufa, and Kufa – as we know historically – was founded on the ruins of Ḥīrah and is today situated in western Iraq. Along with the Christians who lived in Ḥīrah were also various tribes of Arabs, and monasteries of east Syrian monks were spreading from here to there. The Muslims of Kufa would encounter these people, and perhaps some of them may even have pretended to embrace Islam, in order to conspire against it.

Just as the Jews permeated their ideologies in Madinah through narrations of stories and legends, so the Christians did the same in Kufa, spreading their extravagant creeds by furnishing fabricated traditions in support of them.

The Imams of the Ahl al-Bayt (A) explicitly repulsed them and vehemently criticized their ideas, rejecting them outright and forbidding anyone to believe them or to transmit their traditions.

Al-Qāḍī al-Nuᶜmān, in his book *Daᶜāʾim al-Islām*, says:

> There are so many people who deviated and perished from among those who persisted in this matter [i.e. extremism] that the list of their names would exceed the bounds of this book; though it is essential that we mention some points about this:
>
> Among these is the following report on the authority of ᶜAlī ibn

[17] Ibid., p. 189.

Abī Ṭālib (A), that a group of his companions, who had pledged allegiance to him, appointed him and professed his Imāmah (leadership), subsequently deviated from him, were disloyal to him and wronged him, so he fought them all, defeating the disloyal ones, killing the deviators and warring against those who wronged him. So they kept well away from him and he from them.

Another group took extreme measures with regard to him when Shaitan tempted them with his guiles and trickery, saying, 'He is the prophet, but Jibraʿīl made a mistake when he brought the message, for he actually intended him when he came to Muḥammad (S)'.

How deficient are their brains and how corrupted their souls and how fanciful their notions, for if one of them were to send a messenger with a list of dates to someone, and this messenger went and gave it to someone else, he would never allow such a thing, and he would send the message again to the intended recipient or take it back from whoever wrongfully took it. So how can they make such iniquitous claims about the Lord of the universe and about Jibraʿīl, the trustworthy archangel, who descended with the revelation at the time of the Prophet (S) directly to him and about the Qurʾān revealed to him? Then they have the audacity to say that this is the Magnificent Word when they are uttering slanderous lies that Satan, in his dishonesty and enmity, has insinuated to them, leading them into thinking that they are fair.

Others among them foolishly, and in obvious error, claimed that ʿAlī (A) was in the clouds. A group of people, like the ones described above whom Satan had caused to stumble, came to him (A) once, grossly inflating him in their praise, saying, 'You are our god, our creator and our provider, and from you we come and to you we will return'. So Imam ʿAlī (A)'s face turned pale, and he started sweating profusely and trembling like the leaves of a date palm, in awe of Allah's Glory and in fear of Him. Then he became furious, called those around him, and commanded them to dig a ditch, which they did, and he said, 'Today I am going to beat you, flesh and hide!' So when they realized that he was going to fight them, they went so far as to say, 'If you kill us, you will bring us back to life.' He asked them to repent, but they persisted in their error, so he ordered them to be decapitated and burnt them in a fire built in the ditch. This is a famous report about him (A).

During the time of the Imams from his lineage, this kind of thing happened so often that to mention all the incidents would take up a great deal of time and space. Examples of these extremists are al-Mughīrah ibn Saʿīd – may Allah curse him – who used to be a companion of Abū Jaʿfar Muḥammad ibn ʿAlī (A), until Satan caused him to slip, so he became an infidel and claimed prophethood for himself, alleging that he could revive the dead and that the 5th Imam was a god – May Allah the Lord of the universe be exalted – and he claimed that he (the 5th Imam) had sent him as a prophet. Many of his companions followed him and they were called al-Mughīrīyyah, after him.

When Imam Muḥammad al-Bāqir (A) heard this, he had no authority or position as Imam ʿAlī (A) had had, whereby he could kill them as Imam ʿAlī had killed those who had apostasized in his time, so he cursed al-Mughīrah and his followers, disclaimed any association with him, his claims and his followers, and wrote to a group of his friends and his true Shīʿa commanding them to rebuke these people, to seek refuge in Allah from them and to curse him and his followers, which they did, calling them 'al-Mughīrīyyah al-Rāfiḍah' (dissenters)[18] because of their deserting the Imam and accepting what al-Mughīrah said – may Allah curse him.

Al-Mughīrah and his companions sought to challenge the Imam and his companions and to compete with them. They permitted everything that was prohibited and allowed people to commit unlawful deeds. They stopped people from following legal rulings and they themselves abandoned them. They detached themselves from true Islam and all true Shīʿa and stopped following the Imams. Imam Muḥammad al-Bāqir (A) explicitly cursed them and disclaimed all association with them.

Then there was Abū al-Khaṭṭāb at the time of the Imam Jaʿfar ibn Muḥammad al-Sādiq (A), who used to be one of his greatest advocates, until he, like al-Mughīrah, began to disbelieve and claim prophethood, and he claimed that Imam Jaʿfar al-Ṣādiq (A) was a god – may Allah be exalted above these vain statements – and he permitted and authorized all unlawful acts. Whenever his followers did not feel like carrying out an obligatory act, they would come to him asking him to exempt them from it, upon

[18] The word 'Rāfiḍah' in Arabic comes from the root *rafaḍa*, which means to reject, deny, and abandon.

> which he would command them to abandon the act, until they had abandoned all the obligatory acts, permitted all unlawful acts and committed all forbidden acts. He allowed them all to give false testimonies and said, 'Whoever has recognized their Imam, everything that was previously prohibited for him is now lawful for him.'
>
> When Imam Jaʿfar al-Ṣādiq (A) heard of this, he too was in no position to do other than to curse him and disclaim any association with him. So he gathered all his companions and wrote to nearby cities, informing them of this and urging them to curse him and to disassociate themselves from him. This was the most that he was able to do in spite of finding it grievous, abominable, and horrific.[19]

The following reports are accounts of the stances that the Imams took against extremist apostates and their claims:

On the authority of Ibn Miskān, on the authority of the companion who narrated it to him, on the authority of Abū ʿAbdallah (A), who said,

> I heard him (A) say, 'May Allah curse al-Mughīrah ibn Saʿīd, who used to slander my father, and may He make him taste the hottest punishment. May Allah curse anyone who claims things about us that we ourselves do not profess, and may Allah curse those who stop us from worshipping Allah who created us, to whom we will return and who holds us by our forelocks!'

On the authority of Muḥammad ibn ʿĪsā ibn ʿUbayd, on the authority of Yūnus ibn ʿAbd al-Raḥmān, who said,

> Some of our companions asked him [Yūnus], while I was also present, 'O Abū Muḥammad, what do you despise most in *ḥadīth*, and what makes you dislike what our Companions narrate, causing you to reject traditions?' So he said, 'Hishām ibn al-Ḥakam narrated to me that he heard Abū ʿAbdallāh (A) saying, "Do not accept any tradition about us, unless it is compatible with the Qur'ān and the Sunnah, or if it has a certified basis in some of our previous traditions, for al-Mughīrah ibn Saʿīd – may Allah curse him – tampered with the traditions in the books belonging to my father's companions, and added traditions that my father

[19] Al-Qāḍī al-Nuʿmān, *Daʿāim al-Islām*, vol. I, pp. 48–50.

> had never narrated. So guard yourselves with Allah, and do not accept anything about us that contradicts the Word of Our Lord and the practice of our Prophet Muḥammad (S), for when we narrate something, we only say: Allah, Mighty and Exalted, said... or the Prophet (S) said...."'

On the authority of ʿAbd al-Raḥmān ibn Kathīr, who said,

> Abū ʿAbdallāh (A) said to his companions one day, 'May Allah curse al-Mughīrah ibn Saʿīd, and may He curse the Jews whose company he used to frequent and from whom he learnt sorcery, magic and trickery. Verily, al-Mughīrah slandered my father, so Allah stripped him of his belief; and Allah will chastise the people who slandered ʿAlī with the hottest fire. By Allah, we are nothing but servants of the One who created us and chose us. We have no power to harm or benefit. If He is to have Mercy on us, then it is by virtue of His Mercy, and if He is to punish us, then it is as a result of our sins. Verily, by Allah, we have no authority or claim over Allah, and indeed we will die and be buried, then resurrected and raised up and questioned. Woe unto them! What is wrong with them! May Allah curse them! They have offended Allah and the Prophet (S) in his grave, and the Commander of the Faithful, and Fāṭimah, Ḥasan, Ḥusayn, ʿAlī ibn Muḥammad, and Muḥammad ibn ʿAlī (A). And here I stand among you, the flesh and blood of the Prophet of Allah – when I sleep in my bed at night, I am fearful and apprehensive, and they feel secure and sleep soundly in their beds, while I am terrified, sleepless, vigilant and agitated. I seek refuge in Allah from what the disfigured tool-cutter Abū al-Khaṭṭāb – may Allah curse him – claims about me to the Banū Asad. By Allah, if they were to try to test us, and if we commanded them to do so, they would surely decline, for how can they accept when they see me scared and vigilant?! I ask Allah for assistance against them, and I seek refuge in Allah from them. Witness that I am but a man, born from the Prophet's (S) lineage, and I have no excuse before Allah; if I obey Him, He has mercy on me, and if I disobey him, he will punish me severely, with the harshest of punishments.[20]

On the authority of ʿAnbasah ibn Muṣʿab, who said,

> Abū ʿAbdallāh asked me, 'What have you heard Abū al-Khaṭṭāb say?' He replied, 'I heard him say that you placed your hand on

[20] *Muʿjam Rijāl al-Ḥadīth*, vol. XVIII, pp. 275–77.

> his chest and said to him, "Remember and never forget," and that you have knowledge of the unseen, and that you told him that he was the repository of your knowledge and the place of your secrets and a trustee over the living and the dead among us.'
>
> The Imam replied, 'No, by Allah, no part of my body has ever touched any part of his, except for his hand. As regards his claim that I supposedly said that I have knowledge of the unseen, by Allah, who is the only god and there is no other god but Him, I have no knowledge of the unseen, nor has Allah entrusted me with authority over the dead, nor sanctioned me over the living, even if I was to tell him any such thing.'
>
> He [ʿAnbasah] said, '...I had a contract with ʿAbdallāh ibn al-Ḥasan to distribute some land equitably between ourselves. His share happened to be the meadows and streams, while mine was in the mountain; so had I known the unseen, I would have ended up with the meadows and streams, and he with the mountainous area. As for his claim that I referred to him as the repository of our knowledge and the place of our secrets and the trustee over the living and the dead, verily, Allah has not entrusted me with authority over the dead, nor sanctioned me over the living, even if I was to ever appoint him over anything.'

On the authority of ʿImrān ibn ʿAlī, who said,

> I heard Abū ʿAbdallāh (A) say, 'May Allah curse Abū al-Khaṭṭāb and those who have been killed with him and those from among his followers who still remain, and may Allah curse whoever has sympathy for them in his heart.'

On the authority of Muṣādif, who said,

> When the people of Kufa, in their *talbiyah*,[21] called out Imam Jaʿfar al-Ṣādiq's name instead of Allah's, I went to Abū ʿAbdallah (A) and informed him of that, whereupon he fell prostrate and crushed his chest to the floor and wept and began to wring his hands, saying repeatedly, 'Indeed a lowly slave of Allah.' Then he raised his head and his tears were flowing on to his beard. So I regretted informing him about it, and asked him, 'May I be your sacrifice, what is it that has affected you so much?' So he replied,

[21] An obligatory phrase that pilgrims say when they enter the state of *iḥrām* in *hajj*, whose wording is, 'Here I am O Allah, here I am...' (in answer to Allah's call).

> 'O Muṣādif, if Jesus (A) had remained silent with regard to what the Christians were claiming about him, Allah would have had every right to render him deaf and blind. And if I am to remain silent about what Abū al-Khaṭṭāb has claimed concerning me, then Allah will have every right to deafen me and blind me.'

On the authority of Abū Baṣīr, who said,

> Abū ʿAbdallāh (A) said to me, 'O Abū Muḥammad, disclaim association from him who claims that we are gods,' so I said, 'I seek refuge in Allah from such a person.' Then he said, 'Disclaim association from him who claims that we are prophets,' to which I replied, 'I seek refuge in Allah from him.'

On the authority of Murāzim, who said,

> Abū ʿAbdallāh (A) said, 'Tell the extremists to seek repentance from Allah, for they are corrupt, infidels and polytheists.'

On the authority of Ibn Abī ʿUmayr, on the authority of Ibn al-Mughīrah, who said,

> I was with Abū al-Ḥasan (al-Kāẓim) (A), along with Yaḥyā ibn ʿAbdallāh ibn al-Ḥasan, when Yaḥyā said, 'May I be your sacrifice, they are claiming that you have knowledge of the unseen.' So he (A) replied, 'Glory be to Allah, put your hand on my head, for by Allah, all the hairs on my body and on my head are standing on end. By Allah, I know only the practice of the Prophet (A).'

On the authority of Abū Baṣīr, who said,

> I said to Abū ʿAbdallāh (A), 'They are saying things about you.' He replied, 'And what are they saying?' So I said, 'They are saying that you know the number of raindrops and stars and leaves on trees and the weight of all that is in the sea and the number of grains of sand.' So he lifted his hands to the sky and said, 'Glory be to Allah, Glory be to Allah; no, by Allah, no one but Allah knows these things.'

On the authority of al-Ḥasan al-Washāʾ, on the authority of some of our companions, on the authority of Abū ʿAbdallāh (A), who said,

> The curse of Allah is upon whoever claims that we are prophets

> or has doubt [that we are not prophets].[22]

On the authority of al-Mufaḍḍal ibn Yazīd, who said,

> When mention was made of the companions of Abū al-Khaṭṭāb and the extremists, Abū ʿAbdallāh (A) said, 'O Mufaḍḍal, do not sit in their company, do not trust them, do not sit to have a drink with them, do not shake hands with them, and do not bequeath them anything.'[23]

We are able to draw the following conclusions from the above reports:

i. These fabricated traditions are based on certain notions that either liken the Creator to the Creation, as in anthropomorphic traditions, or that liken the Creation to the Creator, as in extremist traditions. These marked the beginnings of the Jewish digression, when the Jews debased the Creator by likening him to the Creation, as well as of the Christian digression, when they inflated the Creation (Jesus) by likening him to the Creator.

ii. The Jews were also involved in the polluting and scheming thoughts of the extremists. This is denoted by the report of ʿAbd al-Raḥmān ibn Kathīr, which pointed out al-Mughīrah ibn Saʿīd's frequent meetings with Jews. We know that historically the Jews used to live in settlements to the east of Kufa, between Kufa and Baghdad, although some of them may have even lived in Kufa itself.

iii. The term *Rāfiḍah* ('dissenters') was used to describe the extremists by Imam Muḥammad al-Bāqir (A) himself, because they 'rejected' (the literal meaning of the verb *rafaḍa*) his statements and adhered to the claims of al-Mughīrah ibn Saʿīd.

It seems that the then governments feared the *imāmī* (Shīʿa Ithna ʿAsharī) opposition to their oppressive and unjust policies so much that they exploited the use of this term *Rāfiḍah* (which has a pejorative connotation and was used to alienate and estrange anyone to whom it was applied) and applied it to the *imāmīs*, in order to ruin their reputation, to incite other Muslims to combat them and because (here the term was used in another sense, invented for the purpose) the *imāmīs* had 'rejected' the caliphate of Abū Bakr or had 'rejected' following Zayd ibn ʿAlī who had accepted Abū Bakr's caliphate (or so

[22] *Muʿjam Rijāl al-Ḥadīth*, vol. XIV, pp. 248–54.
[23] *Tanqīḥ al-Maqāl*, vol. III, p. 190.

it was claimed).

It is not at all surprising that unstable governments such as these may do such a thing, but what is surprising is how so many authors among our Sunni brothers have resorted to using sensitive issues to hit the spot where it hurts, when they know full well that this discussion has certain limits and boundaries that require objectivity and fairness on their part and that they cannot just speak out without any restraints, enraging the *imāmīs* by calling them heretics, and incriminating them for rejecting their leaders while they themselves refuse to follow their own leaders. At the same time, they turn a blind eye to the heresy of *isrāʾīlī* anthropomorphism that repeatedly pervades the Friday sermons, the study circles and the pages of books and journals, as if they are unaware that justice must be impartial.

c) The sectarian motivation

This is the motivation that incited adherents of various Islamic sects to fabricate traditions supporting their school of thought, its ideologies, and its advocates. Among these fabricated traditions are the following.

A report was narrated on the authority of Ibn Lahīʿah, that he heard an ex-Khārijī shaikh saying, after he had repented, 'Verily, these traditions are your very religion, so be careful from whom you accept your religion, for it was our practice, when we wished to bring something into effect, simply to make up a tradition for it.'

Al-Ḥāfiẓ ibn al-Ḥajar said,

> By Allah, this is a mortal blow to people who take *mursal* ('hurried') traditions as authoritative proof,[24] because the Khārijī heresy occurred at the birth of Islam when there were many Companions still alive, then at the time of the Followers, and thereafter. And these people [the Khārijīs], if it was their opinion that something was correct, made up a tradition about it and proliferated it. So it could well be that someone would hear such a tradition from them and narrate it, omitting the name of whoever narrated it to him, preferring not to speculate, and someone else would then narrate it on his authority. Then,

[24] These 'hurried' traditions were often narrated by the Followers, missing out the name of the Companion who had narrated it.

someone using broken traditions such as this one as authoritative proof would come along and use it to derive a ruling, when its origin had been fabricated as mentioned above.[25]

Abū al-ʿAbbās al-Qurṭubī said,

> Some jurists from among the Ahl al-Ra'y[26] have deemed it permissible to attribute a ruling derived by clear-cut *qiyās* ('analogical reasoning') to the Prophet (S). This is why you see their books filled with traditions whose contents clearly indicate that they are just rulings given by jurists, and for which they have not even provided a chain of transmission.[27]

Al-ʿAqīlī reported on the authority of Ḥammād ibn Zayd, saying, 'The atheists have fabricated 14,000 traditions against the Prophet (S).'[28]

d) The Islamic propagation motivation

What is meant by this is that the fabricator would make up a tradition in order to promote religion, especially in advocating rewards for actions and in matters pertaining to achieving nearness to Allah.

Ibn al-Ṣalāḥ in his *Muqaddimah* said,

> There are various kinds of fabricators, the most destructive of whom are a group from among the advocates of asceticism, who fabricated traditions that evaluated rewards for things, and people believe their fabrications because they trust them and rely upon them.[29]

Al-Shahīd al-Thānī said in his *Dirāyah*,

> Fabricators are of various kinds, the most destructive of whom are those who advocate asceticism and goodness without any knowledge; they claim that making up such traditions will bring them closer to Allah, so people believe their fabrications because they trust them from their outward conduct.

This scandalous habit of concoction has even reached the point

[25] Abū Rayyah, *Abū Hurayrah*, p. 118.
[26] These were proponents of the use of personal opinion to derive legal rulings.
[27] ʿUlūm al-Ḥadīth, p. 268.
[28] *Al-Dirāyah*, p. 58.
[29] Al-Taqyīd wa al-Īḍāḥ, p. 131.

where the Karrāmiyyah (who are a sub-sect of the anthropomorphists) hold that it is actually permissible to fabricate traditions in order to generate desire (for Heaven) and terror (of Hell) in people.

Ibn al-Ṣalāḥ said, 'From what we have quoted on the authority of the religious teacher Abū Bakr al-Samʿānī, some of the Karrāmiyyah held that fabrication of traditions generating desire and terror was permissible.'[30]

This type of fabrication has become widespread in the Sunnah, because of people who outwardly advocate asceticism and goodness.

Al-Shaikh al-Amīnī said,

> Yaḥyā ibn Saʿīd al-Qaṭān said, 'The most dishonest act we have seen good-doers commit is to fabricate traditions'; and also, 'There is no more dishonest thing that good people can do than to fabricate traditions'; and, 'I have never seen a more dishonest thing than that committed by ascetics and good-doers'.[31]

Al-Qurṭubī said,

> There is no room for considering the lies that the fabricators have fabricated and the work of forgers in concocting fake traditions about the merits of chapters of the Qurʾān or the merits of other good deeds. Many people have done such a thing and have fabricated traditions so that they will be rewarded – or so they claim – for calling people's attentions to the merits of good deeds. An example illustrating this is the report on the authority of Abū ʿIṣmah Nūḥ ibn Abī Maryam al-Marwazī, Muḥammad ibn ʿAkkāshah al-Kirmānī, Aḥmad ibn ʿAbdallāh al-Juwaybārī and others, that Abū ʿIṣmah was asked, 'Where did you get the information you narrated on the authority of ʿIkrimah, on the authority of Ibn ʿAbbās, about the individual merits of each chapter of the Qurʾān?' He replied, 'I saw people abandoning the Qurʾān and being preoccupied with Abū Ḥanīfa's jurisprudence and Muḥammad ibn Isḥāq's battle accounts instead, so I made up this tradition to get a reward.'[32]

Al-Qurṭubī also said,

[30] Ibid., p. 132.
[31] *Al-Ghadīr*, vol. V, p. 275.
[32] *Al-Tidhkār*, p. 155.

> Al-Ḥākim and other such great *Ḥadīth* scholars said that a man, one of the ascetics, was charged with fabricating traditions about the merits of the Qur'ān and its chapters, so he was asked, 'Why did you do such a thing!?' He replied, 'I saw people being averse to the Qur'ān, so I wanted to awaken their desire for it.' So he was told, 'But the Prophet (S) said, "Whoever intentionally lies about me has taken his seat in Hell'." So he replied, 'I have not lied about him, I have lied for him.'[33]

May Allah have mercy upon al-Sayyid al-Musawī al-Hindī for the following verses he composed:

> How many a caller propagates his religion in the name of the law,
> when the law itself condemns him
>
> He excels in the ways of deception and deceives mankind with his
> abstention
>
> Can you see any calamity more agonizing than this very
> misfortune befalling anyone?'

Al-Ḥāfiẓ Ibn Ḥajar, in the biography of Muḥammad ibn 'Akkāshah al-Kirmānī, said,

> Al-Ḥākim has listed him among the weak reporters, and said, 'Among them is a group who have fabricated, in order to call people's attention to the merits of good deeds, or so they claim, such as Abū 'Iṣmah and Muḥammad ibn 'Akkāshah al-Kirmānī.' Then he quotes on the authority of Sahl ibn al-Sary al-Ḥāfiẓ that he used to say, 'Aḥmad ibn al-Juwaybārī, Muḥammad ibn Tamīm and Muḥammad ibn 'Akkāshah fabricated more than 10,000 traditions about the Prophet (S).'[34]

In the biography of Aḥmad ibn 'Abdallāh al-Juwaybārī, he says that Ibn 'Uady said,

> He used to fabricate traditions for Ibn Karrām about whatever he wanted, for Ibn Karrām quoted them in his books on his authority. Among these traditions arc: 'Ibn Karrām narrated to us that Aḥmad ibn Abī Yaḥyā the teacher narrated to us on the authority of Ḥumayd, on the authority of Anas: "There will be a man from my *ummah* called Abū Ḥanīfah through whom Allah

[33] Ibid., p. 156.
[34] *Lisān al-Mīzān*, vol. V, p. 288.

will revive my Sunnah."'

Ibn Ḥibbān said, 'He is Abū ʿAlī al-Juwaybārī, one of the swindlers who narrated thousands of traditions on the authority of the Imams, which they have never uttered.'

Al-Bayhaqī said, 'As for al-Juwaybārī, I know him very well for his fabrication of traditions on the authority of the Prophet (S), for he has fabricated more than a thousand such traditions.'[35]

e) The social motivation

This refers to the vile, disgraceful motivation that drove the class of preachers to fabricate traditions in favour of oppressive rulers, in their sycophancy of a ruler or governor and in their desire to obtain a higher social position.

Dr Ṣāliḥ says,

> A shrewder and more bitter motivation than this [i.e. the sectarian motivation] is the one that leads some scholars of evil in every generation to fabricate traditions in order to become on more intimate terms with the ruling class, and in order to gain favourable positions with them. An example of this is Ghiyāth ibn Ibrāhīm al-Nakhaʿī al-Kūfī's forgery, when he came to the caliph Mahdī. Mahdī used to love doves and would play with them, so when Ghiyāth came to him, he was told to narrate a tradition to the caliph. So Ghiyāth said, 'x narrated on the authority of y, on the authority of z, that the Prophet (S) said, 'Competition is not permissible, except with arrows, horses, camels and birds.' [He added 'birds' to an existing tradition]. So Mahdī gave him a gift of a pouch of coins and said to Ghiyāth when he stood up to leave, 'I swear by your stature that you are nothing but a liar about the Prophet (S).' But then Mahdī said, 'I was the one who led him to do such a thing,' and ordered the doves to be slaughtered.[36]

I do not know why Dr Ṣāliḥ condemned Giyāth ibn Ibrāhīm for lying about the Prophet (S), yet did not follow it with any reproach of Mahdī for presenting him with a gift of money!? Is this not an indication that he was encouraging fabrication and lying!? And lying, indeed, about none other than the Prophet (S), and collusion on the

[35] Ibid., vol. I, p. 193.
[36] 'Ulūm al-Ḥadīth, p. 268.

part of none other than the caliph of the Muslims, the keeper of their wealth and destinies! Does he not consider this to be the most despicable, the most unscrupulous and most bitter of offences? This is nothing less than saying that they perpetrated the crime jointly!

f) The economic motivation

We saw above how the social motivation may be an economic motivation at the same time, for just as the fabricator may profit from proximity to the subject of his fabrication, so he may profit from monetary gifts from him too.

Just as the economic motivation is sometimes linked to the social motivation, it is very often also linked to the political motivation. This is clearly illustrated by Muʿāwiyah ibn Abī Sufyān's undertakings, for the propaganda to consolidate the foundation of his Umayyad kingdom was not enough for him, so

> he made up stories to fortify his propaganda, which had never been heard before his time. He employed thousands of people and sent them to every part of the Muslim empire to tell stories about him to strengthen his government and maintain his rule, as well as to spread legends and superstitions to corrupt the minds of the Muslims and to manipulate the opinions that others held, encouraging them to doubt the foundations of the religion, as mentioned by Professor Imām.[37]

These stories were based on the *isrāʾīlīyyāt* and legends of past nations interposed in forged traditions. Rabbis and monks who pretended to be Muslims, such as Kaʿb al-Aḥbār and Wahb ibn Munabbih, would be the ones to furnish the details of these myths. The government paid every one of these storytellers. In his book *Fajr al-Islām*, Aḥmad Amīn explains the method used by the storyteller to carry out his task:

> The storyteller would sit in the mosque, surrounded by people. He would first remind them of Allah, then narrate to them stories, traditions, myths and legends of past nations, and other such things, used for the desire or fear they evoked in people rather than for the truth in them.

[37] Abū Rayyah, *Abū Hurayrah*, p. 203.

Al-Layth ibn Saʿd said,

> There were two types of stories: general stories and special stories. General stories were the ones told to the general public to warn them and remind them, which they would make up according to their audiences. Special stories were the ones that Muʿāwiyah would specifically make up and appoint someone to personally narrate it. The storyteller would begin narrating as soon as he had finished his dawn prayer, when he would sit down and begin by mentioning Allah, praising Him, glorifying Him, blessing the Prophet (S), then he would pray for the caliph, his courtiers, his retinue and his army and curse his opponents and all the polytheists.[38]

g) The personal motivation

This is when an unlearned person would feign learnedness by inventing traditions to strengthen his position. In the books of *Ḥadīth* studies, this has been termed 'feigning scholarship'.

Ibn al-Jawzī has reported with a chain of narration going back to Abū Jaʿfar ibn Muḥammad al-Ṭayālisī, who said, 'Aḥmad ibn Ḥanbal and Yaḥyā ibn Maʿīn were praying in al-Raṣāfah mosque when a storyteller stood up in front of them and said that Aḥmad ibn Ḥanbal and Yaḥyā ibn Maʿīn had said,

> ʿAbd al-Razzāq has narrated to us on the authority of Maʿmar, on the authority of Qatādah, on the authority of Anas, who said that the Prophet (S) said, 'Whoever says that there is no god but Allah, for every word he utters, creates a bird with a golden beak and feathers of coral... ' and so on until his story was long enough to fill up twenty pages. So Aḥmad ibn Ḥanbal and Yaḥyā ibn Maʿīn looked at each other, and Yaḥyā said to Aḥmad, 'Did you narrate such a thing?!', to which he replied, 'By Allah, I have never heard it before this very hour.' After he had finished his story and collected money from people, he sat down to wait for the rest of the contributions when Yaḥyā ibn Maʿīn motioned for him to come nearer. So he went, presuming he was going to receive a gift, when Yaḥyā asked him, 'Who narrated this tradition to you?' He replied, 'Aḥmad ibn Ḥanbal and Yaḥyā ibn Maʿīn.' So Yaḥyā said, 'I am Yaḥyā ibn Maʿīn and this is Aḥmad ibn Ḥanbal, and

[38] Ibid., p. 403.

neither of us has ever heard this tradition of the Prophet's.' So he replied, 'I have always heard that Yaḥyā ibn Maʿīn is an idiot, but this has not been proven until just now. You speak as if there are no other Yaḥyā ibn Maʿīn and Aḥmad ibn Ḥanbal apart from you two, while I have written about seventeen different Yaḥyā ibn Maʿīns and Aḥmad ibn Ḥanbals.' Upon hearing this, Aḥmad ibn Ḥanbal covered his face in disdain and said, 'Let him get out of here.' So he stood up and went off scoffing at them.

3. The Method of Fabricating Traditions

Some of the authors of books on *Ḥadīth* studies have set themselves the task of explaining the method of fabrication, based on what they have gathered from the bulk of fabricated traditions. Explaining this method, as if it were a historical phenomenon, can help to indicate how to recognize fabricated traditions. Fabrication is basically a type of personal demeanour, projected on to either the content or the chain.

In terms of the content, fabrication may be carried out in one of two ways:

i the reporter would make up his own content, by composing and putting together words and expressions of *ḥadīth* to make up whatever he desires. An example of this is the famous fabricated tradition, 'My Companions are like the stars; whichever one of them you follow you will be guided.'[39]

ii the reporter would take the statement of a wise person or scholar and attribute it to a *maʿṣūm*. An example of this is the famous proverb, 'The stomach is the seat of the ailment, and diet is the best of all remedies', which is a proverb by al-Ḥārith ibn Kildah al-Thaqafī that a reporter falsely attributed to the Prophet (S).

The actual wording of the proverb, as quoted in the book *ʿUyūn al-Anbā*[40] under al-Ḥārith ibn Kildah's biography, is, 'The belly is the

[39] Al-Shaikh al-Albānī, *Silsilah al-Aḥādīth al-Ḍaʿīfah wa al-Mawḍūʿah*, vol. 1, p. 78, no. 58.

[40] P. 165.

seat of the ailment, and diet is the best remedy'. Perhaps the first statement was taken from this one or from another narration of it.

In terms of the chain, fabrication may also be done in one of two ways:

- the reporter would invent a chain for his forged tradition, by stringing together names of false reporters.
- the reporter would adopt an existing chain of transmission and superimpose his fabricated tradition on to it.

4. Characteristics of Fabrication

These are the clues that reveal that a tradition is fabricated. They are of three types:

i) Clues of fabrication from the reporter

- When the reporter himself admits to having fabricated the tradition, such as Abū ʿIṣmah Nūḥ ibn Abī Maryam's confession to having fabricated traditions about the merits of chapters of the Noble Qurʾān on the authority of Ibn ʿAbbās.

Another example of when the reporter himself admits to fabricating a tradition is the one that al-Ḥāfiẓ al-ʿIrāqī has mentioned in his book *al-Taqyīd wa al-Īḍāḥ*, with reference to the chain of a long tradition about the merits of the chapters of the Qurʾān that was narrated on the authority of Ubay ibn Kaʿb, on the authority of the Prophet (S). He says,

> We reported on the authority of Mu'ammil ibn Ismāʿīl, that he said, 'A shaikh narrated this tradition to me,' so I asked the shaikh who narrated it to him. So he said, 'A man in Madāʾin narrated it to me, and he is still alive,' so I went to him and asked him who narrated it to him. He replied, 'A shaikh in Wāsiṭ narrated it to me, and he is still alive,' so I went to him and asked him who narrated it to him, and he said, 'A shaikh in Basra narrated it to me,' so I went to him, and he said that a shaikh from Abadan narrated it to him, so I went to him. He took me by the hand and made me enter a house, in which was a group of Ṣūfīs with their shaikh. The man told me, 'This is the shaikh who narrated it to me,' so I asked him, 'O shaikh, who narrated it to you?' So he replied, 'Nobody narrated it to me, but we saw that people were

> turning away from the Qur᾿ān, so we made up this tradition for them in order to turn their hearts to the Qur᾿ān.'[41]

- if the reporter is well known among scholarly circles for his fabrication.
- if the source biographical dictionaries state him to be a fabricator.
- if the report is linked to specific evidence proving that the reporter is a fabricator.

ii) Clues of fabrication in the chain

- if the chain is entirely made up of unheard-of reporters and fabricators.
- if the chain contains a single fabricator in it.
- if the chain contains names of people who have not been mentioned in the biographical dictionaries.
- if biographers have textually stated that the sequence of reporters in the chain is wrong.

iii) Clues of fabrication in the content

- if the purport of the tradition contradicts the literal meaning of the Qur᾿ān, and the use of *ta᾿wīl* (allegorical interpretation of the Qur᾿ān) to conform with the tradition is unacceptable.
- if the purport of the tradition contradicts the literal meaning of the established Sunnah, and the use of *ta᾿wīl* to conform with the tradition is unacceptable.
- if the purport of the tradition contradicts the fundamental truths of reason and common sense.

An example of this is mentioned in Dr Ṣāliḥ's book *ʿUlūm al-Ḥadīth*:

> ʿAbd al-Raḥmān ibn Zayd was once asked, 'Didn't your father narrate to you on the authority of your grandfather that the Prophet (S) said, "Verily, the ark of Noah circumambulated the Kaʿbah and prayed two units behind *Maqām Ibrāhīm* ['the Station of Abraham']?"' To which he replied, 'Yes'.

[41] P. 134.

- if the purport of the tradition contradicts the laws of science, the realities of life, the results of empirical investigations and visible truths.

An example of this has been reported in the book *al-Haft wa al-Aẓillah*,[42] where it is stated that the *maʿṣūm* Imam is born from his mother's thigh, in a long tradition that al-Mufaḍḍal ibn ʿUmar al-Juʿfī[43] narrates on the authority of Imam Jaʿfar al-Ṣādiq (A), from which we have selected the following example:

> Al-Mufaḍḍal narrates that he himself said, 'Tell me, O my master, about the birth of the *awṣiyāʾ* [vicegerents].'
>
> Al-Ṣādiq replied, 'The first wonder is that the mothers of the *awṣiyāʾ* are male, and not female.'
>
> So I said, 'O master, Glory be to Allah, how can that be?'
>
> Al-Ṣādiq replied, 'The angels are in the form of women... Allah makes the bodies of the *awṣiyāʾ* grow as thighs on the angels, until they reach a certain extent. The angels are completely pure, as I told you. So when Allah wants to expose the Imam in the external world to discipline His creation, he sends a spirit from

[42] *Al-Haft wa al-Aẓillah* is one of the books deemed sacred by the Mufaḍḍaliyyah sect, which is an offshoot of the Khaṭṭābiyyah extremists following their eponym al-Mufaḍḍal ibn ʿUmar al-Juʿfī al-Ṣayrafī. The book has been ascribed to him, and is narrated – or so they claim – on the authority of Imam Jaʿfar al-Ṣādiq (A). The version edited by ʿĀrif Tāmir was published in 1960, and in 1964 with an edition by Muṣṭafā Ghālib, entitled *al-Haft al-Sharīf.*

[43] Ibn al-Ghaḍāʾirī said, with reference to him, that, 'he is weak, outrageous, exaggerates in his sayings and is a Khaṭṭābī'. Al-Najāshī described him as 'following a corrupt sect, narrating confusing traditions, and cannot be taken seriously'. He has also been described as being 'a Khaṭṭābī, and he has been credited with writing compilations that cannot be relied upon'. See his biography in *Tanqīḥ al-Maqāl.*

I could not find any mention of the book called *al-Haft* ascribed to him in any of the biographical dictionaries at my disposal. Even if this book has indeed been written by him, there is no doubt that what al-Ghaḍāʾirī has said about him is absolutely correct. And there is also no doubt that this book falsely narrates on Imam al-Ṣadiq's authority and has been forged in order to spread their extremist creed. It is therefore not permissible to believe in any of its contents, nor to rely upon it or refer to it.

> Himself, which enters the newborn, which has been purified of all impurities, and which has not been confined by a womb but rather the spirit has entered it, in order for him to discipline people and expose the truth.

- if the text of the tradition contains *isrā'īlīyyāt* that contradict the tenets of Islam.

An example has been narrated in both *ṣaḥīḥ*s of Bukhārī and Muslim:

> On the authority of Anas, on the authority of the Prophet (S), who said, 'People will be thrown in Hell, and it [Hell] will call out, "Is there any more?", until Allah will put his foot in it, when it will say, "Enough, enough..."' and 'on the authority of Abū Hurayrah, that Hell will be asked, "Are you full yet?", to which it will reply, "Is there any more?" Then the Lord will place his foot inside it, and it will say, "Enough, enough".'[44]

- if the text of the tradition contains any extremist notions.
- if the text of the tradition contains any of the legends of past peoples whose authenticity has not been proved.
- if the text of the tradition talks about any virtue or meritorious quality of an individual, a group or a place that does not befit that virtue or quality.
- if the text of the tradition indicates a miracle or supernatural incident, which has occurred out of context or in a situation that does not require such a thing.

5. The number of fabricated traditions

One fact that can be gathered from examining Sunni *ḥadīth* books and Shīʿa *ḥadīth* books is that the spread and circulation of this phenomenon were much more prominent in Sunni *ḥadīth* literature than in Shīʿa *ḥadīth* literature.

I referred to the *Fihrist* of al-Shaikh al-Ṭūsī, and in spite of finding a number of reporters who had been classified as weak, I did not come across any who had been classified as fabricators. When looking at al-Najāshī's *Fihrist*, better known as *Rijāl al-Najāshī*, I came across four

[44] Ta'ammulāt al-Ṣaḥīḥayn, p. 202.

people who had been dubbed fabricators, who are:

1. Jaʿfar ibn Muḥammad ibn Mālik ibn ʿĪsā ibn Sābūr, the client of Asmāʾ ibn Khārijah ibn Haṣīn al-Fazārī al-Kūfī. He [al-Najāshī] described him as being 'weak in his traditions'. Aḥmad ibn al-Husayn al-Ghaḍāʾirī described him, saying, 'He used to forge traditions intentionally, and narrate on the authority of unheard-of people. And I have heard someone else say that "he followed a corrupt sect and was corrupt in his transmission".'[45]
2. ʿUbayd ibn Kathīr ibn Muḥammad al-Kūfī. He described him, saying, 'The scholars have condemned him and have said that he fabricates traditions. He has a book known as *Kitāb al-Takhrīj fī Banī al-Shayṣabān*, but most of it is fabricated and embellished, and there is very little authentic material from him.'[46]
3. ʿAbd al-Raḥmān ibn Kathīr al-Hāshimī. He described him, saying, 'He was weak, and our scholars have criticized him, saying that he fabricates traditions... and he has a book called *al-Aẓillah*, which is corrupt and disordered.'
4. Muḥammad ibn Mūsā al-Hamadānī al-Sammān.[47] He described him, saying, 'The Qummī scholars have pronounced him weak because of his extremism, and Ibn al-Walīd used to say that he fabricated traditions.'[48]

There may have been others in this book that I did not happen to come across, but the number of fabricators the investigator will come across will certainly not exceed ten. If we refer to the later expanded biographical dictionaries, such as *Tanqīḥ al-Maqāl* and *Muʿjam Rijāl al-Ḥadīth*, the number of fabricators definitely enters double figures.

Dr Ḥasan Ibrāhīm Ḥasan, in his book *Tārīkh al-Islam*, says,

> Bukhārī compiled – as we know – 7,275 traditions in his book, including some repetitions. If we omit the repetitions, the total number of traditions is around 4,000. Bukhārī is said to have selected these 4,000 'authentic' ones out of some 300,000 in his possession. From this, the sheer amount of traditions that were

[45] Vol. I, pp. 302–3.
[46] Vol. II, pp. 43–44.
[47] Vol. II, p. 44.
[48] Vol. II, p. 227.

tampered with is evident.[49]

If we refer to the 'List of Fabricated and Distorted Traditions' from al-Shaikh al-Amīnī's book *al-Ghadīr*, whose statistics reflect Sunni *ḥadīth* literature, we find that the number is even greater than that to which Dr Ḥasan Ibrāhīm Ḥasan has alluded, for the number of forged traditions fabricated by 39 reporters is quoted as being 308,684.[50] He calculates the total number of Sunni fabricators of *ḥadīth* to be more than 600,[51] and gives proofs and examples of fabricated traditions about falsified virtues of the Prophet (S) from 100 traditions.[52] This is all because of Muʿāwiyah ibn Abī Sufyān's political motivation, mentioned previously, as well as the social and economic motivations, where the ruler would favour, encourage, and bestow gifts on fabricators of traditions.

The situation in Shīʿa *ḥadīth* literature, on the other hand, was completely different and fabrication was not spurred by these motivations, but rather by the religious motivation, the result of which was that extremist traditions infiltrated the *imāmī* traditions. I do not disregard the idea that both Umayyad and Abbasid dynasties may have had a hand in this, in their bid to inculpate the Shīʿa to justify persecuting, banishing, and annihilating them. This is especially relevant when we realize that there were a large number of Christians in the Umayyad and Abbasid courts, and it was probably through them that the rulers conspired for extremism to penetrate and infiltrate Shīʿa *ḥadīth* through secret channels. The stances adopted by the Imams in the face of this, however, curbed its influence and prevented the rulers from completely achieving their goals, except in a few insignificant areas.

What is extremely regrettable and unfortunate is that we do not find anyone from among our Sunni brothers to stand up against the anthropomorphic traditions that have infiltrated their collections in the same way. As *ḥadīth* collections are the most precious religious treasures we Muslims possess after the Qurʾān, it would have been ideal if they had done this, so that there be nothing therein to destroy

[49] Vol. I, p. 516.
[50] Vol. V, p. 288.
[51] Vol. V, pp. 209–75.
[52] Pp. 297–330.

Islam's reputation by damaging the very tenet of Divine Unity (*tawḥīd*).

6. Works about fabricated traditions

A great scholarly achievement carried out by *Ḥadīth* scholars of the Ahl al-Sunnah is their contribution to works on fabricated traditions, the most important of which are:

- *Kitāb Tadhkirat al-Mawḍūʿāt* (*Treatise on Fabricated Traditions*) by Abū al-Faḍl Muḥammad ibn Úāhir al-Maqdisī (d. 507 AH)
- *Kitāb al-Abāṭīl* (*Book on Trivialities*) by Abū ʿAbdallāh al-Ḥasan ibn Ibrāhīm al-Hamadānī al-Jawzaqī al-Ḥāfiẓ (d. 543 AH)
- *Kitāb al-Mawḍūʿāt* (*Book on Fabricated Traditions*) by Abū al-Faraj ʿAbd al-Raḥmān ibn ʿAlī ibn al-Jawzī (d. 597 AH)
- *Al-Qawl al-Musaddad fī al-Dhabb ʿan Musnad al-Imām Aḥmad* (*The Definitive Argument in Defence of Aḥmad b. Ḥanbal's Musnad*) by al-Ḥāfiẓ Ibn Ḥajar al-ʿAsqalānī (d. 852 AH)
- *Kitāb al-Laʾālī al-Maṣnūʿah fīl Aḥādīth al-Mawḍūʿah* (*Book on the Artificial Pearls in Fabricated Traditions*) by al-Ḥāfiẓ Jalāl al-Dīn al-Suyūṭī (d. 911 AH)
- *Kitāb Tanzīh al-Sharīʿah al-Marfūʿah ʿan al-Akhbār al-Shanīʿah al-Mawḍūʿah* (*Reinstating the Position of the Eminent Law from Abominable Fabricated Reports*) by Abū al-Ḥasan ʿAlī ibn Muḥammad al-Katānī (d. 963 AH)
- *Tadhkirah al-Mawḍūʿāt* (*Treatise on Fabricated Traditions*) by Jamāl al-Dīn al-Fatanī (d. 986 AH)
- *Al-Fawāʾid al-Majmūʿah fī al-Aḥādīth al-Mawḍūʿah* (*Sum of Benefits Collected in Fabricated Traditions*) by Abū ʿAbdallāh Muḥammad ibn ʿAlī al-Shawkānī al-Yamānī (d. 1250 AH)
- *Silsilah al-Aḥādīth al-Ḍaʿīfah wa al-Mawḍūʿah* (*Series of Weak and Fabricated Traditions*) by Nāṣir al-Dīn al-Albānī (contemporary).

Note: These books were written after the Sunni *ḥadīth* collections – the *ṣiḥāḥ* as well as others had already been compiled. This is why they did not dare to tackle the two *ṣaḥīḥ* strongholds, Bukhārī and Muslim, which continued to be venerated and revered in the hearts of the Ahl al-Sunnah even in such late times. If these books had been written before the canonical collections, their influence would definitely have been stronger and they would have had greater use, for they would probably have prevented the *isrā'īliyyāt* from penetrating these collections.

A Shī'a work on fabricated traditions is *Kitāb al-Mawḍū'āt fīl Āthār wa al-Akhbār* (*Book on Fabricated Works and Reports*) by al-Sayyid Hāshim Ma'rūf al-Ḥasanī (contemporary).

CHAPTER TEN

WHO CAN RELATE *ḤADĪTH*?

1. Importance of this Subject

This subject is considered among the most important subjects within the science of *ḥadīth* because it is the reporter's competence in transmissions and the qualifications that he must possess that allow valid traditions to be distinguished and differentiated from invalid traditions. It is also important because this is what biographers rely upon when carrying out the task of qualifying the reporters in terms of veracity, or defaming them, commending them or deprecating them, in order that the extent of the validity or invalidity in the chain can be ascertained in light of the qualities they mention about the reporters, and subsequently so that the standard of the chain can be established in terms of whether it is *authentic, good, dependable* or *weak*. This is also useful when measuring the preponderance among contradictory reports, where the chains can be classified in terms of high, low, or middle standard.[1]

2. Legitimacy of the Subject Matter

From what al-Shahīd al-Thānī has written by way of an introduction to this subject in *al-Bidāyah*, it seems that question arises here as to the legal permissibility of such an investigation, insofar as it may entail the infamy of reporters by disclosing hidden traits and making their private conduct public.

Al-Shahīd al-Thānī himself dealt with this question comprehensively and exhaustively, saying,

[1] Translator's Note: This science of evaluating reporters to assess their veracity or to defame them is termed 'the science of *jarḥ wa taʿdīl*' (lit. 'defamation and authentication'), which is how we will refer to it hereafter.

> This investigation is permitted, even though it may entail calumnizing a Muslim with a seemingly blameless record and publicizing vile deeds of believers, for the sake of preserving the pure Islamic law from the infiltration of alien elements into it, and in order to keep mistakes and lies well away from it.

One of the scholars is said to have been asked, 'Do you not fear that these people whose traditions you have rejected may stand up against you in complaint to Allah on the Day of Judgement?', to which he replied, 'I would much prefer them to stand up against me rather than the Prophet (S), who would ask me, "Why did you not guard my *ḥadīth* against lies?"'

It has been reported that someone heard one of the scholars defaming in this manner, and said to him, 'O shaikh, scholars must not be slandered.' He replied, 'Woe unto you! This is advice, not slander.'

This is an indisputable and evident matter, and is in fact one of the prerequisites of this science and a principle in the science of *ḥadīth*. Nonetheless, it is true that the investigator, in his inspection and defamation of someone, must ascertain the truth with care and precision so that he does not calumnize a good and blameless person, assuming him to be blameworthy and defaming him with a bad reputation that tarnishes him forever. Such a mistake has been committed by many a person, where they have discredited great and notable reporters on the basis of criticism they have heard about them that is either dubious or has not been verified properly.

So whoever wishes to base his investigations on the true circumstances of reporters should refer to the biographical dictionary of al-Kashshī. We have an adequate supply of *jarḥ wa taʿdīl* literature from our pious classical scholars from the works that they have compiled, such as Ibn al-Ghaḍāʾirī's book listing weak reporters, or works that contain both defamation (*jarḥ*) as well as authentication (*taʿdīl*) of reporters, such as the biographical dictionaries of al-Najāshī, al-Shaikh Abū Jaʿfar al-Ṭūsī, al-Sayyid Jamāl al-Dīn Aḥmad ibn Ṭāwūs, al-ʿAllāmah Jamāl al-Dīn ibn al-Muṭahhir, al-Shaikh Taqī al-Dīn ibn Dāwūd and others.

It is up to the adept investigator, whom Allah has endowed with the best of skills, to ponder over their writings and carefully consider their verdicts, for he may find many things that they have failed to notice, and come across directives of commendation and defamation that they have neglected, for we too have come across many such things, which we have noted in various places, especially when it comes to conflicting defamatory reports. Such conflicting reports have survived about many of the classical reporters. Al-Kashshī has quoted all the conflicting reports in his book, without weighing them up for preponderances, but has commented on them afterwards. The scholars have differed greatly with regard to determining which defamatory report gains preponderance over its counterpart. Therefore, the investigator should not blindly follow whatever has been written, but should use the faculties with which Allah has endowed him, for every scholar has been given his share of skills. Many people consider the method of combining these conflicting criticisms to be imprecise, because its methodology and principles differ from one to the other when dealing with authentic reports or good reports or dependable reports, and when discarding some or all of them, for sometimes there may not be an authentic report on either side, and combining reports would be unnecessary. Instead the investigator should look to rely upon the authentic reports as his basis, especially if some of the criticisms have come from authentic reports and their opposites from good or dependable reports; and he can rely on the combining method when the reports are not compatible with the previous method, etc.

Often scholars will happen to authenticate reporters using reports that are not suitable for authentication, as can be seen in their books, especially in *Khulāṣah al-Aqwāl*, which is the quintessence of biographical studies.[2]

3. Defining the Subject Matter

Some authors have called this section of *ḥadīth* studies 'Those Whose Transmission Can Be Accepted and Those Whose Transmission Is Rejected'. Others have called it 'The Attributes of a Reporter' or 'Prerequisites of a Reporter'. All the names describe the same aim, namely, to elucidate the reporter's competence in receiving and transmitting the report. Competence – as we know – is a person's aptitude to carry out a function, responsibility or task with which he

[2] *Al-Bidāyah*, p. 62.

has been entrusted. Hence, the reporter's competence is his aptitude and suitability for implementing the reception and transmission of a report, for which he needs to fulfil certain necessary requirements.

4. Personal Qualifications

These are attributes that a person must possess in order to be competent at receiving and transmitting a report. In other words, they are prerequisites in a person that must be fulfilled in order for him to be suitable as a reporter executing the task of reception and transmission. These prerequisites are as follow.

i. Islam

The reporter must be a Muslim when transmitting the report, though not necessarily when receiving it.

Al-Shahīd al-Thānī said,

> The leading scholars of *ḥadīth* and the principles of jurisprudence have agreed that adherence to Islam is a requirement of a reporter at the time of transmission, even though he may not have been a Muslim at the time of receiving the report.[3]

His son, al-Shaikh Ḥasan al-ʿĀmilī, said,

> We do not doubt that this is a prerequisite, in accordance with Allah's statement, 'If a corrupt person comes to you with any news, ascertain the truth...' and this includes unbelievers [i.e. non-Muslims] as well as others.[4]

The requirement, stipulated in recent times, that the reporter be a Muslim, carries with it, by unanimous agreement, the rule that the report of an unbeliever (*kāfir*) is not acceptable.

ii. Reason

The reporter must be sane. This is a self-evident and unanimously agreed requirement for competence.

[3] *Al-Bidāyah*, p. 64.
[4] *Al-Maʿālim*, pp. 352–53.

iii. Maturity

The reporter must have reached the legal age of maturity, the age at which he has legal rights and obligations, when he transmits the report, though not necessarily when he receives it. The scholars are unanimous on this point.

iv. Faith

The reporter must be an *imāmī* Shīʿa (Ithnā ʿAsharī). Al-Shaikh al-ʿĀmilī said, 'This prerequisite is well known among our associates [i.e. Shīʿa scholars]'.[5]

Some of our scholars will also consider the opposite, that is, they will accept the report of a *non-imāmī* from either Shīʿa or Sunni sects, if they consider him to be dependable – as explained under the definition of the *muwaththaq* ('dependable') tradition.

This is the opinion held by al-Shaikh al-Ṭūsī, according to his detailed exposition of the issue, the conclusion of which is that:

1 The report of a Sunni is acceptable, if he has been deemed dependable by our scholars – not just in his own school of thought – and if he has narrated on the authority of one of our Imams (A), provided that none of our traditions contradicts his.

He said in *al-ʿUddah*,[6]

> If he differs in his belief of the principles of our faith, in spite of which he narrates on the authority of the Imams (A), his report is inspected as follows:
>
> If there is something in the reliable sources that contradicts his report, then it must be rejected.
>
> If there is nothing contradictory that causes us to reject it, and there are other reports that confirm what he has said, then it must be accepted and implemented.
>
> If there is no report from our correct school of thought with which his report agrees nor any that it contradicts, nor do the scholars know anything averse to it, it must be accepted and

[5] *Al-Maʿālim*, p. 353.
[6] See pp. 379–80.

> implemented, according to a narration on the authority of Imam al-Ṣādiq (A), who said, 'If you are faced with a situation for which you cannot find any ruling from us, then look into what they [the Ahl al-Sunnah] have narrated on the authority of Imam ʿAlī (A), and implement it'.

According to what we have mentioned above, the Shīʿa have accepted and implemented the reports of Ḥafṣ ibn Ghiyāth, Ghiyāth ibn Kulūb, Nūḥ ibn Darrāj, al-Sakūnī and other Sunnis who have narrated reports on the authority of our Imams (A) that they have not denied and that are not countered by any contradictory reports from them.

2 The report of a non-*imāmī* Shīʿa is acceptable, if he has been deemed dependable by our scholars – not just in his own school of thought – provided that:

- there is nothing by way of contradiction to his report in our reports;
- his report is linked to evidence that boosts its acceptability;
- our reports contain information corroborating his report.

He said (pp. 380–81),

> If the reporter is from one of the Shīʿa sects such as al-Faṭḥiyyah or al-Wāqifah or al-Nāwūsīyyah or any others, his report must be inspected as follows:
>
> If there is associated evidence or another reliable report that backs up his report, then it must be accepted and implemented.
>
> If there is another reliable report that contradicts his report, the dubious content of his report must be rejected and the report of the reliable person only must be implemented.
>
> If there is no reliable report to counter his report, and if the *imāmī* scholars do not know of anything to disparage it, then it must be accepted and implemented, as long as the reporter is conscientious about his narration and is trusted as reliable, even though he may be erring in his school of thought.
>
> In accordance with these principles, our school of thought has implemented the reports of adherents of the Faṭḥiyyah, such as ʿAbdallāh ibn Bukayr and others, the reports of some of the Wāqifah, such as Samāʿah ibn Mahrān, ʿAlī ibn Abī Ḥamzah,

ʿUthmān ibn ʿĪsā, and of those that came after them, among them Banū Faḍḍāl, Banū Samāʿah, al-Ṭāṭarīyyūn – their reports having been uncontested by other established ones.

3 As regards the acceptance or rejection of reports narrated by the extremist sects (*ghulāt*), suspect and weak reporters, he said:

> As for the extremists: if they are such that their state of righteousness can be distinguished from their state of deviation, then whatever they have narrated during their righteous state can be implemented and whatever they narrate during their extremist state is rejected. This is why our school of thought has implemented what Abū al-Khaṭṭāb Muḥammad Abū Zainab narrated when he used to be righteous and has rejected whatever he narrated after his deviation. The same stance has been adopted with regard to reports from Aḥmad ibn Hilāl al-ʿAbartāʾī, Ibn Abī ʿAdhāfir and others. Whatever extremists narrate during their state of extremism cannot be implemented in any case whatsoever.
>
> The same goes for suspect and weak reporters, although if there is anything to support their narration that proves its authenticity, then it must be implemented. And if there is no such certification for its authenticity, then the report must be discarded.
>
> This is why the great scholars discarded the reports of many such people, and they neither transmitted them nor quoted them in their indexes and compilations.

v. Veracity

We have spoken at length above about veracity, the concept of it and the different opinions about it, so we will go on to deal with the means of ascertaining veracity and infamy.

The Means of Ascertaining Veracity and Infamy

How can we ascertain whether this reporter, whose report we would like to furnish as evidence for deducing legal rulings and extrapolation, can be described as veracious or not? The scholars have listed three means of doing so.

i) Widespread repute

This means that the veracity or infamy of a reporter is well known within scholarly circles, be it in the field of *ḥadīth* or in other scholarly fields. The scholars have affirmed the veracity of 'our classical scholars from the time of al-Shaikh Muḥammad ibn Yaʿqūb al-Kulaynī up to the present day using their widespread repute... such that it was not necessary for any of these classical scholars' integrity to be stipulated textually, nor was their veracity called into question, for their reliability, accuracy and piety in addition to their veracity was famed in all ages.'[7]

ii) Testimony

This is when two veracious persons testify to the integrity of a reporter or defame him, by uttering statements about him such as: 'he is reliable' or 'he is a liar', etc. Testimony is required for ascertaining the veracity or infamy of reporters who are not widely reputed to be such in scholarly circles. This is carried out by reference to the source biographical dictionaries, such as the works of the scholars of Baghdād, like al-Kashshī, al-Najāshī, al-Ṭūsī and subsequent scholars, and of the scholars of Ḥillah, such as Ibn Ṭāwūs, al-ʿAllāmah and Ibn Dāwūd.

iii) The Evidence of a Single Veracious Person

Our famous scholars believe that it suffices to rely upon a single reporter in order to accept a report. Ascertaining the reporter's integrity constitutes a subsidiary investigation into the acceptance of a report; and just as number had no consequence in the initial investigation – which was concerned with accepting the report (i.e. of one person) – it is also of no consequence in the subsidiary investigation – which is ascertaining the integrity or lack of integrity of the reporter.

Others believe that a single witness is not enough, because ascertaining integrity and infamy fall under legal testimony, and testimony in turn must involve numbers.

Al-Fāḍil al-Qummī put it excellently when he said,

> Ascertaining integrity is a subject to do with individual rational speculation, not fact and testimony. The criterion here is to arrive at valid speculation, however this may be achieved – and why not? For the scholars who go about ascertaining this integrity never met the Companions of our Imams (A), but relied upon

[7] *Al-Bidāyah*, p. 69.

statements such as those narrated by al-Kashshī.[8]

The conclusion of the above is that if the biographers' evaluation of reporters, from both reliable biographical dictionaries and the faculties of jurisprudential reasoning that the researcher possesses, generates speculation about the worth of the reporter, this speculation can be depended on and relied upon and the report can be evaluated in light of it.

Combination of Both Veracity and Infamy

From the previous issue stems the question: what would happen if there were both statements attesting to the veracity of the reporter and statements defaming him? The authors of *ḥadīth* works have treated the subject as a general incident that may happen in everyday life situations. This would be correct if one were laying down guidelines for future study and investigation to help those who were likely to come across actual living reporters; and we would benefit from such explanations if we wanted to evaluate a contemporary reporter. However, when we are dealing with reporters who have passed into history, we cannot evaluate their characters, except through whatever has been written about them in biographical dictionaries, and these are merely quoted statements resulting from investigations dating centuries back, or from studies that scholars who lived before the biographical authors' time undertook, whose conclusions alone were available to the biographers.

The solution for us, therefore, lies in elucidating the method of dealing with the characteristics listed in the biographical dictionaries, the treatment of this subject being based on our knowledge of the individual methodologies carried out by the biographers. For example, if we compare the biographical dictionaries of al-Najāshī and al-Ṭūsī objectively, we find that al-Najāshī is more detailed and more precise in his evaluations. This being so, if al-Najāshī's evaluation of someone clashed with al-Ṭūsī's, al-Najāshī's would predominate.

Similarly, if the evaluation of the Baghdādī biographers (al-Kashshī, al-Najāshī, and al-Ṭūsī) clashed with the Ḥillī (Ibn Ṭāwūs, al-ʿAllāmah, and Ibn Dāwūd) biographers' evaluation, the Baghdādī

[8] *Al-Miqbās*, vol. II, p. 173.

evaluation would predominate, because they based their evaluations on what they had gained from the scholars immediately preceding their generation, who were closer in time and better acquainted with the lives and circumstances of the reporters.

Ultimately, this issue is based largely on personal judgement and investigation, stemming from the investigator's own methodology and from the basic principles that lead him to this.

vi. Accuracy

This means that the reporter must have memorized whatever he is narrating, 'and if he is narrating from memory, he must be attentive and not heedless. If he is writing it or dictating it to someone, he must be accurate and guard against any mistakes, grammatical errors, or misspellings. And if he is narrating the meaning, he must be aware of anything that could distort the meaning'[9] – according to those who permit this.

5. Narration by Women

Following what he said previously, al-Shahīd al-Thānī said, 'It is not a prerequisite of a reporter that he be male, because it was not originally so stipulated and because the pious predecessors and their descendants are all unanimous about accepting the report of a woman.'[10]

Hence, we encounter the names of a significant number of female reporters, narrators, and *ṣāḥibāt al-ijāzāt* (women who have been specially authorized to transmit traditions) in biographical dictionaries, history books, and catalogues of reporters. The names of some of these women are listed in the remaining pages of this chapter.

[9] *Al-Bidāyah*, pp. 65–66.
[10] *Al-Dirāyah*, p. 66.

— *from among the Ṣaḥābiyyāt (women who lived at the time of the Prophet)*

- The mother of the believers Khadījah bint Khuwaylid al-Qurashiyyah.
- The mother of the believers Umm Salamah bint Umayyah ibn al-Mughīrah al-Makhzūmiyyah – who narrated 378 traditions on the authority of the Prophet (S).
- The mother of the believers ʿĀʾishah bint Abū Bakr al-Tamīmiyyah – on whose authority 2210 traditions have been narrated.
- The mother of the believers Ḥafṣah bint ʿUmar ibn al-Khaṭṭāb al-ʿAdawiyyah – Bukhārī and Muslim have quoted 60 traditions of hers.
- Arwā bint Anīs – who narrated on the authority of the Prophet (S).
- Asmāʾ bint Abū Bakr Dhāt al-Niṭāqayn.
- Asmāʾ bint ʿUmays al-Khathʿamiyyah.
- Umm Ayman: Barakah bint Thaʿlabah al-Ḥabashiyyah.
- Umm Ḥudhayfah ibn al-Yamān – whose son Ḥudhayfah narrated on her authority.
- Umm al-Khaṭṭāb, the wife of ʿUthmān ibn Maẓʿūn – whose son Khaṭṭāb narrated on her authority.
- Umm Saʿd bint Saʿd ibn al-Rabīʿ al-Anṣāriyyah – Dāwūd ibn al-Ḥaṣīn narrated on her authority.
- Umm Sulaym bint Malḥān – who narrated on the authority of the Prophet (S), and whose son Ibn ʿAbbās and others narrated on her authority.
- Umm Sumbulah al-Aslamiyyah – ʿĀʾishah narrated on her authority.
- Umm ʿAbdallāh ibn Masʿūd – who narrated on the authority of the Prophet (S), and whose son ʿAbdallāh narrated on her authority.
- Umm Farwah al-Anṣāriyyah – whose nephew al-Qāsim ibn Hanām narrated on her authority.
- Umm al-Faḍl: Lubābah bint al-Ḥārith al-Hilāliyyah, wife of al-ʿAbbās ibn al-Muṭṭalib – who narrated on the authority of the Prophet (S), and whose two sons Tamām and ʿAbdallāh narrated on her authority.
- Umm al-Karām al-Salamiyyah – who narrated on the authority of the Prophet (S).
- Umm Naṣr al-Muḥāribiyyah.
- Umm Hānī al-Anṣāriyyah.
- Jumrah bint al-Nuʿmān al-ʿAdawiyyah.
- Darrah bint Abī Salamah al-

Makhzūmiyyah.

- Sā'ibah, the Prophet's (S) slavegirl – who narrated on his authority, and Ṭāriq ibn ʿAbd al-Raḥmān narrated on her authority.
- Sabīʿah al-Aslamiyyah – who narrated on the authority of the Prophet.
- Laylā, the wife of Abū Dharr al-Ghaffārī – Umāmah bint al-Ṣalat narrated on her authority.
- Nasībah bint al-Kaʿb al-Anṣāriyyah, the mother of ʿĀmmārah.

— *from among the Tābiʿiyyāt (women in the second generation of Muslims known as the Followers)*

- Asmā' bint ʿAbd al-Raḥmān ibn Abī Bakr.
- Umm Jamīlah al-Saʿdiyyah – who narrated on the authority of ʿĀ'ishah.
- Umm Ḥafṣ bint ʿUbayd ibn ʿĀzib – who narrated on the authority of her uncle al-Barrā' ibn ʿĀzib
- Umm Ḥamīd bint ʿAbd al-Raḥmān – who narrated on the authority of ʿĀ'ishah.
- Umm ʿAmr bint Khawāt ibn Jubayr – who narrated on the authority of ʿĀ'ishah.
- Umm ʿĪsā ibn ʿAbd al-Raḥmān – who narrated on the authority of ʿĀ'ishah.
- Umm Kulthūm al-Laythiyyah – who narrated on the authority of ʿĀ'ishah, and ʿAbdallāh ibn ʿUbayd al-Laythī narrated on her authority.
- Umm Maskīn bint ʿĀṣim ibn ʿUmar ibn al-Khaṭṭāb – who narrated on the authority of Abū Hurayrah.
- Barzah Umm al-Zubayr ibn ʿArabī – who narrated on the authority of ʿĀ'ishah.
- Tabālah bint Yazīd – who narrated on the authority of ʿĀ'ishah.
- Jumānah bint al-Musayyib ibn al-Najiyyah al-Fazārī – who narrated on the authority of Ḥudhayfah ibn al-Yamān.
- Dhafrah bint Ghālib al-Rāsibiyyah al-Baṣriyyah – who narrated on the authority of ʿĀ'ishah
- Zubaybah bint al-Nuʿmān – who narrated on the authority of Abū Hurayrah.
- Zaynab bint Kaʿb, wife of Abū Saʿīd al-Khudrī – whose authority was attested by Ibn Ḥibbān.
- Zaynab bint Nabīṭ al-Anṣāriyyah.
- Sārah bint ʿAbdallāh ibn Masʿūd – who narrated on the authority of her father.
- Sakīnah bint Quraysh – who

narrated on the authority of ʿĀʾishah, and Muslim al-Jaramī narrated on her authority.

- Salmā, the slavegirl of Bakr ibn Wāʾil – who narrated on the authority of Umm Salamah and others.
- Sumā al-Anṣariyyah – who narrated on the authority of Umm Salamah.
- Sīrīn bint ʿAbdallāh ibn Masʿūd – who narrated on the authority of her father.
- Ṣafiyyah bint Shaybah ibn ʿUthmān al-ʿAbdariyyah – whose authority was attested by Ibn Ḥibbān.
- Karīmah bint Hammām – who narrated on the authority of ʿĀʾishah, and ʿAlī ibn Mubārak and Yaḥyā ibn Abī Kathīr narrated on her authority.
- Maryam bint Ayyās al-Anṣāriyyah.
- Hind bint al-Ḥārith – who narrated on the authority of Umm Salamah.
- Hind bint Shurayk al-Baṣriyyah – who narrated on the authority of ʿĀʾishah.

— *from among the Imāmiyyāt (the women of the Ahl al-Bayt and the companions of the Imams)*

- Fāṭimah al-Zahrāʾ (A) – who narrated on the authority of her father (S).
- Zaynab bint ʿAlī ibn Abī Ṭālib (A).
- Fāṭimah bint ʿAlī ibn Abī Ṭālib – who narrated on the authority of her father.
- Fāṭimah bint al-Ḥasan ibn ʿAlī ibn Abī Ṭālib.
- Fāṭimah bint al-Ḥusayn ibn ʿAlī ibn Abī Ṭālib – who narrated on the authority of her father and her brother Zayn al-ʿĀbidīn (A), and her son ʿAbdallāh ibn al-Ḥasan al-Muthannah narrated on her authority.
- Fāṭimah bint ʿAlī ibn al-Ḥusayn ibn ʿAlī ibn Abī Ṭālib – who narrated on the authority of her aunt Fāṭimah bint al-Ḥusayn.
- Fāṭimah bint Muḥammad al-Bāqir (A).
- Fāṭimah bint Jaʿfar al-Ṣādiq (A).
- Fāṭimah bint Mūsā al-Kāẓim (A).
- Fāṭimah bint ʿAlī al-Riḍā (A) – who narrated on the authority of Fāṭimah bint Mūsā al-Kāẓim, who narrated in turn on the authority of Fāṭimah bint Jaʿfar al-Ṣādiq, who narrated in turn on the authority of Fāṭimah bint Muḥammad al-Bāqir, who narrated in turn on the authority of Fāṭimah bint ʿAlī

Zayn al-ʿĀbidīn, who narrated in turn on the authority of Fāṭimah bint al-Ḥusayn, who narrated on the authority of Umm Kulthūm bint ʿAlī ibn Abī Ṭālib, who narrated on the authority of Fāṭimah al-Zahrāʾ (A).

- Umm Kulthūm bint ʿAlī ibn Abī Ṭālib.
- Āminah Baygum bint Muḥammad Taqī al-Majlisī.
- Asmāʾ bint ʿĀbis ibn Rabīʿah al-Kūfiyyah – who narrated on the authority of her father, and on whose authority Ibn Mājah narrated.
- Umm Abīhā bint ʿAbdallāh ibn Jaʿfar al-Ṭayyār.
- Umm al-Aswad bint Aʿyan, sister of Zurārah – who was the first woman to become a Shīʿa from the clan of Aʿyan.
- Umm al-Ḥasan Fāṭimah bint Muḥammad ibn Makkī al-Shahīd al-Awwal – whom her father and Sayyid Ibn Maʿiyyah gave permission to transmit on their authority.
- Umm al-Ḥasan ibn ʿAlī ibn Ziyād al-Washāʾ – whose son al-Ḥasan narrated on her authority.
- Umm Salamah the mother of Muḥammad ibn al-Muhājir – Muḥammad ibn Abī ʿUmayr narrated on her authority on the authority of Imam Jaʿfar al-Ṣādiq (A).
- Umm Farwah Fāṭimah bint al-Qāsim ibn Muḥammad ibn Abī Bakr, the mother of Imam al-Ṣādiq (A) – who narrated on the authority of Imam Zayn al-ʿĀbidīn (A).
- Umm Mūsā Ḥabībah, the slavegirl of Amīr al-Mu'minīn (A) – on whose authority she narrated.
- Umm Hānī al-Thaqafiyyah – who narrated on the authority of Imam Muḥammad al-Bāqir (A).
- Ḥabābah bint Jaʿfar al-Asadiyyah al-Wālibiyyah Umm al-Nidā.
- Ḥakīmah bint Mūsā al-Kāẓim (A).
- Ḥakīmah bint Muḥammad al-Jawād (A).
- Ḥamādah, sister of Abī ʿUbaydah al-Ḥadhāʾ – who narrated on the authority of Imam al-Ṣādiq (A).
- Ḥamīdah, the mother of Imam Mūsā al-Kāẓim (A).
- Khadījah bint ʿUmar ibn ʿAlī ibn al-Ḥusayn – who narrated on the authority of her uncle Imam Muḥammad al-Bāqir (A).
- Al-Rabāb, wife of Imam al-Ḥusayn (A).
- Saʿīdah bint ʿUmayr – who narrated on the authority of Imam al-Ṣādiq (A).
- Sakīnah bint al-Ḥusayn ibn ʿAlī ibn Abī Ṭālib.

- ʿAliyyah bint ʿAlī ibn al-Ḥusayn Zayn al-ʿĀbidīn – who wrote a book.
- Fāṭimah bint al-Sayyid Raḍī al-Dīn ʿAlī ibn Ṭāwūs – who had permission from her father to transmit on his authority.
- Kulthūm bint Sulaym – who narrated on the authority of Imam al-Riḍā (A), and Muḥammad ibn Ismāʿīl ibn Bazīʿ narrated on her authority.
- Māriyah al-ʿAbadiyyah.
- Munah bint Abī ʿUmayr – who narrated on the authority of Imam al-Ṣādiq (A).
- Al-Hāshimiyyah al-Ispahāniyyah bint al-Sayyid Muḥammad ʿAlī Amīn al-Tajjār, the jurisconsult and *mujtahidah* (scholar capable of independent legal deduction) – who had authorized permission from leading scholars to exercise her independent legal reasoning (*ijtihād*).

— *Others*

- Āsiyah bint Jārallāh al-Shaybānī al-Ṭabarī (796–835 AH) – whom al-Ḥāfiẓ al-ʿIrāqī and others permitted to narrate on their authority, and al-Suyūṭī took traditions from her, and she in turn gave Shams al-Dīn Muḥammad ibn ʿAbd al-Raḥmān al-Sakhāwī permission to transmit on her authority.
- Āminah bint Abī al-Ḥarb, from among the authoritative associates of Abī Ṭāhir al-Khaṭīb al-Anbārī.
- Āminah bint Mūsā ibn Aḥmad (d. 860 AH) – who permitted the aforementioned al-Sakhāwī to transmit on her authority.
- Āminah bint Naṣrallāh al-Kanāniyyah (770–853 AH) – al-Sakhāwī studied under her, and a group of scholars permitted her to transmit on their authority.
- Umm Aḥmad al-Mirsiyyah (d. 850 AH) – who permitted al-Sakhāwī to transmit on her authority.
- Umm al-Bahāʾ Fāṭimah bint al-Ḥāfiẓ Taqī al-Dīn Muḥammad al-Hāshimiyyah, from among the authoritative associates of al-Suyūṭī.
- Umm al-Khayr bint Yūsuf – from whom al-Suyūṭī took traditions.
- Khadījah bint Ismāʿīl ibn ʿUmar – who permitted al-Suyūṭī to transmit on her authority.
- Darrah bint Ṣāliḥ (d. 607 AH)

– who narrated on the authority of al-Armawī with his permission.

- Ruqayyah bint Aḥmad – who obtained permission to transmit on the authority of Zaynab al-Shiʿriyyah in the year 669 AH.

CHAPTER ELEVEN

GENERAL AUTHENTICATIONS

When a reader investigates the books of *ḥadīth*, the biographical dictionaries and the books of deductive jurisprudence, he will come across certain expressions that seem to be traditionist (i.e. to do with *ḥadīth*) precepts or criteria derived from *ḥadīth* studies and biographical studies. However, they have not been recorded in the works of the classical scholars as perceptions or investigations, but as conclusive results of investigations that were carried out and put aside, and that have not reached us.

Later scholars, especially the contemporary ones, have attempted to study these expressions in light of the principles and fundamentals of *ḥadīth* and biographical studies, in order to derive the results of the proofs and documented evidence therein.

I decided to term this study 'general authentications' because it is in actual fact an authentication of a group of traditions within a specific framework, from which I have chosen to look at the most crucial and most comprehensive, which are:

- the authentication of *aṣḥāb al-ijmāʿ*'s reports;
- the authentication of the three principal transmitters of *mursal* ('hurried') traditions: Ibn Abī 'Umayr, Ṣafwān ibn Yaḥyā and Aḥmad ibn Muḥammad ibn Abī Naṣr al-Bizanṭī;
- the authentication of traditions from the Four Books.

I will proceed to deal with each one of them as thoroughly and as comprehensively as possible, given the limitations of time and space.

1. Authentication of the Reports from the *Aṣḥāb al-Ijmāʿ*

Al-Shaikh Abū ʿAmr al-Kashshī, in his famous biographical dictionary known as *Rijāl al-Kashshī*, said that our scholars are in *unanimous agreement* (*ijmāʿ*) about authenticating the traditions of 18 reporters from among the companions of the Imams (A).

This is why they have been termed *aṣḥāb al-ijmāʿ*.[1]

a. Their Names

These companions are divided into three groups, and each of the groups contains six reporters, divided between Companions of four of the Imams, as follows:

i. From Among the Companions of Imam al-Bāqir and Imam al-Ṣādiq (A)

- Zurārah ibn Aʿyan al-Shaybānī al-Kūfī
- Maʿrūf ibn Kharrabūdh al-Makkī
- Barīd ibn Muʿāwiyah al-ʿAjalī
- Al-Fuḍayl ibn Yasār al-Baṣrī
- Muḥammad ibn Muslim al-Ṭāʾifī al-Kūfī
- Abū Baṣīr ʿAbdallāh ibn Muḥammad al-Asadī or Abū Baṣīr Layth ibn al-Bakhtarī al-Murādī

ii. From Among the Companions of Imam al-Ṣādiq (A)

- Jamīl ibn Darrāj al-Nakhaʿī
- ʿAbdallāh ibn Muskān al-ʿAnazī
- ʿAbdallāh ibn Bukay ibn Aʿyan al-Kūfī
- Ḥammād ibn ʿĪsā al-Juhnī
- Ḥammād ibn ʿUthmān al-Nāb
- Abān ibn ʿUthmān al-Aḥmar al-Bajalī

iii. from among the companions of Imam al-Kāẓim and Imam al-Riḍā (A)

- Yūnus ibn ʿAbd al-Raḥmān
- Ṣafwān ibn Yaḥyā al-Bajalī Bayyāʿ al-Sābirī
- Muḥammad ibn Abī ʿUmayr al-Azdī al-Baghdādī
- ʿAbdallāh ibn al-Mughīrah al-Bajalī

[1] Translator's Note: *ijmāʿ* in Arabic means 'unanimous agreement' or 'consensus'; hence, the phrase means 'the agreed-upon companions'. As the English phrase is quite cumbersome, we will continue to refer to them by their Arabic appellation.

- Aḥmad ibn Muḥammad ibn Abī Naṣr al-Bizanṭī al-Kūfī
- Al-Ḥasan ibn Maḥbūb al-Sarrād al-Kūfī or Al-Ḥasan ibn ʿAlī ibn Faḍāl and Faḍālah ibn Ayyūb al-Azdī or ʿUthmān ibn ʿĪsā al-Rawāsī

b. The Wordings in al-Kashshī's Expressions

i) When referring to the jurisconsults from among the companions of Imam al-Bāqir and Imam al-Ṣādiq (A), he said,

> The body of Shīʿa scholars (*ʿiṣābah*)[2] have reached a consensus attesting the honesty of these foremost companions of Abū Jaʿfar (al-Bāqir) and Abū ʿAbdallāh (al-Ṣādiq) (A), and have examined them with regard to their jurisprudence, saying, the six most skilled at jurisprudence out of these foremost companions are: Zurārah, Maʿrūf ibn Kharrabūdh, Barīd, Abū Baṣīr al-Asadī, al-Fuḍayl ibn Yasār and Muḥammad ibn Muslim al-Ṭāʾifī. The most skilled of them all is Zurārah. Some of the scholars have said that instead of Abū Baṣīr al-Asadī, the companion so designated is Abū Baṣir Layth ibn al-Bakhtarī al-Murādī.[3]

ii) In reference to the jurisconsults from among the companions of Imam al-Ṣādiq (A), he said,

> The body of Shīʿa scholars have reached a consensus authenticating the soundness of whatever is narrated on their authority and attesting the truth in their statements. They have confirmed the juristic capacity of six more companions in addition to those six companions previously listed and named, who are: Jamīl ibn Darrāj, ʿAbdallāh ibn Miskān, ʿAbdallāh ibn Bukayr, Ḥammād ibn ʿĪsā, Ḥammād ibn ʿUthmān, and Abān ibn ʿUthmān. They have said that the jurisconsult Abū Isḥāq – i.e. Thaʿlabah ibn Maymūn – asserted that the most skilled at jurisprudence out of these six was Jamīl ibn Darrāj, and that they have all narrated the most traditions from Imam Jaʿfar al-Ṣādiq (A).[4]

[2] In Shīʿa sources there are frequent references to the consensus of *al-ʿiṣābah*, indicating that band of the Imams' Companions who were invested with the authority of giving *fatwā*. The *ʿiṣābah*, or 'body of scholars', by practising the binding authority of *ijmāʿ* ('consensus'), determined the course and character of Shīʿite sectarianism.

[3] Al-Wasāʾil, vol. XX, p. 79: Appendix VII.

[4] Ibid., p 80.

iii) As regards the jurisconsults from among the companions of Imam Mūsā al-Kāẓim and Imam al-Riḍā (A), he said,

> Our scholars have reached a consensus authenticating the soundness of whatever is narrated on their authority and attesting to their honesty, and have confirmed their juristic capacity and knowledge, and they are yet another six people in addition to those mentioned above: Yūnus ibn ʿAbd al-Raḥmān, Ṣafwān ibn Yaḥyā Bayyāʿ al-Sābirī, Muḥammad ibn Abī ʿUmayr, ʿAbdallāh ibn al-Mughīrah, al-Ḥasan ibn Maḥbūb and Aḥmad ibn Muḥammad ibn Abī Naṣr. Some of the scholars have replaced the name of al-Ḥasan ibn Maḥbūb with al-Ḥasan ibn ʿAlī al-Faḍāl or Faḍālah ibn Ayyūb, whereas others have substituted say ʿUthmān ibn ʿĪsā for Faḍālah ibn Ayyūb. The most skilled of all these jurists were Yūnus ibn ʿAbd al-Raḥmān and Ṣafwān ibn Yaḥyā.[5]

The Significance of al-Kashshī's Statements

There are three different opinions about the degree of significance that can be derived from the above statements.

- that they denote the authentication of the *aṣḥāb al-ijmāʿ* and the attestation of their honesty in all the reports that they transmit, for example when they say, 'x narrated to me...' or 'I heard x saying...'
- that they denote the authenticity of the reports that the *aṣḥāb al-ijmāʿ* themselves narrate directly on the authority of the Imams, be it a 'supported' narration or a 'hurried' narration, and whether the intermediaries between the *aṣḥāb al-ijmāʿ* and the Imams are veracious or dependable or indeed in the absence of any intermediaries.
- that they denote the authenticity of whatever is reported on their (the *aṣḥāb al-ijmāʿ*'s) authority.

In other words, it can mean the authentication of:

- everything that the *aṣḥāb al-ijmāʿ* narrate, or
- everything that the *aṣḥāb al-ijmāʿ* narrate on the authority of the Imam, or
- everything that is narrated on the *aṣḥāb al-ijmāʿ*'s authority.

[5] Ibid.

According to the first opinion, with the exception of the *asḥāb al-ijmāʿ*, all reporters are subject to evaluation, as a result of which their reports may be deemed valid and acceptable or invalid and unacceptable.

According to the second opinion, the *aṣḥāb al-ijmāʿ* 's narrations on the authority of the Imam are regarded as valid, but the subsequent reporters' narrations on the authority of the *aṣḥāb al-ijmāʿ* are subject to evaluation, and may be found to be valid and acceptable or invalid and unacceptable.

According to the third opinion, the reports are considered to be valid and acceptable on all accounts and are exempt from evaluation.

If we re-examine the wording of al-Kashshī's statements – given that the statements all mean the same thing, the exact wording being as follows: 'The body of Shīʿa scholars have reached a consensus attesting the honesty of these... '

'The body of Shīʿa scholars have reached a consensus authenticating the soundness of whatever is narrated on their authority, and attesting the truth in their statements... '

'Our scholars have reached a consensus authenticating the soundness of whatever is narrated on their authority, and attesting to their honesty... '

We find that the first statement indicates the attestation of their honesty, which encompasses both their honesty in terms of their personal integrity and the truth of whatever they say and transmit. This correlates with the second opinion, which regards their transmission on the authority of the Imam as valid, whether it is 'supported' or 'hurried' and whether the chain is made of veracious or weak reporters. We can see that the second and third statements both hold same meaning as the first statement, and can thus conclude as follows:

Only the chain of transmission between the subsequent reporter and the *aṣḥāb al-ijmāʿ* needs to be validated for the entire report to be considered valid, as the *aṣḥāb al-ijmāʿ* have already been authenticated as honest in their transmission between the Imam and themselves.

c. Nature of *Ijmāʿ* ('General Consensus')

There are two different opinions with regard to the nature of the general consensus mentioned by al-Kashshī in the above statements:

i) that it is the legally binding consensus that constitutes one of the sources in the principles of jurisprudence, whose doctrinal justification rested on the presence of the Imam and which disclosed the Imam's opinion.

Al-Ḥurr al-ʿĀmilī is of this opinion, and says in his *Wasāʾil*,

> Know that in these noble traditions [i.e. al-Kashshī's statements], the *maʿṣūm* or even two *maʿṣūms* (A) enter into this noble consensus conveyed by this eminent reliable authority or another. Not to mention the fact that in this noble consensus, whose transmission and chain have been established, there is decisive evidence that every single tradition narrated by one of the above-mentioned scholars, be it 'supported' or 'hurried', narrated by a veracious, weak or unknown reporter, is authentic because of the statement and the consensus.[6]

ii) that consensus here simply denotes mutual agreement and unanimity with regard to something.

Al-Mīrzā al-Nūrī mentions this opinion in his *Mustadrak*, saying,

> The consensus of 'the body of scholars' about the authenticity of the traditions of this group of companions is a consensus that hinges on the conjunction of their traditions with evidence that leads to their authentication.[7]

He supports the view that consensus here means the consensus of opinions, and not the consensus achieved from adding the *maʿṣūm*'s opinion into the equation. According to al-Mīrzā al-Nūrī, the word *ijtamaʿat* ('reached a consensus') in al-Kashshī's statement is synonymous with the word *ajmaʿat* ('agreed unanimously').

Furthermore, *ijmāʿ* or 'consensus', in its legal and technical sense, did not become prominent as legal evidence and as one of the sources of *imāmī* legislation until after the Minor Occultation of the 12th Imam, i.e. during the time of al-Shaikh al-Mufīd and his students. Therefore, only three sources of legislation have historically been listed by al-Sayyid al-Murtaḍā in *al-Dharīʿah* and al-Shaikh al-Ṭūsī in

[6] Vol. 20, pp. 80–81.
[7] Vol. 3, p. 759.

al-ʿUddah. Al-Shaikh al-Kashshī, who conveys this 'consensus', died in the year 340 AH, which means that this 'consensus' of religious scholars can have taken place only during the Minor Occultation, which ended in 329 AH. This reinforces the fact that this was not a legal consensus resting on the presence of the Imam, for there was no need yet for such a legal consensus to disclose the Imam's opinion.

d. Another Opinion

A contrasting opinion held by some scholars is that it is not permissible to accept whatever has been authenticated as sound from the reports of the *aṣḥāb al-ijmāʿ*. One of the proponents of this view is al-Sayyid al-Khūʾī, in his book *Muʿjam Rijāl al-Ḥadīth*. In light of what we have just concluded, that the consensus conveyed by al-Kashshī was not the legal consensus but was a unanimous agreement based on the existence of certain proofs that led the scholars so to conclude, he believes that since the beginning of the Major Occultation, these associated proofs began to disappear, such that it was no longer possible for later scholars to accept what earlier scholars had accepted. This was because they had had certain pieces of evidence at their disposal, which had aided their investigations and to which later scholars no longer had recourse.

In light of what we have seen so far, this issue is a matter of personal judgement, in which the proofs and the extent of their capacity for extrapolation of rulings must be examined carefully.

2. Authentication of the Three Principal Transmitters of Mursal Traditions

These three are:

i) Muḥammad ibn Abī ʿUmayr al-Azdī al-Baghdādī (d. 217 AH)

Al-Najāshī described him as being 'of esteemed ranking and eminent position, according to us as well as to our opponents'.

Al-Qummī said,

> He was the most dependable person according to both Shīʿā and Ahl al-Sunnah, and the most ascetic of them all, the most pious, the best worshipper, and the best-acquainted with Imam Mūsā al-Kāẓim and the two Imams after him (A). He was one of the *aṣḥāb*

> *al-ijmāʿ*, of esteemed ranking and eminent position. Our scholars rely upon his *mursal* ('hurried') reports because he used to forward reports only on the authority of reliable people.[8]

ii) Ṣafwān ibn Yaḥyā al-Bajalī al-Kūfī (d. 210 AH)

Al-Najāshī called him 'reliable, reliable, distinguished. His father used to narrate on the authority of Abū ʿAbdallāh (A), and he narrated on the authority of Imam al-Riḍā (A) with whom he had an eminent position.'

Al-Shaikh al-Ṭūsī said that he was 'the most reliable person of his time and the best worshipper of all, according to the traditionists'.[9]

We mentioned previously that al-Kashshī included him among the *aṣḥāb al-ijmāʿ*.

iii) Aḥmad ibn Muḥammad ibn Abī Naṣr al-Bizanṭī al-Kūfī (d. 221 AH)

Al-Shaikh al-Ṭūsī said of him, 'He is reliable; he met al-Riḍā (A) and had an esteemed position with him'.[10]

We mentioned previously that al-Kashshī included him too among the *aṣḥāb al-ijmāʿ*.

What is meant by 'authentication' here is that if these three people forwarded a tradition on the authority of the Imam, it would be accepted and considered as a valid tradition, and would not be subject to the usual criteria for evaluation of a *mursal* ('hurried') tradition.

The first person to say this was al-Shaikh al-Ṭūsī, in his *ʿUddah*. When explaining the preponderance of a reporter over another, he said,

> If one of the reporters narrates 'supported' traditions going back to the *maʿṣūm*, and the other forwards traditions on the authority of the *maʿṣūm*, the circumstance of the second reporter should be looked into. If he is someone who is known to forward traditions on the authority of reliable persons only, then another report cannot gain preponderance over his report. Because of this, the body of Shīʿa scholars (*ṭāʾifah*)[11] treated the narrations of Muḥammad ibn Abī ʿUmayr, Ṣafwān ibn Yaḥyā and Aḥmad ibn Muḥammad ibn Abī Naṣr and other such reliable people on the

[8] *Al-Kunan wa al-Alqāb*, vol. I, pp. 199–200.
[9] Muʿjam Rijāl al-Ḥadīth, vol. IX, p. 124.
[10] Ibid., vol. II, p. 231.
[11] Synonymous with *ʿiṣābah*.

> same footing as the 'supported' narrations of other reporters, for they knew that these people narrated and forwarded reports only on the authority of reliable and dependable people. They therefore implemented their *mursal* reports, even if they were different from other reports.[12]

What we can conclude from the above:

- That regarding a *mursal* report as valid is not restricted to the narrations of these three individuals, but applies to all such reliable reporters who are known to narrate on the authority of reliable people only.
- That the scholars, from the word *ṭā'ifah* [the body of Shīʿa scholars] in the above paragraph, have concluded it to mean a consensus of scholars.
- Hence, this issue is dealt with in the same way as the previous one about the traditions of the *aṣḥāb al-ijmāʿ*. It is strongly believed that the consensus to which al-Shaikh al-Ṭūsī alluded – when he said that the body of Shīʿa scholars (*ṭā'ifah*) had treated the hurried reports the same as others – is the same *ijmāʿ* ('consensus') that al-Kashshī conveyed, especially since these three reporters are included among the *aṣḥāb al-ijmāʿ*.
- These three reporters were quoted by al-Shaikh al-Ṭūsī in his above statement, as part of an example he was giving to make his point, which further supports the idea that this ruling is generalized and applied to every reliable reporter who is known to forward traditions on the authority of reliable people only. Based on this, the two above issues are treated as one and the same. Similarly, the consensus to which al-Shaikh al-Ṭūsī alluded is not the legally binding consensus but the consensus of opinion, since the legal consensus became prominent as a source of legislation only at the time of al-Shaikh al-Mufīd and his students, and al-Shaikh al-Ṭūsī points out that this particular consensus was arrived at before that time.

In the same respect, this issue is also a matter of personal judgement, which the investigator must make based on his knowledge of the evidence and on the extent of its demonstrative power.

[12] Vol. I, p. 386.

3. Authentication of the Traditions in the Four Books

a. The Four Books

Al-Kāfī by Abū Jaʿfar Muḥammad ibn Yaʿqūb al-Kulaynī al-Rāzī (d. 329 AH)

Man Lā Yaḥḍuruhu al-Faqīh Abū Jaʿfar Muḥammad ibn ʿAlī ibn al-Ḥusayn ibn Mūsā ibn Bābawayh al-Qummī (d. 381 AH)

Tahdhīb al-Aḥkām Abū Jaʿfar Muḥammad ibn al-Ḥasan al-Ṭūsī (d. 460 AH)

Al-Istibṣar also by Abū Jaʿfar al-Ṭūsī

b. The Issue

What is meant by authentication here is whether all the traditions quoted on the authority of the Ahl al-Bayt (A) in these Four Books can be considered valid and established as having originated from a *maʿṣūm*. This issue is the subject of much controversy among scholars, as also of quite elaborate discussions and debate.

The main point of controversy is whether the statements of the three eminent scholars about the authenticity of their traditions and the reliability of their reporters constitute a testimony on their part, whereby they can be accepted, based on the validity of one veracious person's testimony (i.e. the author's) in such a matter, or whether these statements are merely an 'independent judgement' (*ijtihād*) on their part, based on their own individual methodologies, which then means that they are not authoritative for anyone other than themselves.

The author of *al-Mafātīḥ* said,

> Al-Kulaynī's assertion that everything he has written in *al-Kāfī* is authentic can arise from a standpoint of his certainty about them and his decisive knowledge that they have come down from the Imams (A), in which case they can be relied upon, as is the case with all statements of veracious people; or his assertion may arise from a judgemental standpoint about them and how they appear to him, even if it be by means of speculative evidence. In this

> second case, it would not be permissible to rely upon them, as the speculation of a jurisconsult is not authoritative proof, and this is deemed self-evident by the scholars, not to mention by all sensible people. There would, therefore, be no possibility of giving preference to the first alternative, which would have obligated reliance upon these reports.[13]

The origin of all this stems from the discussion that al-Mīrzā Muḥammad Amīn al-Astarābādī al-Akhbārī raised in his book entitled *al-Fawā'id al-Madaniyyah*,[14] entitled 'Section 9: About the authentication of the traditions in our books, from my understanding of them by the help of Allah, the King the All-Knowing, and by the guidance of the Ahl al-Dhikr [i.e. the Ahl al-Bayt] (A), and by the permissibility of referring to them because they have been successively attributed to their author'. He then goes on to list twelve reasons for accepting the authenticity of the traditions in the Four Books. The most important and weightiest of these reasons are the statements that the three shaikhs themselves have made in the prefaces of their books, asserting their belief that all the traditions contained therein are traditions that have been narrated on the authority of the Imams (A).

A large group of our scholars and the majority of the Akhbārī scholars followed him in this respect, and al-Ḥurr al-ʿĀmilī, for example, formulated the sixth appendix of his book *al-Wasā'il*[15] in accordance with this, saying, 'Appendix Six: about the attestation of a large group of our scholars as to the authenticity of the aforementioned books and similar books, their multiple successive attribution to their respective authors, and the confirmation that the traditions contained in them have come down from the *maʿṣūms*'.

Then he quoted what each of the three shaikhs said about their conviction that everything they had quoted in their books was authentically from the Ahl al-Bayt (A). He continued by quoting the assertions of other scholars.

In the ninth appendix, he mentioned 22 proofs of the decisive origin of the traditions in the Four Books and other such books written by our classical scholars on the authority of the Ahl al-Bayt

[13] Dirāsāt fī al-Ḥadīth wa al-Muḥaddithīn, pp. 135–36.
[14] P. 181.
[15] Vol. XX, p. 61.

(A), including the proofs listed by al-Mīrzā al-Astarābādī. Here too, the most important and weightiest of proofs was the attestations of the three shaikhs themselves in the prefaces of their books, asserting their conviction about the authenticity of the traditions quoted therein on the authority of the Ahl al-Bayt (A).

The reason why this discussion was brought up in the first place was al-Sayyid Ibn Ṭāwūs's four-part classification of reports, affirmed by his student, al-ʿAllāmah al-Ḥillī, which served to promote the opening up of this issue for discussion and exhaustive study. The impetus was what had happened to the whole phenomenon of the *imāmī* faith after the Major Occultation of the 12th Imam (A) when the associated proofs denoting the validity or invalidity of traditions began to disappear, and a great number of the four hundred *uṣūl* source collections were lost.

Al-Shaikh al-Ṭarīḥī says,

> The reason for this, according to some of the later scholars, is that such a long period of time elapsed between the first centuries of Islam and the later scholars. This all goes back to the destruction of some of the reliable source material because of the oppression of cruel and tyrannical governors and the widespread terror to which people were subjected when they wanted to expose or transcribe this source material. Moreover, some of the source collections were joined together with famous collections of the time. The result was that the traditions that had been taken from the reliable source material got mixed up with the traditions that had not been taken from such reliable sources; and the frequently quoted traditions became obscured by the infrequently quoted traditions. Hence, most of the proofs that had allowed scholars of the past to rely upon many of these traditions were now missing and unavailable for the later scholars, and they were not able to follow in the classical scholars' footsteps in distinguishing the reliable from the unreliable. So they began to need regulations to enable them to distinguish valid and reliable traditions from the rest, so they established for us – may Allah reward them for their efforts – a new system of classification, and brought closer what had become distant, and classified the traditions quoted in books of deductive jurisprudence in terms of authenticity, commendability, and dependability.[16]

[16] *Jāmiʿ al-Maqāl*, pp. 36–37.

As long as it is the case that extraneous material infiltrates into matters pertaining to precautionary aspects of religion and formulation of the noble Sunnah, it is essential to re-examine the whole phenomenon of reports. Al-Mīrzā al-Astarābādī and other Akhbārīs who followed him did not see any such significant effect in the development of *imāmī ḥadīth* literature that necessitated re-examination.

In order for us to be able to examine the true state of affairs and respond to the requirements of this study in a systematic manner, we must first quote the relevant passages from the introductions of their books and then attempt to examine them more closely in order to comprehend their import or at least what is evident from them.

i) From al-Kāfī*'s Introduction*

> You wanted a book to be handy, comprehensive and inclusive of all knowledge about your religion – a book on which a student of religion could safely rely, to which a seeker of light and guidance could turn and from which a student seeking the knowledge of religion could derive full benefit and act on *the traditions of the truthful Imams (A).*

This is al-Kulaynī's testimonial passage from which we can derive his assertion that the contents of his book *al-Kāfī* are the 'traditions of the truthful Imams'.

Al-Sayyid al-Khū'ī – may Allah sanctify him – disputed this derived significance, saying:

> In objection to what has been said about Muḥammad ibn Yaʿqūb al-Kulaynī's testimony that all the traditions in his book are authentic reports of the truthful Imams, I say as follows. First, Muḥammad ibn Yaʿqūb was asked to compile a book that would include all the authentic reports of the truthful Imams (A). However, there was no condition imposed on him to the effect that he should not quote anything other than authentic traditions or traditions on the authority of anyone other than the Imams (A) in addition. Muḥammad ibn Yaʿqūb produced what he had been asked, and wrote a book that comprised the authentic traditions of the Imams in all facets of religious knowledge, albeit containing other inauthentic traditions from them (A) or authentic traditions from other people too, in the process of broaching the subjects and achieving maximum benefit. So it would be possible for the investigator to contrive the authenticity

of a report that had not been deemed authentic by the author, or had not been established as such.

Accordingly, we must note that Muḥammad ibn Yaʿqūb did quote many traditions in *al-Kāfī* on the authority of non-*maʿṣūms*, a few of which we will mention here:

The report on the authority of ʿAlī ibn Ibrāhīm, on the authority of some of his associates, on the authority of Hishām ibn al-Ḥakam, who said, 'Things can be perceived through two means only...'[17]

The report with its chain on the authority of Abū Ayyūb al-Naḥawī, who said, 'Abū Jaʿfar al-Manṣūr sent for me in the middle of the night...'[18] He also quoted it on the authority of ʿAlī ibn Ibrāhīm, on the authority of his father, on the authority of al-Naḍr ibn Suwayd.[19]

The report with its chain on the authority of Usayd ibn Ṣafwān, the Companion of the Prophet (S), who said, 'When the day of Amīr al-Mu'minīn (A)'s death dawned, the whole place shook with weeping'.[20]

The report with its chain on the authority of Idrīs ibn ʿAbdallāh al-Awadī, who said, 'When al-Ḥusayn (A) was killed, the people wanted to trample their horses on him.'[21]

The report with its chain on the authority of Fuḍayl, who said, 'The virtues of kindness and good character bring about love'.[22]

The report with its chain on the authority of Ibn Miskān, on the authority of Abū Ḥamzah, who said, 'The believer blends in compassion in his deeds...'[23]

The report with its chain on the authority of al-Yamān ibn ʿUbaydallāh, who said, 'I saw Yaḥyā ibn Umm al-Ṭawīl standing by the church... '[24]

[17] *Al-Kāfī*, vol. I, book 3, ch. 9: On the Refutation of Seeing Allah, number 12.

[18] *Al-Kāfī*, vol. I, book 4, ch. 71: The Sign and the Warrant for Abū al-Ḥasan Mūsā (A), number 13.

[19] *Al-Kāfī*, vol. I, book 4, ch. 71: The Sign and the Warrant for Abū al-Ḥasan Mūsā (A), number 14.

[20] *Al-Kāfī*, vol. I, book 4, ch.112: On the Birth of Amīr al-Mu'minīn (A), number 4.

[21] *Al-Kāfī*, vol. I, book 4, ch.115: On the Birth of al-Ḥusayn ibn ʿAlī (A), number 8.

[22] *Al-Kāfī*, vol. II, book 1, ch.50: On Good Character, number 5.

[23] *Al-Kāfī*, vol. II, book 1, ch.55: On Compassion, number 2.

[24] *Al-Kāfī*, vol. II, book 1, ch.163: On Social Interaction with the Deviated

The report with its chain on the authority of Isḥāq ibn ʿAmmār, who said, 'Condolences must be given at the graveside only...'[25]

The report with its chain on the authority of Yūnus, who said, 'Every adulterous act is fornication, but every act of fornication is not adultery...' and this is a long tradition to which Muḥammad ibn Yaʿqūb allocated a separate chapter.[26] He also narrated a report with its chain on the authority of Yūnus, in which he said, 'the reason why shares are to be divided into six, no more or less...' and 'Bequests have been divided into six portions...'[27] Muḥammad ibn Yaʿqūb also allocated separate chapters for these two traditions.

The report with its chain on the authority of Ibrāhīm ibn Abī al-Bilād, who said, 'al-ʿAbbās ibn Mūsā censured me...'[28]

The report from the book of Abū Nuʿaym al-Ṭaḥḥān, which he narrated on the authority of Shurayk, on the authority of Ismāʿīl ibn Abī Khālid, on the authority of Ḥakīm ibn Jābir, on the authority of Zayd ibn Thābit, in which he said, 'It was customary in the pre-Islamic period for men to leave no inheritance to women.'[29]

The report with its chain on the authority of Ismāʿīl ibn Jaʿfar, who said. 'Two men disputing about a cow came to Dāwūd (A)...'[30]

Second: Given that Muḥammad ibn Yaʿqūb attested to the authenticity of all the traditions in *al-Kāfī*, then such an attestation is inconceivable, for if by it he meant that all the traditions individually meet the conditions of authoritativeness, then this is definitely false, for among them are *mursal* traditions, chains containing unknown persons and well-known fabricators of traditions such as Abū al-Bakhtarī. And if by his attestation he meant that in spite of these traditions lacking authoritativeness in themselves, there are external

Communities, number 16.

[25] *Al-Kāfī*, vol. III, book 3, ch. 70: On Condolences and the Duties of the Bereaved, number 3.

[26] *Al-Kāfī*, vol. III, book 3, ch. 70: On Condolences and the Duties of the Bereaved, number 3.

[27] *Al-Kāfī*, vol. VII, book 2, ch. 11: On the Reason Why Shares Are No More Than Six, number 1.

[28] *Al-Kāfī*, vol. VI, book 6, ch. 134: On *Ushnān* and *Suʿd* [types of plants], number 5.

[29] *Al-Kāfī*, vol. VII, book 2, ch. 2: On the Explanation of Obligatory Acts in the Qurʾān, number 2.

[30] *Al-Kāfī*, vol. VII, book 6, ch. 19: On Unusual Matters, number 21.

proofs that determine their authenticity and their reliability, then although this is possible, it cannot lead us to consider them as one hundred per cent correct nor to attribute authenticity to so many such traditions that do not even meet the requirements of validity.

It is extremely improbable that all these sources should contain marks of truth, and furthermore, Muḥammad ibn Yaʿqūb's assertion about the authenticity of everything in his book was not a testimony, but rather his own personal judgement, based on what he believed to be proofs of their soundness. If we had access to the factors that he took to be proofs of authenticity, they may not even generate speculation for us, let alone certitude.

Third: There are some unusual traditions to be found in *al-Kāfī* that would be deemed reliable had we not definitely proved that they have not originated from *maʿṣūms*. Therefore, how can the allegation be true that all the traditions in *al-Kāfī* are definitely authentic and that they have all come down from *maʿṣūms*? Our point that not all the traditions in *al-Kāfī* are authentic is further supported by the fact that al-Shaikh al-Ṣadūq did not believe them to be so, and nor did his teacher, Muḥammad ibn al-Ḥasan ibn al-Walīd.

The conclusion, therefore, is that not only has the authenticity of all the traditions in *al-Kāfī* not be established, but there is also no doubt that some of them are weak, and some of them are believed to have come down from non-*maʿṣūms*; and Allah knows best about the inner particularities of matters.[31]

If we were to continue reading the preface of *al-Kāfī*, we would find that al-Shaikh al-Kulaynī did not firmly believe that everything in his book was authentic, but rather he hoped that he had compiled the book according to the demands made of him, as we can see from his statement:

> Thus has Allah made the task of selecting and collecting the traditions easy. All praise is due to Allah, that He has enabled me to compile the book that you have requested. I hope that this book will serve your purpose. Whatever deficiency there may be in this work of mine, know that there is none in the sincerity of my intention to counsel my people, which is essential, especially in the case of our brethren and fellow Shīʿa.

[31] *Muʿjam Rijāl al-Ḥadīth*, vol. I, pp. 89–92.

His 'hoping' here is not a result of his modesty, but rather points to the fact that it was not a product of decisive certitude and that he had tried his utmost to accomplish what was asked of him, and thereafter could only hope that his labours had been satisfactory.

If he had indeed been sure that he had accomplished what he had been asked to do, he would have affirmed this explicitly because this is a matter that pertains to legal affairs. Instead he speculated and even implied that his book might contain substandard material, such as his reports on the authority of non-Imams, as well as weak, unknown and forging reporters. He would have known all this perfectly well for he was a scholar of biographical studies, who even compiled biographical works himself. This is especially pertinent because the proofs or authenticity that may have existed and aided previous scholars to accept these reports were no longer extant during his time.

Al-Sayyid al-Ḥasanī says,

> It is obvious from al-Kulaynī's statement, 'Thus has Allah made the task of selecting and collecting the traditions easy. I hope that this book will serve your purpose' that he was relying upon his personal judgement and his studies in selecting the traditions that he compiled in his *al-Kāfī*.[32]

ii) From* al-Faqīh*'s Introduction

> I have not set out to quote everything that other authors quote in such works, but rather to quote only those traditions on the basis of which a legal verdict (*fatwā*) can be given with a degree of certainty, and those that are deemed authentic; and I believe that so far as authoritativeness of a tradition is concerned, it is a matter between me and my Lord – may His Remembrance be hallowed and His Might exalted – and everything in my book has been taken from the famous books whose authenticity is agreed upon and accepted by all.

It is clear from al-Shaikh al-Ṣadūq's statement that he believes in the authenticity of everything in his book, and that he sees its authoritativeness as a matter between himself and Allah. It is also clear that this is his personal judgement based on his individual methodology, which al-Sayyid al-Khū'ī defined as being 'following

[32] Dirāsāt fī al-Ḥadīth wa al-Muḥaddithīn, vol. II, p. 138.

his teacher al-Shaikh Muḥammad ibn al-Ḥasan ibn al-Walīd al-Qummī in deeming traditions weak or authentic', and that he himself did not investigate whether a reporter was reliable or not, as witnessed by his own assertion in *al-Faqīh* (in the chapter on voluntary fasting and its rewards):

> As regards the report about the prayer of the Day of Ghadīr Khum and the reward stipulated for whoever fasts on that day, our shaikh Muḥammad ibn al-Ḥasan did not authenticate it, saying that it came down on the authority of Muḥammad ibn Mūsā al-Hamadhānī, who was not reliable. All the reports that the shaikh *has not authenticated and has not established as such are discarded by us and deemed inauthentic.*

Personal judgement is not a testimony that can be taken as authoritative proof over something else. Al-Sayyid al-Khū'ī says,

> Al-Shaikh al-Ṣadūq's assertion that the reports in his book are authentic and authoritative is an assertion based on his opinion and personal judgement, which has no authority over anything else.

iii) From* al-Tahdhīb*'s Introduction

I set out the issue as it was and sought information about it, from the literal wording of the Qur'ān, its explanation, its significance, import or meaning; from the Sunnah that has been established by way of *mutawātir* reports or reports linked to evidence proving their authenticity; from the consensus of Muslims if it exists concerning this particular matter; or from the consensus of the correct sect. Then I quoted any famous traditions of our scholars about the matter, and then investigated into traditions that opposed or contradicted these. I went on to elucidate the common ground between them, either through the interpretation derived by combining both conflicting traditions or by indicating the point of disparity between them, any weaknesses in the chain or any assertion that the body of scholars have acted in opposition to the content of such a tradition. If there was no reason to prefer one of two conflicting reports, then I clarified that the implementation of an action must be in accordance with what is found in the *aṣl* (*ḥadīth* source collection), and whatever goes against this should be discarded. As long as I was able to interpret traditions without disparaging their chains, I did so, and exercised my independent judgement in quoting a tradition whose content supported my interpretation of it, either from its literal meaning or its significance, until I had reached a verdict based upon the interpretation of the report; and even though this may not be incumbent upon us, it is discernible through adherence to traditions. I have adopted this method throughout the book, and have elucidated matters clearly so that it is not left ambiguous for the investigator in any way.

This statement, though long, contains no explicit indication on the author's part that the contents of his book are authentic. Rather, what is discernible explicitly is that the book may contain inauthentic material, as per his statement: 'or by indicating the point of disparity between them, any weaknesses in the chain or any the assertion that the body of scholars have acted in opposition to the content of such a tradition'.

iv) From* al-Istibṣār *'s Introduction

Al-Istibṣār is an abridgement of *al-Tahdhīb*, i.e. a summary of it, as the author mentioned in his introduction, saying, 'So they asked me to summarize it [*al-Tahdhīb*], and devote care to its compilation and abridgement...'

He used the same methodology in both books, explaining, 'I have adopted this method in my large book mentioned earlier'.

Just as there is nothing in *al-Tahdhīb* to suggest that the author believed that all the traditions in his book were authentic, so there is nothing in this book to suggest it either.

Conclusion: The contents of the Four Books are no different from the contents of other *ḥadīth* books, in that it is just as essential that they be subject to the standards of evaluation of the reporter and the narration.

CHAPTER TWELVE

MANNER OF RECEIVING AND TRANSMITTING *ḤADĪTH*

1. Reception and Conveyance

While reading about the reporter's competence at narrating, we frequently come across the words 'reception' (*taḥammul*) and 'conveyance' (*adāʾ*) of *ḥadīth*, as two technical terms in the science of *ḥadīth*. They are defined as follows:

- Reception denotes the reporter's receipt of the tradition from another reporter who narrated it to him, and the receiving reporter's subsequent learning of it, whether it be learning by heart or by use of a book or written record. Reception, therefore, means carrying the tradition, though the *ḥadīth* scholars have preferred to use 'reception' as a technical term instead of 'carrying', because the word 'reception' implies a certain responsibility, and there is no doubt that receiving and passing on *ḥadīth* involve some degree of responsibility in guarding it against infiltration or distortion from external material.
- Conveyance denotes a reporter's narration of the tradition to another reporter who takes it from him.

2. Transmission

It is a well-known fact that the *ḥadīth* represents the noble Sunnah, which is the second source in Islamic legislation after the Qurʾān. Islamic legislation remains authoritative for all Muslims, present and future, until the end of time. Because of this, it is essential that *ḥadīth* be transmitted from one generation to the next. In order for it to be transmitted intact, the scholars have laid down certain criteria for this transmission, which are:

- competence in conveying

- competence in receiving
- means of transmission.

Because we have already treated the subject of competence in conveying, we shall concentrate on the other two subjects. In light of the above, we can define transmission as the passage of the tradition from one reporter to the next, with the purpose of implying the existence of its chain between the generations of Muslims.

3. Competence in Reception

This refers to the attributes or prerequisites that must be met by a person who wishes to receive *ḥadīth*. They are:

a. Reason

As explained previously under the attributes required by a reporter, reason is a self-evident prerequisite, because receiving *ḥadīth* is a responsibility, and responsibility, in terms both of Islam and the law, can be borne only by a sane person who knows what he is doing.

b. Distinction

According to al-Shahīd al-Thānī's definition of it, this means that

> the bearer of the tradition must be able to differentiate between the tradition he is narrating and any other, if he hears it from an authenticated source.[1]

This prerequisite has also been referred to as *samāʿ*, or 'hearing', or by similar terms within the 'means of transmission'.

c. Accuracy

This we have already defined under the qualities of a reporter. It is also a prerequisite here for the reporter to distinguish his report from among other traditions, if he has not heard it from an authenticated source.

[1] *Al-Dirāyah*, p. 82.

4. Means of Transmitting *Ḥadīth*

Scholars of *ḥadīth* have adhered to these means of transmission and have also required them to pertain in transmission between one reporter to the next, although not between the first reporter and the *maʿṣūm*, as this method of transmission was invariably through 'hearing'. Some scholars list eight different means, treating *waṣiyyah* as a separate category, whereas others treat it as part of *iʿlām*, thus listing only seven.

a. *Samāʿ* ('Hearing')

A reporter can be described as 'hearing the tradition' or 'listening to the tradition' or 'hearing someone narrating' or 'listening to someone narrating'. *Samāʿ*, therefore, literally means 'to hear' or 'to listen'. It also has a technical meaning, viz. to learn, by heart or from a book, for example when a student hears the tradition from his teacher and learns it. There are two subsidiary methods of 'hearing': *imlāʾ* ('dictation') and *taḥdīth* ('narration of traditions').

imlāʾ ('dictation'): This is when the teacher dictates the tradition to his student, either reading out from his book or from memory, and the student writes it down.

taḥdīth ('narration of traditions'): This is when the teacher narrates traditions, either from a book or from memory, and the student listens to him.

b. *Qirāʾah* ('Reading')

This is when the student reads back to the teacher the tradition that his teacher has narrated to him, or when someone else rereads the tradition and the student listens. There is no differentiation between reading from memory and from a book, provided that the teacher confirms and certifies that the tradition has been read out correctly. This method is also termed *ʿarḍ* ('presentation'), since the student is presenting his understanding of the tradition to his teacher in order to check the accuracy of the chain and content.

c. *Munāwalah* ('Handing Over')

This is when the teacher hands over his book of traditions to his student or to any other person who wishes to narrate on his authority. This is divided into two types:

Munāwalah with permission to transmit from it: i.e. when the teacher gives his book to his student or to a person wishing to narrate on his authority, he explicitly indicates or utters his permission, allowing him to narrate on his authority, saying something like, 'this is what I have heard/this is my report, narrate it on my authority' or 'I allow you to narrate it on my authority'.

Munāwalah without permission to transmit from it: i.e. when the teacher hands over his book, he does not utter permission, but merely says words to the effect of 'this is what I have heard' or 'this is my report', and leaves it at that.

d. *Kitābah* ('Writing Down')

This is when the teacher writes down his tradition, either in his own hand or ordering someone else to write it (provided that the text has some kind of indication to this). Then he sends the text to whoever wishes to narrate on his authority. This is also divided into two types:

Kitābah with permission to transmit it:, i.e. when the teacher writes to the person wishing to narrate the written tradition on his authority, permitting him to do so.

Kitābah without permission to transmit it, i.e. when the written tradition is unaccompanied by written permission to transmit.

e. *Iʿlām* ('Declaration')

'This means that the teacher would declare and inform the student that this book or this tradition is his report or a result of his hearing a certain report from someone, without actually saying words to the effect of "narrate on my authority" or "I permit you to narrate it".'[2]

f. *Waṣiyyah* ('Will')

This is when a reporter instructs a person, before a journey or his

[2] *Al-Dirāyah*, p. 106.

death, to narrate his book of traditions or some other traditions on his authority.

g. *Wijādah* ('Finding Traditions')

This has been defined in *ḥadīth* terminology as obtaining knowledge from a manuscript, without having heard it (*samāʿ*), without having been given it (*munāwalah*) and without permission to transmit it. The word itself was not originally part of the Arabic language (although its root was), but was coined specifically for this usage.

It occurs when the reporter comes across a book or a written tradition of a reporter from whom he did not hear the tradition, whose permission he does not have to transmit it on his authority, and which was not given to him by the author. In explaining the origin of the report, 'he would probably say, "I found it and read it in the handwriting of x/in x's book in his own handwriting, on the authority of..."'[3]

h. *Ijāzah* ('Permission to Transmit the Tradition')

This is expressed in works of traditions by words such as 'the teacher permitted the student' or 'the teacher allowed the student', meaning he permitted him to transmit traditions on his authority. One may also find such expressions as 'the student asked permission from his teacher', meaning he asked him for permission to transmit on his authority. *Ijāzah* is, therefore, permission and authorization to narrate traditions on one's authority.

Al-Shaikh al-Ṭihrānī defined it as 'the utterance of a person who possesses a written composition, permitting the transmission of traditions on his authority after having declared the reports in their entirety'.[4]

Ijāzah is also of two types:

Oral *ijāzah*, where the teacher would utter his permission to the student, saying words to the effect of 'I give you permission to transmit the traditions I have heard and have in my possession' or 'I allow you to transmit the traditions I have heard and have in my

[3] Ibid., p. 108.
[4] *Al-Dharīʿah*, vol. I, p. 131.

possession, on my authority'.

Written *ijāzah*, where the teacher would give his student written permission to transmit on his authority. Written permission is further divided into three types:

- Brief *ijāzah*: where the teacher would simply give permission to narrate on his authority, writing, for example, 'I give x permission to narrate the traditions that I deem correct, on my authority'.
- Intermediate *ijāzah*: when the person giving permission would quote one of the chains of transmission in full, in demonstrating the blessedness of the chain that has come down intact from the Ahl al-Bayt (A).
- Extensive *ijāzah*: this is when the person giving permission would mention, as part of his permission, all his authoritative sources and their respective chains of transmission going back to the *maʿṣūms*, along with the biographies of all the notable reporters and other features that would benefit the case.

Examples of extensive *ijāzah* are:

al-ʿAllāmah al-Ḥillī's *ijāzah* to the sons of Zahrah al-Ḥalabiyyīn, which al-Shaikh al-Majlisī has quoted in *Biḥār al-Anwār* (107:6).

The *ijāzah* of al-Shaikh al-ʿĀmilī, author of *al-Maʿālim*, given to al-Sayyid Najm al-Dīn al-Ḥusaynī and his two sons, also mentioned in *Biḥār al-Anwār* (109:3).

The *ijāzah* of al-Muḥaddith al-Baḥrānī, the author of *al-Ḥadāʾiq*. The *ijāzah* is entitled *Luʾluʾah al-Baḥrayn fī al-Ijāzah li Qurratay al-ʿAyn*, and was published in India and in Najaf, edited by al-Sayyid Muḥammad Ṣādiq Baḥr al-ʿUlūm.

The *ijāzah* of al-Sayyid ʿAbdallāh al-Jazāʾirī entitled *al-Ijāzah al-Kabīrah*, published in Qum, edited by Muḥammad al-Samāḥī al-Ḥāʾirī, supervised by al-Sayyid Maḥmūd al-Marʿashī, with introduction by al-Sayyid al-Marʿashī al-Najafī – may Allah sanctify him.

The *ijāzah* of al-Sayyid Ḥasan al-Ṣadr al-Kāẓimī, entitled *Baghyah al-Wuʿāt fī Ṭabaqāt Mashāyikh al-Ijāzāt.*

The benefits of the *ijāzah*, as outlined by al-Shaikh al-Ṭihrānī , are:

The consecutive link between chains of transmissions of books and traditions to each other, and their intact formulation without breaks or omissions.

The good fortune of being able to trace a chain of transmission back to the Ahl al-Bayt (A), and the blessedness of having a chain include notable scholars and descendants of the Prophets narrating on their authority (A).

Reference to the recorded *ijāzahs*, especially the extensive ones, enables one to find the biographies of reporters and scholars, their conduct and methodologies, the names of their books, libraries, and encyclopedias, the centres of scholarly knowledge, their environments and eras and many other such useful information.

All Praise is due to Allah, the Lord of the Universe.

GLOSSARY

adāʾ: conveyance, denoting a reporter's narration of the tradition to another reporter who takes it from him.

ʿadālah: veracity. See Introduction.

ʿādil: veracious – lexically means just, equitable and reliable. In jurisprudence, this designates a person of irreproachable reputation and veracity whose testimony is valid.

ʿadl: equitable.

āḥād or khabar al-wāḥid: solitary report – refers to any report that is not *mutawātir*.

akhbārīs: Shīʿa traditionists whose legal and ritual understanding was primarily based on the literal traditions of the Imams.

ʿālim (pl. *ʿulamāʾ*): a scholar well versed in the knowledge of the Qurʾān, the traditions, and Islamic jurisprudence.

āmālī: dictations.

ʿāmmah: majority, or commoners, referring to the Ahl al-Sunnah.

aṣḥāb al-ijmāʿ: since *ijmāʿ* in Arabic means unanimous agreement or consensus, the phrase means 'the agreed-upon companions', denoting their unanimously agreed upon reliability. The phrase denotes eighteen reporters from among the companions of the Imams (A).

athar (pl. *āthār*): report of a companion, though the Shīʿa do not accept these as *ḥadīth*, so it is used synonymously with *khabar*.

ḍaʿīf: weak – a tradition that does not fit into the categories of authentic, good or dependable. It is therefore a 'weak' tradition.

ḍaʿīf al-munjabar: the reinforced weak report.

dirāyat al-ḥadīth: critical and contextual study and criticism of traditions.

fāsiq: corrupt – antithesis of *ʿādil*, according to some scholars, or synonymous with *kāfir* (disbeliever) according to others.

fatwā: juridical or legal verdict pronounced by a jurisconsult.

fiqh: science of jurisprudence.

ghālī (pl. *ghulāt*): extremist sect, see *ghuluww* below.

ghuluww: extremism – refers to certain sects' exaggeration and overestimation of the vicegerent of Allah, or their extreme neglect in underestimating and degrading him below his decreed status. It also refers to reports that were narrated by Christian converts to pollute *ḥadīth* literature with messianic thought.

ḥadīth (pl. *aḥādīth*): tradition or report, specifically the traditions of the Prophet (S) and the infallible Imams (A), i.e. their sayings, actions and tacit approvals of others' actions, or the narrations of these. Throughout the course of this book, I have used the word '*ḥadīth*' to refer to the bulk of tradition literature and the general concept, and the word 'tradition' or 'report' to refer to individual narrations.

ḥāfiẓ: is a term that recurs throughout the book, usually prefixed or suffixed to someone's name. It literally means 'memorizer' and is used as a title in *ḥadīth* terminology to describe a scholar who has an excellent memory and has memorized a great number of traditions.

ḥalāl: permissible.

ḥarām: prohibited.

ḥasan: good – a tradition where all the transmitters in its chain are *imāmī* and veracious, or some of them are *imāmī* and commendable and the rest are non-*imāmī* but commendable.

iʿlām: declaration – one of the means of receiving traditions, where the teacher would declare and inform the student that this book or this tradition is his report or a result of his hearing a certain report from someone, without actually saying words to the effect of: 'narrate on my authority' or ' I permit you to narrate it'.

ijāzah: permission and authorization to narrate traditions on someone's authority.

ijmāʿ: legal consensus of scholars.

ijtihād: independent jurisprudential investigation when deducing legal rulings from sharīʿah sources. Also refers to a scholar's personal judgment when investigating matters.

ʿilm: literally means knowledge, but in this field refers to the legal knowledge of traditions and jurisprudence. Also refers to the 'certitude' attained about the report's origin.

ʿilm al-dirāyah: the science of critical study of the content of the *ḥadīth*, i.e. the science of Islamic legal knowledge, which includes the narrators of a *ḥadīth*, its text, its chain of transmission, the manner of transmission, etc. This term is often interchangeable with *uṣūl al-ḥadīth* (principles of *ḥadīth*).

ʿilm al-rijāl: biographical studies – the science of *ḥadīth* reporters in which the circumstances of reporters are analysed and classified.

ʿilm uṣūl al-fiqh: the science of the principles of jurisprudence.

imāmī: Shīʿa Ithna ʿAsharī or a follower of the twelve Imams, who adheres to the Jaʿfarī school of jurisprudence.

imlāʾ: dictation of traditions.

irsāl: the act of 'forwarding' traditions on the authority of the *maʿṣūm*, without mentioning the intermediary source(s) in between.

ʿiṣābah: in Shīʿa sources there are frequent references to the consensus of *al-ʿiṣābah*, which points to those of the Imams' companions who were invested with the authority of giving *fatwā*. The *ʿiṣābah*, or the 'body of scholars', by practising the binding authority of *ijmāʿ*, determined the course and character of Shīʿa sectarianism. This word is synonymous with the word *ṭāʾifah*.

isnād or *sanad*: chain of transmission.

isrāʾīliyyāt: traditions and legends narrated by Jewish converts to Islam, which infiltrated and perverted *ḥadīth* literature with concepts and ideas that were not originally present therein. These traditions are rife in Sunni *ḥadīth*, and have penetrated into their most sacred *ḥadīth* collections, 'the authentic (*ṣaḥīḥ*) canonical collections'.

jāmiʿ: comprehensive compilation of traditions encompassing traditions on all matters of religion from juristic matters to contracts and interpretation of the Qurʾān, as well as historical accounts.

jarḥ wa taʿdīl: defamation and authentication of reporters.

khabar (pl. *akhbār)*: report.
khabar al-wāḥid or āḥād: solitary report – refers to any report that is not *mutawātir.*
khabar al-wāḥid al-maqrūn: linked solitary report.
khabar al-wāhid ghayr al-maqrūn: unlinked solitary report.
kitābah: writing down – one of the means of receiving traditions, whereby the teacher would write down his tradition, either in his own hand or by ordering someone else to write it, then send it to the reporter who has requested it.
maʿṣūm: infallible – referring specifically to the Prophet (S) and the Imams (A).
makrūh: undesirable act.
marfūʿ: 'traceable' – refers to any tradition that can be traced back to a *maʿṣūm*, regardless of the continuity in its chain of transmission.
marjaʿ al-taqlīd: grand jurisconsult who is the most learned in the field of jurisprudence and extrapolation of legal rulings, who has the legal capacity to pronounce juristic verdicts (*fatwa*), and is followed (*taqlīd*).
mashhūr: famous. The word *mustafīḍ* implies extensiveness and abundance on all the levels, whereas *mashhūr* implies general fame and prevalence, not necessarily attained on all the levels.
matn: content or text of a tradition.
mawḍūʿ: fabricated, invented, forged.
muʿallaq: suspended – describes a chain of transmission in which the names of some or all of the reporters have been intentionally omitted by the author of a compilation for brevity, and subsequently appended at the back of the book.
muḍmar: ambiguous – refers to a chain of transmission in which the name of the *maʿṣūm* is not mentioned, but rather a personal pronoun referring to him, such as 'he'. Its opposite is *muṣarraḥ* ('explicit'), where the name of the *maʿṣūm* is mentioned frankly. This is also referred to as *maqṭūʿ* ('disconnected').
muḥaddith: traditionist; jurist who transmits traditions.
mujtahid: a jurisconsult who attempts to deduce legal rulings from the sources according to a certain discipline.
mukallaf: legally responsible person, i.e. one who has reached the Islamic legal age of maturity, and thus has become responsible for performing Islamic duties.
munāwalah: handing over. This is when the teacher would hand over (give) his book of traditions to his student or to whoever wishes to narrate on his authority.
mursal: hurried -- a tradition whose complete chain of transmission is unknown, i.e. the names of one or more of its narrators are missing or unknown. The word '*mursal*' literally means 'forwarded on' because often the tradition is forwarded on by a Follower, missing out the name of the Companion who narrated it to him.
muṣarraḥ: explicit – refers to a chain of transmission in which the *maʿṣūm* is explicitly mentioned by name. This is also referred to as *mawṣūl* ('connected').
musnad (pl. *masānīd)*: refers to works of *ḥadīth* categorized according to the first narrator in the chain after the Prophet (S) (i.e. a Companion).
musnad: supported – a tradition supported by a known chain of transmission that goes all the way back to the Prophet (S).
mustafīḍ: extensively narrated.
mustaḥab: legally recommended act.
mutawātir: a tradition from the Prophet (S) or an infallible Imam, repeatedly and widely narrated in an uninterrupted sequence, through successive reliable narrators. In the absence of a single English word to express this very specific

meaning, this has been left as *mutawātir* in the text. See Introduction.

muwaththaq: dependable – a tradition in which some or all of the transmitters in its chain are non-imāmī, but it has been established that they are dependable by our scholars' standards.

naql: the act of transmission.

naṣṣ: textually explicit legal statement.

qarīnah (pl. *qarāʾin*): external evidence linked to a report, which proves the soundness of its origin.

qawī: strong. Classification of *ḥadīth* similar to *muwaththaq*; it refers to a tradition transmitted by an *imāmī* who has been neither commended nor criticized in the biographical dictionaries.

qirāʾah: reading – one of the means of receiving traditions, whereby the student would read out his teacher's tradition back to him, for verification.

qiyās: analogical reasoning.

Rāfiḍah: dissenters – a term used to describe certain extremist sects because of their desertion of the Imam and rejection of his statements.

rāwī (f. *rāwiyah*, pl. *rāwūn*): narrator, reporter.

rāwiyyah: reporter of many traditions.

rijāl works: biographical dictionaries of Muslim dignitaries and narrators of traditions.

riwāyah: narration or transmission.

ṣaḥābī (pl. *ṣaḥābah*): 'Companion' refers to the Companions of the Prophet (S). In earlier times the term was restricted to his close friends who had close contact with him. Later the term was extended to include the believers who had seen him, even if only for a brief moment or at an early age.

ṣāḥib (pl. *aṣḥāb*): Companion – as a general term used to refer to Companions of Imams, of other people and of the Prophet.

ṣaḥīfah (pl. *ṣuḥuf*): literally means journal or manuscript, and here refers to small personal *ḥadīth* collections of people who lived at the time of the Prophet (S).

ṣaḥīḥ (pl. *ṣiḥāḥ*): refers to works of *ḥadīth* compiled to include only authentic traditions from the Prophet (S).

ṣaḥīḥ: authentic – a tradition in which all the transmitters in its chain are *imāmī* and veracious. This is the highest grade of *ḥadīth*.

samāʿ: hearing – one of the means of receiving traditions, in which the reporter would hear the tradition and subsequently learn it, by heart or from a book.

sanad or *isnād*: chain of transmission.

shādh: unusual tradition.

sunan: work of traditions that is mainly to do with matters of jurisprudence that a Muslim encounters in everyday life.

ta'wīl: allegorical interpretation of the Qurʾān.

tābiʿī (pl. *tābiʿūn*): 'Follower' or 'Successor' – refers to the second generation of Muslims who came after the Companions, who did not know the Prophet (S) but who knew his Companions.

taḥammul: reception – refers to the reporter's receipt of the tradition from another reporter who related it to him, and the hearer's subsequent learning of it, whether by heart or by use of a book or written record.

taḥdīth: narration of traditions.

taqiyyah: dissimulation of one's faith when faced with a life-threatening situation.

taqlīd: the legal imitation or following of a *mujtahid* – a veracious legal authority in matters of jurisprudence.

tarjīḥ: preponderance – a field of study within the science of *ḥadīth* in which contradictory reports are weighed up and evaluated in terms of their authenticity in order to determine which of them prevails over the rest.

tawātur: recurrent multiple successive transmission, i.e. the path of a *mutawātir* report.

thiqah: reliable.

uṣūl (sing. aṣl): the Arabic term for books in which Shīʿa *ḥadīth* scholars at the time of the Imams recorded the traditions directly received by them. There were four hundred such source collections, termed *al-uṣūl al-arbaʿumi'ah*, in which *uṣūl* literally means 'principles', 'fundamentals' or 'roots', to indicate that they are a primary source for scholars to refer to and rely upon.

uṣūl al-fiqh: principles of interpreting Islamic law, namely: the Qurʾān, the Sunnah of the Prophet and the Ahl al-Bayt (A), reason (*ʿaql*) and legal consensus.

uṣūlīs: the rational segment of *imāmī* jurists who favoured the incorporation of the semantic–exegetical methodology in jurisprudence.

wājib: obligatory.

waṣiyyah: will – one of the means of receiving traditions, whereby a reporter would instruct a person, before a journey or his death, to narrate his book of traditions or some other traditions on his authority.

wijādah: finding traditions – one of the means of receiving traditions. This has been defined in *ḥadīth* terminology as: obtaining knowledge from a manuscript, without having heard it (*samāʿ*), without having been given it (*munāwalah*) and without permission to transmit it.

ẓann: valid conjecture or speculation of a jurist about the soundness of a report's origin, which does not entail more than a probability.

BIBLIOGRAPHY

All dates given in common era unless specified.

Al-Adab al-Siyāsī fī al-Nizāʿ bayna ʿAlī wa Muʿāwiyah, Dr Naẓmī ʿAbd al-Badīʿ Muḥammad (Cairo: al-Amānah Publishers, 1982).

Ahādīth Umm al-Mu'minīn ʿĀ'ishah, al-Sayyid Murtaḍā al-ʿAskarī (Beirut: Dār al-Zahrā', 1405 AH/1985), first edition.

Al-ʿAmal al-Abqā fī Sharḥ al-ʿUrwah al-Wuthqā, al-Sayyid ʿAlī al-Husaynī Shabbar (Najaf: al-Najaf Publishers, 1383 AH).

Anwār al-Wasā'il, al-Shaikh Muḥammad Ṭāhir Āl Shabbīr al-Khāqānī (Najaf: Najaf Publishers, 1377 AH/1957).

Biḥār al-Anwār, al-Shaikh al-Majlisī (Beirut: Mu'assasah Ahl al-Bayt, 1409 AH/1989) third edition.

Dirāsāt fī al-Ḥadīth wa al-Muḥaddithīn, al-Sayyid Hāshim Maʿrūf al-Ḥusaynī (Beirut: Dār al-Taʿāruf, 1398 AH/1978) second edition.

Al-Dirāyah, al-Shaikh Zayn al-Dīn al-ʿĀmilī al-Shahīd al-Thānī (Najaf: al-Nuʿmān Publishers, n.d.).

Durūs fī Fiqh al-Imāmiyyah, ʿAbd al-Hādī al-Faḍlī.

Daʿā'im al-Islām, al-Qāḍī al-Nuʿmān al-Maghribī, edited by Āṣif ibn ʿAlī Aṣghar Fayḍī (Beirut: Dār al-Aḍwā', 1411 AH/1991).

Dalā'il al-Ṣidq, al-Shaikh Muḥammad Ḥasan al-Muẓaffar (n.p., 1409 AH/1989).

Dalīl al-ʿUrwah al-Wuthqā, Lectures of al-Shaikh Husayn al-Ḥillī, recorded by his student al-Shaikh Ḥasan Saʿīd (Najaf: Maktabah al-Najaf, 1379 AH).

Al-Dharīʿah ilā Uṣūl al-Sharīʿah, al-Sharīf al-Murtaḍā, edited by Dr Abū al-Qāsim Gorjī (Tehran: Tehran University, n.d.) [my own personal manuscript].

Al-Dharīʿah ilā Taṣānīf al-Shīʿah, al-Shaikh Āghā Buzurg al-Ṭihrānī (Beirut: Dār al-Aḍwā', 1403 AH/1983) third edition.

Al-Fikr al-Manhajī ʿInda al-Muḥaddithīn, Dr. Hammām ʿAbd al-Raḥīm Saʿīd (Doha: Kitāb al-Ummah, 1408 AH) first edition.

Al-Fihrist, Ibn al-Nadīm (Beirut: Dār al-Maʿrifah, n.d.).

Al-Fihrist, al-Shaikh al-Ṭūsī, edited by al-Sayyid Muḥammad Ṣādiq Baḥr al-ʿUlūm (Sayhat: Maktabah al-Zawād, 1403 AH/1983) third edition.

Fawāʾid Rijāliyyah, al-Shaikh Muḥammad Āṣif Muḥsinī (Iran, n.d.).

Al-Fawāʾid al-Madaniyyah, al-Shaikh Muḥammad Amīn al-Astarābādī (n.p., Dār al-Nashr Li Ahl al-Bayt, 1405 AH).

Al-Ghadīr, al-Shaikh al-Amīnī (Beirut: Dār al-Kitāb al-ʿArabī, 1403 AH/1983) fifth edition.

Al-Ḥadāʾiq al-Nāḍirah, al-Shaikh Yūsuf al-Baḥrānī, edited by al-Shaikh Muḥammad Taqī al-Ayrawānī (Beirut: Dār al-Aḍwāʾ, 1405 AH/1985) second edition.

Ḥadīqah al-Rawḍah, Ḥawāshī al-Rawḍah al-Bahiyyah – see *al-Rawḍah al-Bahiyyah* .

Al-Haft wa al-Aẓillah, al-Mufaḍḍal al-Juʿfī, edited by Dr ʿĀrif Tāmir (Beirut: Maktabah al-Hilāl, 1401 AH/1981).

Ḥaqāʾiq al-Uṣūl, al-Sayyid Muḥsin al-Ḥakīm (Najaf: al-ʿIlmiyyah Publishers, 1372 AH).

Al-Istibṣār, al-Shaikh Muḥammad ibn al-Ḥasan al-Ṭūsī, edited by al-Sayyid Ḥasan al-Kharsān (Beirut: Dār al-Aḍwāʾ, 1406 AH/1985) third edition; revised edition by Muḥammad Jaʿfar Shams al-Dīn (Beirut: Dār al- Taʿāruf, 1412 AH/1991).

Jāmiʿ al-Maqāl, al-Shaikh Fakhr al-Dīn al-Ṭarīḥī, edited by Muḥammad Kāẓim al-Ṭarīḥī (Tehran: Ḥaydarī Publishers, n.d.).

Jawāhir al-Kalām, al-Shaikh Muḥammad Ḥasan al-Najafī, edited by al-Shaikh ʿAbbās al-Qūjānī (Beirut: Dār Iḥyāʾ al-Turāth al-ʿArabī, 1981) seventh edition.

Al-Kāfī, al-Shaikh Muḥammad ibn Yaʿqūb al-Kulaynī, edited by al-Shaikh ʿAlī Akbar al-Ghaffārī (Beirut: Dār al-Aḍwāʾ, 1405 AH/1985); revised edition by Muḥammad Jaʿfar Shams al-Dīn (Beirut: Dār al-Taʿāruf, 1411 AH/1990).

Al-Kashshāf, Jārallāh al-Zamakhsharī (Tehran: Intishārāt Āftāb, n.d.).

Kifāyah al-Uṣūl, al-Shaikh Muḥammad Kāẓim al-Khurāsānī (Beirut: Muʾassasah Āl al-Bayt, 1411 AH/1990) first edition; see also *Ḥaqāʾiq al-Uṣūl*.

Kitābah al-Baḥth al-ʿIlmī wa Maṣādir al-Dirāsāt al-Islāmiyyah, Dr ʿAbd al-Wahhāb Ibrāhīm Abū Sulaymān (Jeddah: Dār al-Shurūq, 1400 AH/1980) first edition.

Kulliyyāt fī ʿUlūm al-Rijāl, al-Shaikh Muḥammad Jaʿfar al-Subḥānī (Beirut: Dār al-Mīzān, 1401 AH/1990) first edition.

Al-Kunan wa al-Alqāb, al-Shaikh ʿAbbās al-Qummī (Beirut: Muʾassasah al-Wafāʾ, 1403 AH/1983) second edition.

Lisān al-Mīzān, Ibn Ḥajar al-ʿAsqalānī (Hyderabad: Maktabah Majlis Dāʾirah al-Maʿārif al-Niẓāmiyyah, 1329 AH) first edition.

Maʿālim al-Dīn, al-Shaikh Ḥasan al-ʿĀmilī, edited by ʿAbd al-Ḥusayn Muḥammad ʿAlī al-Baqqāl.

Maʿālim al-Madrasatayn, al-Sayyid Murtaḍā al-ʿAskarī (Beirut: Muʾassasah al-

Nuʿmān, 1410 AH/1990).

Maʿārij al-Uṣūl, al-Muḥaqqiq al-Ḥillī, edited by Muḥammad Ḥusayn al-Raḍawī.

Mabādiʾ al-Wuṣūl, al-ʿAllāmah al-Ḥillī, edited by ʿAbd al-Ḥusayn Muḥammad ʿAlī al-Baqqāl (Beirut: Dār al-Aḍwāʾ, 1406 AH/1986) second edition.

Mafātīḥ ʿUlūm al-Ḥadīth, Muḥammad ʿUthmān al-Khasht (Cairo: Maktabah al-Qurʾān, n.d.).

Majmaʿ al-Bayān, al-Shaikh Abū ʿAlī al-Ṭabarsī (Beirut: Dār Maktabah al-Ḥayāt, n.d.).

Man Lā Yaḥḍuruhu al-Faqīh, al-Shaikh al-Ṣadūq, edited by al-Sayyid Ḥasan al-Kharsān (Beirut: Dār al-Aḍwāʾ, 1405 AH/1985) first edition; revised edition of al-Shaikh Ḥusayn al-Aʿlamī (Beirut: Muʾassasah al-Aʿlamī, 1406 AH/1986) first edition; revised edition of al-Shaikh Muḥammad Jaʿfar Shams al-Dīn (Beirut: Dār al-Taʿāruf, 1411 AH/1990).

Al-Milal wa al-Niḥal, al-Shahrastānī (Beirut: Dār al-Maʿrifah, 1404 AH/1984).

Miqbās al-Hidāyah, al-Shaikh ʿAbdallāh al-Māmaqānī, edited by al-Shaikh Muḥammad Riḍā al-Māmaqānī (Beirut: Muʾassasah Āl al-Bayt, 1411 AH/1991) first edition.

Al-Mufradāt, al-Rāghib al-Iṣfahānī, edited by Muḥammad Sayyid Kaylānī (Beirut: Dār al-Maʿrifah, n.d.).

Muʿjam Alfāẓ al-Qurʾān al-Karīm, Arabic Language Association of Cairo (Cairo: Dār al-Surūq, n.d.).

Muʿjam al-Firaq al-Islāmiyyah, Sharīf Yaḥyā al-Amīn (Beirut: Dār al-Aḍwāʾ, 1406 AH/1986) first edition.

Al-Muʿjam al-Mufahras li Alfāẓ al-Qurʾān al-Karīm, Muḥammad Fuʾād ʿAbd al-Bāqī (Cairo: Dār al-Shaʿb, n.d.).

Muʿjam Rijāl al-Ḥadīth, al-Sayyid Abū al-Qāsim al-Khūʾī (Qum: Madīnah al-ʿIlm, 1409 AH/1989) fourth edition.

Al-Muʿjam al-Wasīṭ, Arabic Language Association of Cairo (Cairo: Dār al-Maʿārif, 1392 AH/1972) second edition.

Al-Muʿtabar, al-Muḥaqqiq al-Ḥillī (Iran: lithographic print, n.d.).

Muḥīṭ al-Muḥīṭ, al-Muʿallim Buṭrus al-Bustānī (Beirut: Maktabah Lubnān, 1977).

Muqaddimah Ibn al-Ṣalāḥ, see *al-Taqyīd wa al-Īḍāḥ*.

Murūj al-Dhahab, Abū al-Ḥusayn al-Masʿūdī, revised by Yūsuf Asʿad Dāghir (Qum: Dār al-Hijrah, 1409 AH).

Mustadrak al-Wasāʾil, al-Mīrzā al-Nūrī (Iran: lithographic print, n.d.).

Mustamsik al-ʿUrwah al-Wuthqā, al-Sayyid Muḥsin al-Ḥakīm (Beirut: Dār Iḥyāʾ al-Turāth al-ʿArabī, 1391 AH) fourth edition.

Mustaṭrafāt al-Sarā'ir, al-Shaikh Ibn Idrīs al-Ḥillī (Qum: Amīr Publishers, 1408 AH/1987) first edition.

Al-Muwāfaqāt, Abū Isḥāq al-Shāṭibī (Cairo: al-Maktabah al-Tijāriyyah al-Kubrah, n.d.).

Nash'at al-Fikr al-Falsafī fil Islām, Dr ʿAlī Sāmī al-Nashshār (Cairo: Dār al-Maʿārif, 1977) seventh edition.

Qawāʿid al-Ḥadīth, al-Sayyid Muhyī al-Dīn al-Gharīfī (Beirut: Dār al-Aḍwā', 1406 AH/1986) second edition.

Al-Qawānīn, al-Mīrzā al-Qummī (Iran: lithographic print, n.d.).

Qirā'ah fī Kitāb al-Tawḥīd, ʿAbd al-Hādī al-Faḍlī.

Al-Rawḍah al-Bahiyyah, al-Shahīd al-Thānī (Iran: lithographic print, n.d.).

Rijāl al-Najāshī, edited by al-Shaikh Muḥammad Jawad al-Nā'īnī (Beirut: Dār al-Aḍwā', 1408 AH/1988) first edition.

Risālah fī al-Tasāmuḥ fī Adillah al-Sunan wa al-Makrūhāt, al-Shaikh Murtaḍā al-Anṣārī, as part of *Majmūʿah Rasā'il Fiqhiyyah wa Uṣūliyyah*, edited by al-Shaikh ʿAbbās al-Ḥajiyānī (Beirut: Mu'assasah Ahl al-Bayt, 1407 AH/1987).

Sharḥ Nahj al-Balāghah, Ibn Abī al-Ḥadīd (photocopy of the first edition in Egypt).

Shaikh al-Maḍīrah Abū Hurayrah, al-Shaikh Maḥmūd Abū Rayyah (Cairo: Dār al-Maʿārif, n.d.) third edition.

Silsilah al-Aḥādīth al-Ḍaʿīfah wa al-Mawḍūʿah, al-Shaikh Muḥammad Nāṣir al-Dīn al-Albānī (Riyaḍ: Maktabah al-Maʿārif, 1408 AH/1988) first edition .

Ta'ammulāt fī al-Ṣaḥīḥayn, Muḥammad Ṣādiq Najamī, translated by Ḥasan Murtaḍā al-Qazwīnī (Beirut: Dār al-ʿUlūm, 1408 AH/1988) first edition .

Ta'sīs al-Shīʿah li ʿUlūm al-Islām, al-Sayyid Ḥasan al-Ṣadr (Beirut: Mu'assasah al-Nuʿmān, 1411 AH/1991).

Tahdhīb al-Aḥkām, al-Shaikh al-Ṭūsī, edited by al-Sayyid Ḥasan al-Kharsān (Beirut: Dār Ṣaʿab – Dār al-Taʿāruf, 1401 AH/1981).

Al-Tanqīḥ fī Sharḥ al-ʿUrwah al-Wuthqā, Lectures of al-Sayyid Abū al-Qāsim al-Khū'ī, recorded by his student al-Shaikh ʿAlī al-Gharawī (Beirut: Mu'assasah Ahl al-Bayt, n.d.).

Tanqīḥ al-Maqāl, al-Shaikh ʿAbdallāh al-Māmaqānī (Iran: lithographic print).

Tanwīr al-Ḥawālik, Jalāl al-Dīn al-Suyūṭī (Beirut: Dār al-Fikr, n.d.).

Al-Taqyīd wa al-Īḍāḥ: Sharḥ Muqaddimah Ibn al-Ṣalāḥ, al-Ḥāfiẓ Zayd al-Dīn al-ʿIrāqī, edited by ʿAbd al-Raḥmān Muḥammad ʿUthmān (n.p.: Dār al-Fikr al-ʿArabī, n.d.).

Tarājim Aʿlām al-Nisā', al-Shaikh Muḥammad Ḥusayn al-Aʿlāmī al-Ḥā'irī (Beirut: Mu'assah al-Aʿlamī, 1407 AH/1987) first edition.

Tārīkh al-Fiqh al-Islāmī, Dr ʿUmar Sulaymān al-Ashqar (1402 AH/1982) first edition.

Tārīkh al-Islām, Dr Ḥasan Ibrāhīm Ḥasan (Cairo: Maktabah al-Nahḍah al-Miṣriyyah, 1979) ninth edition.

Tārīkh al-Tashrīʿ al-Islāmī, ʿAbd al-Hādī al-Faḍlī.

Al-Tashrīʿ wa al-Fiqh fīl Islām, al-Shaikh Manāʿ al-Qaṭān (Beirut: Muʾassasah al-Risālah, 1409 AH/1989) tenth edition .

ʿUddah al-Dāʿī, Ibn Fahd al-Ḥillī (Beirut: Muʾassasah Ahl al-Bayt, 1392 AH).

ʿUddah al-Uṣūl, al-Shaikh al-Ṭūsī, edited by al-Shaikh Muḥammad Mahdī Najaf (Beirut: Muʾassasah Āl al-Bayt, 1403 AH/1983) first edition.

ʿUlūm al-Ḥadīth wa Muṣṭalaḥuhu, Dr Ṣubḥī al-Ṣāliḥ (Beirut: Dār al-ʿIlm lil Malāyīn, n.d.) fourth edition.

Uṣūl al-Fiqh, al-Shaikh al-Mufīd (Beirut: Markaz al-Dirāsāt wa al-Buḥūth al-ʿIlmiyyah al-ʿĀliyah, 1408 AH/1988) first edition.

Uṣūl al-Fiqh, al-Shaikh Muḥammad Riḍā al-Muẓaffar (Qaṭīf: Maktabah al-Zawād, n.d.).

Uṣūl al-Ḥadīth wa Aḥkāmuhu, al-Shaikh Jaʿfar al-Subḥānī (Qum: Mehr Publishers, 1412 AH).

ʿUyūn al-Anbāʾ fī Ṭabaqāt al-Aṭibbāʾ, Ibn Abī Uṣaybiʿah (Beirut: Maktabah al-Ḥayāt, 1965).

Al-Wāfī, al-Fayḍ al-Kāshānī (Iran: lithographic print, 1324 AH).

Al-Wajīzah, al-Shaikh Bahāʾ al-Dīn al-ʿĀmilī.

Wajīzah fī ʿIlm al-Rijāl, al-Shaikh al-Mishkīnī, edited by al-Sayyid Zuhayr al-Aʿrajī (Beirut: Muʾassasah al-Aʿlamī, 1411 AH/1991) first edition.

Wasāʾil al-Shīʿah, al-Ḥurr al-ʿĀmilī, edited by al-Shaikh ʿAbd al-Rahīm al-Rabbānī Beirut: Dār Iḥyāʾ al-Turāth al-ʿArabī, 1403 AH/1983) fifth edition.

Journal article

'ʿUlūm al-Ḥadīth: Nashʾatuhā wa Taṭawwuruhā' by Mājid al-Gharbāwī, in *Majallah al-Fikr al-Jadīd*, vol. I, no. 3 (London, 1413 AH/1992)

INDEX

Abān ibn Muḥammad al-Bajalī, 66
Abān ibn Taghlib al-Kūfī, 44, 66, 105
Abān ibn ʿUthmān al-Aḥmar al-Bajalī, 66, 202
al-ʿAbbās ibn al-Muṭṭalib, 154, 155, 195
Abbasid Dynasty, 111, 146, 182
Abdallāh ibn al-Ḥasan al-Muthannah, 197
Abdallāh ibn ʿAmr ibn al-ʿĀṣ, 54, 57
abrogation, 15, 41-43, 55, 62
Abu al-Dardāʾ, 151
Abū al-Khaṭṭāb, 160-61, 163, 165-68, 191
Abū Bakr, 149-50, 156, 157, 168
Abū Baṣīr, 167, 202-3
Abū Dharr al-Ghaffārī, 41, 196
Abū Ḥanīfah, 156, 172
Abū Hurayrah, 54, 151, 154, 155-170, 174, 180, 196
Abū Miqdām, 63
Abū Saʿīd al-Khudrī, 196
Abū Shuʿayb al-Muḥāmilī al-Kūfī, 68
Abū Yaḥyā Ibrāhīm ibn Abī al-Bilād, 67, 215
accuracy, ix, 8, 10, 12, 14, 16-18, 56, 65, 115-16, 120, 138-39, 143-44, 192, 194, 222
ʿādil (veracious), ix, 8, 10, 11, 18, 19, 24, 38-39, 45-47, 64, 83, 103, 116, 118, 120, 125, 127, 131-37, 139, 147, 156, 185, 191-93, 204, 205-6, 210, 211
āḥād, see khabar al-wāḥid
Ahl al-Bayt, vii, x, 8, 57-58, 61-64, 41, 155, 160, 161, 197, 210-12, 225-26
Ahl al-Sunnah, xi, xii, 5, 8, 10, 47, 51, 54, 59, 61, 64, 104, 105, 124, 143-45, 158, 169, 180, 182-83, 189, 190, 208
Aḥmad ibn Ḥanbal, 61, 159, 175, 183
Akhbārī, viii, 104, 211
Allah, vii, 14, 17, 42-43, 56, 77-78, 83, 97-98, 123-124, 130, 134, 141, 144, 155, 158-159, 162-163, 165-67, 169-170, 175, 179-80
al-ʿĀmilī, al-Ḥurr, 73, 75, 92, 94, 126, 146, 211
Āminah Baygum bint Muḥammad Taqī al-Majlisī, 198
Āminah bint Abī al-Ḥarb, 199
Āminah bint Mūsā ibn Aḥmad, 199
Āminah bint Naṣrallāh al-Kanāniyyah, 199
al-ʿĀmulī, Bahāʾ al-Dīn, 48
analogical reasoning (*qiyās*), 97, 156, 170
Anṣār, 58
anthropomorphism, 158, 168-69, 171, 182
al-Armawī, 200
Arwā bint Anīs, 195
Asad ibn Mūsa al-Umawī, 60
asceticism, 17, 170-72, 208
aṣḥāb al-ijmāʿ, 201, 202, 204, 205, 207-9
Āsiyah bint Jārallāh al-Shaybānī al-Ṭabarī, 199
aṣl, see source collection
Asmāʾ bint ʿAbd al-Raḥmān ibn Abī Bakr, 196
Asmāʾ bint ʿĀbis ibn Rabīʿah al-Kūfiyyah, 198
Asmāʾ bint Abū Bakr Dhāt al-Niṭāqayn, 195
Asmāʾ bint ʿUmays al-Khathʿamiyyah, 195

al-Astarābādī, al-Amīn, viii, 211, 212, 213
athar, 5, 49, 50, 51
atheists, 160, 170
authentic, *see ṣaḥīḥ*
authentication, 9, 12, 14, 19, 37, 46, 64, 65, 80-82, 85-87, 90, 92-97, 104-5, 109, 112, 115, 121, 144-45, 180, 185-87, 191, 201, 204-21
authoritativeness, 39, 40, 100, 112, 117-19, 122, 127-28, 135, 216-18; *see also* inauthoritativeness
authority, vii, 8, 13, 15-16, 19-25, 38-45, 54-58, 62, 62-67, 76-77, 87, 90, 94-98, 100, 106-12, 118-19, 123, 126-27, 129-31, 133, 136, 141-42, 146, 148-50, 154-90, 195-226
al-Awzāʿī, 59
ayah al-nabaʾ, 117
Baghdad, 168
Baghdādī biographers, 193
al-Bahāʾī, al-Shaikh (d. 1040 AH), 33-34, 48, 65-66, 69, 80
al-Baḥrānī, Yūsuf, viii, 51, 112, 225
Bakr ibn Wāʾil, 197
Baʿlbak, xii
Banū Faḍḍāl, 191
Banū Samāʿah, 191
Barīd ibn Muʿāwiyah al-ʿAjalī, 202
al-Barrāʾ ibn ʿĀzib, 196
Barzah Umm al-Zubayr ibn ʿArabī, 196
Basra, 14, 59, 177
Battle of Siffīn, 144
al-Bayḍāwi, xi
Bible, 159
al-Bidāyah fī ʿIlm al-Dirāyah, 48
Biḥār al-Anwār, 73, 75
biographical dictionaries, 38-39, 44, 62, 65-66, 116, 135-37, 141-42, 144, 178-79, 181, 186, 192-94, 201-2
biographical sciences (*ʿilm al-rijāl*), vii, 36-40, 44, 62, 65-66, 76, 103, 104, 116, 135-37, 141-42, 144, 178-79, 181, 186-87, 192-94, 201-2, 217
al-Bizanṭī, Aḥmad ibn Muḥammad ibn Abī Naṣr, 201, 203, 208
al-Bukhārī, Muḥammad ibn Ismāʿīl, 60, 61, 155
carelessness, 140, 143
certainty, 39, 65, 84, 121, 128, 135, 210, 217
chain of narration, ix, 5-16, 24, 26, 33-39, 46-47, 51, 59, 64, 67, 72, 76-77, 87, 89, 91, 94, 96, 103, 104-9, 115-29, 136, 144, 146-47, 155, 170, 175, 176-78, 185, 205-6, 214, 215, 218-22, 225-26
Christians, 141, 157, 161, 167-68, 182
commendation, 65, 118, 131, 136-37, 139, 186
common sense, 118, 135, 178
Companions of the Prophet (S), 5, 8, 15, 21, 25, 43, 49, 51, 54-57, 59, 61, 87, 104, 112, 146, 150, 153-54, 156, 160, 164, 169, 176, 192, 195, 202-3
  second generation (*tābiʿūn*), 15, 25, 49, 59, 104, 150, 154, 169, 196
consensus (*ijmāʿ*), 15, 46, 65, 93-4, 96, 202-9, 218
contradictory reports, 44, 46, 122, 129, 145, 147, 185, 189-90
conveyance (*adāʾ*), 220
corruption (*fisq, fāsiq*), 3, 10, 12, 18-19, 62, 98, 117, 128, 132-34, 140-41, 143, 159-60, 167, 174, 179, 181, 188, 191
Daʿāʾim al-Islām, 126, 161
ḍaʿīf (weak), 8, 11-19, 33-34, 47, 60, 101-5, 115, 117-25, 128, 131, 140, 143-44, 146-47, 158, 172, 179-81, 185-86, 191, 205-6, 216-18
ḍaʿīf al-munjabar (reinforced weak report), 119
al-Dāmād, al-Muḥaqqiq (Mir Dāmād), 48, 65, 66
Damascus, xi, 149
Darrah bint Abī Salamah al-Makhzūmiyyah, 196
Darrah bint Ṣāliḥ, 199
Dāwūd ibn al-Ḥaṣīn, 146, 195
declaration (*iʿlām*), 23, 222
dependable, *see muwaththaq*
dependability, ix, 9, 11-12, 15, 18, 33, 47, 52, 103-4, 115-18, 120, 131, 136-39, 143-45, 185, 187, 189-90, 204, 207, 209, 213

Dhafrah bint Ghālib al-Rāsibiyyah al-Baṣriyyah, 196
al-Dharī'ah ilā Uṣūl al-Sharī'ah, 33, 46, 65-67, 207
dictation, 13, 62-63, 194, 222
Dirāsāt fī al-Ḥadīth wa al-Muḥaddithīn, 48, 58, 211, 217
dirāyah, 32
disbelief, 134, 163
disbeliever (*kāfir*), 188
disparagement (*jarḥ*), 9, 19, 185, 186
dissimulation (*taqiyyah*), 111-12
equitable, *see 'ādil*
extremists, *see ghulāt*
fabrication, ix, 6, 12, 17, 19, 23, 45, 80-82, 88-89, 95, 124, 149-84, 216
faith, vii, 8, 11, 18, 65, 68, 152, 189, 212
Fatḥ al-Bārī, 60
Fatḥiyyah, 20, 143, 190
Fāṭimah al-Zahrā' (A), 61, 155, 165, 197, 198
Fāṭimah bint al-Ḥasan ibn 'Alī ibn Abī Ṭālib, 197
Fāṭimah bint al-Ḥusayn, 197-98
Fāṭimah bint 'Alī al-Riḍā (A), 197
Fāṭimah bint 'Alī ibn Abī Ṭālib, 197
Fāṭimah bint 'Alī ibn al-Ḥusayn ibn 'Alī ibn Abī Ṭālib, 197
Fāṭimah bint al-Sayyid Raḍī al-Dīn 'Alī ibn Ṭāwūs, 199
Fāṭimah bint Ja'far al-Ṣādiq, 197
Fāṭimah bint Muḥammad al-Bāqir, 197
Fāṭimah bint Mūsā al-Kāẓim, 197
fiqh, see jurisprudence
four hundred source collections, 8, 63-67, 212
al-Fuḍayl ibn Yasār al-Baṣrī, 202
generations (of reporters), ix, 6, 9, 26, 34-35, 104, 109, 221
Ghadīr Khumm, 58, 171, 218
gharīb (rare), 7, 14
al-gharīb al-lafẓī (strangely worded), 15
Ghinyat al-Qāṣidīn fī Ma'rifat Iṣṭilāḥat al-Muḥaddithīn, 48
Ghiyāth ibn Ibrāhīm al-Nakha'ī al-Kūfī, 173
ghulāt (extremists), 140-41, 157, 160-63, 167-68, 179, 181-82, 191
ghusl (obligatory purification), 107
good, *see ḥasan*
Ḥabābah bint Ja'far al-Asadiyyah al-Wālibiyyah Umm al-Nidā, 198
al-Ḥāfiẓ al-'Irāqī, 177, 199
Ḥafṣah bint 'Umar ibn al-Khaṭṭāb, 195
al-Haft wa al-Aẓillah, 179, 181
ḥajj (pilgrimage), 7, 88
al-Ḥakam ibn 'Uyaynah, 63
Ḥakīmah bint Muḥammad al-Jawād, 198
Ḥakīmah bint Mūsā al-Kāẓim, 198
Ḥall al-Ishkāl Fī Ma'rifat al-Rijāl, 46, 47, 103
Ḥamādah, 198
Ḥamīdah (the mother of Imam Mūsā al-Kāẓim (A)), 198
Ḥammād ibn Abī Sulaymān, 59
Ḥammād ibn 'Īsā, 41, 202-3
Ḥammād ibn 'Uthmān, 202-3
Ḥammām ibn Munabbih, 54
Ḥanafī, xi, xii
Ḥanbal, Aḥmad ibn, 60-61, 159, 175, 183
Ḥanbalī, xii
handing over (*munāwalah*), 224
ḥasan (good), 9, 11, 33, 46-47, 104, 112, 115-18, 131, 137, 139, 144
al-Ḥasan al-Baṣrī, 141
al-Ḥasan ibn Faḍāl, 44
hearing (*samā'*), 6, 9, 21, 53, 54, 85, 117, 176, 221-23
Heaven, 158, 171
Hell, 41, 42, 148, 151, 155, 158, 171-72, 180
Hidāyah al-Akhyār Ilā Fihris Biḥār al-Anwār, 75
Hijaz, xi, 59, 157
al-Ḥillī, al-'Allāmah, 11, 46, 47, 89, 92, 104-5, 119, 129, 132-33, 212, 225
Hind bint al-Ḥārith, 197
Hind bint Shurayk al-Baṣriyyah, 197
Hishām ibn al-Ḥakam, 160, 164, 214
Ḥudhayfah ibn Manṣūr, 130,
Ḥudhayfah ibn al-Yamān, 195
Hushaym ibn Wāsiṭ, 59

hypocrisy, 42, 134
Ibn ʿAbbās, 171, 177, 195
Ibn Abī ʿUmayr, 12, 39, 44, 123, 126-27, 144, 167, 198, 201, 203-4, 207, 209
Ibn al-ʿAwdī, xii
Ibn al-Ghaḍāʾirī, Aḥmad ibn al-Ḥusayn, 66, 142-43, 179, 181, 186
Ibn al-Nadīm, 44
Ibn al-Zubayr, 21
Ibn Bābawayh, Muḥammad ibn ʿAlī (al-Shaikh al-Ṣadūq), 63, 106, 107, 125, 216, 218
Ibn Ḥajar, 60, 172, 183
Ibn Ḥibbān, 173, 196-97
Ibn Jurayj, 59
Ibn Maḥbūb, 77
Ibn Mājah, 198
Ibn Miskān, 164, 214
Ibn Mubārak, 59
Ibn Ṭawūs, Aḥmad ibn Mūsā al-Ḥillī, 47
Ibrāhīm ibn ʿAbd al-Ḥamīd al-Asadī, 67
Ibrāhīm ibn Abī al-Kirām al-Jaʿfarī, 67
Ibrāhīm ibn Hāshim al-Qummī, 12, 39, 145
Ibrāhīm ibn Khālid al-ʿAṭṭār al-ʿAbadī, 67
Ibrāhīm ibn Muhzim al-Asadī al-Kūfī, 67
Ibrāhīm ibn Muslim al-Ḍarīr al-Kūfī, 67
Ibrāhīm ibn Naṣr al-Juʿfī, 68
Ibrāhīm ibn Nuʿaym al-ʿAbdi, 68
Ibrāhīm ibn Ṣāliḥ al-Anmāṭī al-Asadī, 67
Ibrāhīm ibn ʿUthman al-Khazzāz al-Kūfī, 66
Ibrāhīm ibn Yūsuf al-Kindī, 68
ijāzah (permission), 9, 21, 22, 54, 56, 58, 198-200, 223-25
ijmāʿ, *see* consensus
ijtihad, xii, 29, 37, 40, 90, 199, 210
Ikmāl al-Dīn, 160
Imam ʿAlī ibn Abī Ṭālib (A), 41, 43, 57-59, 61-64, 74, 88, 148-57, 162-63, 165, 190, 198, 214
Imam ʿAlī al-Riḍā (A), 26, 74, 98, 127, 199, 202, 204, 208
Imam al-Ḥasan ibn ʿAlī (A), 21, 57, 74, 165
Imam al-Ḥasan al-ʿAskarī (A), 74
Imam al-Ḥusayn (A), 21, 74, 165, 198, 214
Imam Jaʿfar al-Ṣādiq (A), 8, 20, 54, 63, 74, 77, 106-8, 134, 160, 163-64, 166, 179, 190, 198-99, 202-4
Imam al-Mahdī (A), 74, 88, 143, 161, 206, 212
Imam Muḥammad al-Bāqir (A), 8, 63, 68-71, 74, 127, 129, 154-56, 163, 168, 175, 186, 198, 202-3, 210, 214
Imam Muḥammad al-Jawād (A), 74, 127, 163, 165
Imam Mūsā al-Kāẓim (A), 8, 20, 74, 100, 167, 198, 202, 204, 208, 225
imāmī (Shīʿā Ithnā ʿAsharī), 10-12, 18, 38-39, 46-47, 103, 112, 116-17, 135-37, 139, 143-44, 146, 168-69, 182, 189-90, 206, 212-13
Imams (Shīʿā), 6, 8, 10, 29, 32, 37-38, 44, 49, 50, 64-67, 73-74, 105, 111-12, 121, 123, 129, 139, 161, 163-64, 173, 182, 189-90, 192, 197, 202-4, 208, 211, 213, 217
inauthoritativeness, 112, 118, 120, 122, 127-28; *see also* authoritativeness
Iran, xii, 68-69, 72, 75
Isḥāq ibn ʿAmmār al-Sābiṭī, 67, 215
Isḥāq ibn Rāhawayh, 60
Islamic law
  rulings (*fatāwā*), viii, 7, 8, 29, 35, 37, 39-40, 51, 59, 63, 64, 73, 88, 97, 99-100, 111, 112, 118-19, 121-25, 128, 134, 146-47, 154, 163, 170, 191, 207
  sciences, 37; *see also* jurisprudence
isnād, *see* chain of narration
isrāʾīlīyyāt, 157-59, 169, 174, 180
al-Istibṣār fī mā Ikhtalafa min al-Akhbār (al-Istibṣār), 71, 219
Jabal ʿĀmil, xi
Jaʿfar ibn Muḥammad ibn Mālik ibn ʿĪsā ibn Sābūr, 181
Jamāl al-Dīn ibn al-Muṭahhir, 186
Jāmiʿ al-Maqāl fī mā Yataʿallaqu bi

Aḥwāl al-Ḥadīth wa al-Rijāl, 48
Jamīl ibn Darrāj al-Nakhaʿī, 8, 202-3
jarḥ, see disparagement
Jarīr ibn ʿAbd al-Ḥamīd, 60
Jārūdiyyah, 143
Jerusalem, xi, 58
Jews, 57, 141, 157, 159, 161, 165, 168-69, 174, 180; *see also isrāʾīlīyyāt*
Jibraʿīl, 63, 162
Jumānah bint al-Musayyib ibn al-Najiyyah al-Fazārī, 196
Jumrah bint al-Nuʿmān al-ʿAdawiyyah, 195
jurisprudence (*fiqh*), vii-ix, xi-xii, 10-11, 13, 15, 18, 23, 29, 37-40, 45, 51-52, 62, 67-68, 71, 73, 77, 89, 96, 104-5, 110, 117-19, 131, 133-34, 136, 147, 171, 188, 201, 203-4, 206, 213
Kaʿb al-Aḥbār, 58, 157, 159, 174, 178
Karīmah bint Hammām, 197
Karrāmiyyah, 171
al-Kāshānī, al-Fayḍ (Muḥsin), viii, 72
al-Kashshī, 186, 192-93, 202-9
Kaysāniyyah, 143
khabar 5, 49-50
khabar al-wāḥid (solitary report), x, 7, 10, 35, 39-40, 45, 46, 79, 80, 81, 91-130, 135
  linked (*al-maqrūn*), 6, 45-46, 81, 92-96, 100-101
  unlinked (*ghayr al-maqrūn*), 92, 93, 96, 100, 102, 117, 118, 129
Khadījah bint Ismāʿīl ibn ʿUmar, 199
Khadījah bint Khuwaylid, 195
Khadījah bint ʿUmar ibn ʿAlī ibn al-Ḥusayn, 198
al-Khāqānī, 100, 120
Khārijites, 144, 146
al-Khūʾī, Sayyid Abu al-Qāsim, viii, 39, 122, 207, 213, 218
Khurasan, 59
Kifāyat al-Uṣūl, 112
Kitāb ʿAlī (the Book of ʿAlī), 62-64
Kufa, 14, 59, 60, 109, 153, 155, 157, 161, 166, 168
Kulthūm bint Sulaym, 199
Laylā (the wife of Abū Dharr al-Ghafārī), 196
legends, 157-58, 161, 174, 180
liar (*kadhdhāb*), 19, 97, 140, 173, 192
Maʿārij al-Uṣūl, 46
Madinah, 156-57, 159, 161
Mahajjat al-Bayḍāʾ, xii
al-Mahdī, Muḥammad ibn Manṣūr, 173
al-Majlisī, Muḥammad Bāqir, 73, 225
Makkah, 6, 56, 58-59, 149-51
maleness, 159, 179, 194
Mālik ibn Anas, 59
Mālik ibn ʿAṭiyyah, 77
Mālikī, xii
al-Māmaqānī, ʿAbdallāh, 34, 48, 80, 91, 107, 112, 121, 142
Maʿmar, 59, 154, 175
Man lā Yaḥḍuruhū al-Faqīh, 69-70
maqbūl (accepted), 7, 15
maqlūb (altered), 16
maqṭūʿ (broken), 15, 110, 112
mardūd (rejected), 7
marfūʿ (traced), 13, 129
Māriyah al-ʿAbadiyyah, 199
marjaʿ al-taqlīd, 118
Maʿrūf ibn Kharrabūdh al-Makkī, 202-33
Maʿrūf, Hāshim, 48, 58, 80, 91, 184
Maryam bint Ayyās al-Anṣāriyyah, 197
mashhūr (famous), 7, 14, 108, 109
Mashriq al-Shamsayn, 65-66
maʿṣūm (infallible), 5, 8, 10, 11, 13-15, 16, 29, 32, 35, 37, 39, 40, 49-51, 76, 79, 80, 82, 84-85, 87, 90-91, 93, 94, 96, 100, 109-12, 115, 116, 119, 125, 129, 135, 176, 179, 206, 208, 210-11, 214, 216, 222, 225; *see also* Imams, Ahl al-Bayt
matn (text), 5, 76
maturity, 18, 21, 90, 189
mawqūf (stopped), 15
Miqbās al-Hidāyah fī ʿIlm al-Dirāyah, 34-35, 48, 84, 86, 112, 121, 131, 142
al-Miqdād ibn al-Aswad al-Kindī, 41
Moses, 83, 158, 159
muʿallal, 16
muʿallaq (suspended), 13, 106, 125-26
muʿanʿan, 13, 33

Muʿāwiyah ibn Abī Sufyān, 149-55, 157, 174, 175, 182
Muʿāwiyah ibn ʿAmmār al-Dahnī, 38, 39
mudabbaj (prestigious), 25
mudallas (deceptive), 16
muḍmar (ambiguous), 105, 109, 110, 111, 112
mudraj (interposed), 14
muḍṭarib (conflicting), 16
al-Mufaḍḍal ibn ʿUmar al-Juʿfī, 179
al-Mufaḍḍal ibn Yazīd, 168
al-Mufīd, al-Shaikh, 45-46, 93, 103, 207, 209
mufrad (exceptional), 14
al-Mughīrah ibn Saʿīd, 160, 161, 163-65, 167-68, 195, 203-4
al-Muḥaddith al-Fāṣil Bayna al-Rāwī wa al-Wāʿī, 104
Muḥammad ibn ʿAdhāfir, 63
Muḥammad ibn al-Muslim, 112
Muḥammad ibn Ismāʿīl ibn Bazīʿ, 112, 199
Muḥammad ibn Khālid al-Barqī, 44, 127
Muḥammad ibn Miqlāṣ al-Asadī al-Kūfī, 160
Muḥammad ibn Mūsā al-Hamadānī al-Sammān, 181
mukhtalaf (disparate), 15
Munah bint Abī ʿUmayr, 199
mursal (hurried), 9, 14, 16, 33-34, 70, 125-29, 169, 201, 204-6, 208-9, 216
al-Murtaḍā, al-Sharīf, 10, 103, 155, 207
Murūj al-Dhahab, 150
Musaddad ibn Musarhad, 60
muṣaḥḥaf (misspelt), 14
muṣaḥḥaḥ (authenticated tradition), 115
musalsal (sequential), 14
muṣarraḥ (explicit), 109-10
mushtabah (suspect), 7
Muslim ibn al-Ḥajjāj, 155, 158-59, 180, 183, 195
Muslim al-Jaramī, 197
musnad
  type of book, 60
  with a full *sanad*, 13, 70, 105, 115, 125
Musnad Aḥmad ibn Ḥanbal, 55, 61
Mustadrak al-Wasāʾil wa Mustanbiṭ al-Dalāʾil, 75
mustafīḍ (extensively narrated), 7, 108-9, 123
al-Mustarhamī al-Isbahānī, Hidāyat-allāh, 75
mutashābih (similar), 25
mutawātir (widely narrated), viii, ix, 6, 7, 10, 35, 39, 45, 79-93, 95-96, 100, 123, 218
Muʿtazilah, 143
muttafiq wa al-muftariq (same yet different), 25
muttaṣil (consecutive), 13, 33
muwaththaq (dependable), 9, 11, 46, 104, 115-18, 131, 136-37, 139, 144, 189
al-Muwaṭṭaʾ, 59, 61
al-Muẓaffar, Muḥammad Riḍā, 91, 96, 99
Naʿīm ibn al-Ḥammād al-Khuzāʿ, 60
al-Nāʾīnī, Mirza Muhammad Husayn, 100
al-Najāshī, 39, 63, 137, 141, 143, 180-81, 186, 192-93
Nasībah bint al-Kaʿb al-Anṣāriyyah, 196
Nāwūsiyyah, 143
Nihāyat al-Dirāyah, 48
al-Nūrī, al-Mīrzā Ḥūsayn, viii, 75, 206
philosophy, xi, xii, xiii
prayer, xii, 7, 88, 110, 112, 175, 218
preponderance (*tarjīḥ*), 16, 19, 44, 94, 122, 147, 185, 187, 208
proofs (*qarāʾin*), 93-96, 100, 104, 105, 117, 121, 122-23
Prophet Muḥammad (S), vii, x, 3, 5, 6, 15-16, 21, 25, 29, 32, 35, 37, 41-43, 49-64, 74, 79, 83, 85, 87, 91, 124, 130, 148, 150-59, 162, 165, 167, 170, 172-173, 175-78, 180, 182, 186, 195-96, 214
al-Qāḍī al-Rāmahurmuzī, 104
al-Qāḍī al-Nuʿmān, 126
al-Qāsim ibn Hanām, 195
qawī (strong), 11-12, 105, 116, 117
Qum, 48, 225

al-Qummī, al-Mīrzā Abu al-Qasim, 128
Qurʾān, vii, viii, xii, 6, 36, 41, 43, 55, 56, 58-59, 62, 68, 74, 83, 93-94, 96, 98, 117-18, 133-35, 141-42, 151, 153, 162, 164, 171-72, 177-78, 182, 215, 218, 220
al-Rabāb, 198
Rāfiḍah (dissenters), 163, 168
al-Rawāshiḥ al-Samāwiyyah, 48, 65, 112
rāwī, 52
rāwūn, 52
Ray, 60
reliable (*thiqah*), 19, 136, 137
al-Riʿāyah fī ʿIlm al-Dirāyah, 48
rijāl, *see* biographical sciences
riwāyah, 25, 32, 52
Ruqayyah bint Aḥmad, 200
Sabīʿah al-Aslamiyyah, 196
al-Ṣadūq, al-Shaikh, *see* Ibn Bābawayh
Ṣafiyyah bint Shaybah ibn ʿUthmān al-ʿAbdariyyah, 197
Ṣafwān ibn Yaḥyā, 146, 201-2, 204, 208-9
ṣaḥīfah, 61
ṣaḥīḥ (authentic), 9-10, 19, 33, 38, 46, 59, 104, 112, 115, 117-18, 122, 131, 136-37, 139, 144, 158, 183
Ṣaḥīḥ Muslim, xi, 55, 61, 155
Sāʾibah, 196
Saʿīd al-Aʿraj, 77
Saʿīdah bint ʿUmayr, 198
Sakīnah bint al-Ḥusayn ibn ʿAlī ibn Abī Ṭālib, 198
Sakīnah bint Quraysh, 196
Salmān al-Fārsī, 41
Samāʿah ibn Mahrān, 110, 190
Samrah ibn Jundab, 54
sanad, *see* chain of narration
sanity, 18, 188, 221
Sārah bint ʿAbdallāh ibn Masʿūd, 196
Sayyid Ḥasan ibn al-Sayyid Jaʿfār, xii
school of thought, 12, 44, 103, 138-41, 143, 169, 189-91
sects, 12, 143-44, 169, 171, 179, 181, 189-91, 218
shādh (unusual), 11, 14, 129, 130
Shāfiʿī, xi-xii, 68
al-Shahīd al-Awwal, xii
al-Shahīd al-Thānī (Zayn al-Dīn al-ʿĀmilī), xi, 1, 33-34, 47, 80, 91, 105, 112, 119, 146, 185, 194, 221
Shaikh Nāsir al-Dīn al-Milqānī, xi
Shams al-Din ibn Tūlūn al-Ḥanafī, xi
Sharḥ Lumʿah, xii
Sharḥ Uṣūl Dirāyat al-Ḥadīth, 47, 104
Shīʿa Ithna ʿAsharī, *see Imāmī*
Shihāb al-Dīn Aḥmad al-Ramli, xi
Sīrīn bint ʿAbdallāh ibn Masʿūd, 197
solitary report, *see khabar al-wāhid*
source collection (*aṣl*), 8, 63-67, 120, 138, 212, 219
speculation (*ẓann*), 39, 80, 84, 85, 92, 96-97, 100, 119, 122, 125, 128, 192-193, 211, 216
storyteller, 174-75
strength, 8, 11, 12, 14, 34, 59, 65, 105, 116-17, 144-45, 183
al-Subḥānī, Jaʿfar, 48, 81, 91, 95, 128, 133, 144
Sufyān al-Thawrī, 59, 156
Sulaym ibn Qays al-Hilālī, 41
Sumā al-Anṣariyyah, 197
Sunnah, vii, 36-37, 39, 50-51, 53-58, 61, 93-94, 96, 104, 135, 142, 164, 171, 173, 178, 183, 213, 218, 220
Sunnism, *see* Ahl al-Sunnah
al-Suyūṭī, Jalāl al-Dīn, 183, 199
Syria, xi, 59, 149, 150, 157, 161
Tabālah bint Yazīd, 196
al-Ṭabarsī, 97
tacit approval, 5, 13, 29, 50-51, 53-54, 84-85
tafsīr, xi
Tahdhīb al-Aḥkām, 8, 13, 68, 70-71, 106-107, 112, 125, 130, 210, 218-219
Ṭalḥā, 151
taqlīd, 118, 131
al-Ṭarīhī, Fakhr al-Dīn, 48
Ṭāriq ibn ʿAbd al-Raḥmān, 196
tarjīḥ (preponderance), 16, 19, 44, 94, 122, 147, 185, 187, 208
al-Ṭāṭarīyyūn, 191
tawātur, *see mutawātir*

ta'wīl (allegorical interpretation), 178
testimony, 10, 18, 38, 46, 93, 131-32, 134, 153, 192, 210, 213, 216, 218
thiqah (reliable), ix, 8, 10, 11-14, 19-20, 35, 38, 55-56, 65-67, 79, 86, 89, 91, 94, 98-100, 107, 112, 115, 118, 126-127, 132-133, 135-38, 144, 156, 189-190, 192-93, 206, 208-9, 212, 216, 218
al-Ṭihrānī, Muhammad Muhsin (Agha Buzurg), 33-35, 62, 65-67, 73, 224-25
Torah, 57, 158-59
al-Ṭūsī, Abū Jaʿfar Muḥammad ibn al-Ḥasan, viii, xi, 8, 11, 13, 25, 66, 70-71, 93-94, 96, 102, 106-7, 118, 120, 125-26, 130, 132-33, 137, 141, 143, 180, 186, 189, 192-93, 207-10
Ubay ibn Kaʿb, 58, 177
Umāmah bint al-Ṣalat, 196
Umayyid Dynasty, 59, 111, 149, 152, 154, 174, 182
Umm ʿAbdallāh ibn Masʿūd, 195
Umm Abīhā bint ʿAbdallāh ibn Jaʿfar al-Ṭayyār, 198
Umm Aḥmad al-Mirsiyyah, 199
Umm ʿAmr bint Khawāt ibn Jubayr, 196
Umm al-Aswad bint Aʿyan, 198
Umm Ayman, 195
Umm al-Bahā' Fāṭimah bint al-Ḥāfiẓ Taqī al-Dīn Muḥammad al-Hāshimiyyah, 199
Umm al-Faḍl (Lubābah bint al-Ḥārith al-Hilāliyyah), 195
Umm Farwah al-Anṣāriyyah, 195
Umm Farwah Fāṭimah bint al-Qāsim ibn Muḥammad ibn Abī Bakr, 198
Umm Ḥafṣ bint ʿUbayd ibn ʿĀzib, 196
Umm Ḥamīd bint ʿAbd al-Raḥmān, 196
Umm Hānī al-Anṣāriyyah., 195
Umm Hānī al-Thaqafiyyah, 198
Umm al-Ḥasan Fāṭimah bint Muḥammad ibn Makkī al-Shahīd al-Awwal, 198
Umm al-Ḥasan ibn ʿAlī ibn Ziyād al-Washā', 198
Umm Ḥudhayfah ibn al-Yamān, 195
Umm ʿĪsā ibn ʿAbd al-Raḥmān, 196
Umm Jamīlah al-Saʿdiyyah, 196
Umm Kulthūm al-Laythiyyah, 196
Umm Kulthūm bint ʿAlī ibn Abī Ṭālib, 198
Umm al-Karām al-Salamiyyah, 195
Umm al-Khaṭṭāb, 195
Umm al-Khayr bint Yūsuf, 199
Umm Maskīn bint ʿĀṣim ibn ʿUmar ibn al-Khaṭṭāb, 196
Umm Mūsā Ḥabībah, 198
Umm Naṣr al-Muḥāribiyyah, 195
Umm Saʿd bint Saʿd ibn al-Rabīʿ al-Anṣāriyyah, 195
Umm Salamah (the wife of the Prophet (S)), 195
Umm Salamah (the mother of Muḥammad ibn al-Muhājir), 198
Umm Sulaym bint Malḥān, 195
Umm Sumbulah al-Aslamiyyah, 195
unknown narrators, 12, 19, 103, 112, 117, 124-25, 136, 206, 216, 217
unseen, knowledge of the, 166, 167
al-uṣūl al-arbaʿumi'ah, see four hundred source collections
Uṣūlī, viii, 104
ʿUthmān ibn ʿAffān, 151, 153
veracity, *see ʿādil*
Wahb ibn Munabbih, 157, 174
al-Wāfī, 73
al-Wajīzah fī ʿIlm al-Dirāyah, 33, 48
Wāqifah, 20, 143, 190
Wasā'il al-Shīʿah, 72, 75, 98, 126, 134, 146, 203
weak, *see ḍaʿīf*
widely narrated, *see mutawātir*
will (*waṣiyyah*), 222
women, 159, 179, 194-99, 215
wuḍū' (ablution), 107
Wuṣūl al-Akhyār Ilā Uṣūl al-Akhbār, 48
Yaḥyā ibn Abī Kathīr, 197
Yaḥyā ibn Juʿdah, 57
Yaḥyā ibn Maʿīn, 175
Yemen, 58-59, 157
Yūnus ibn ʿAbd al-Raḥmān, 98, 164, 202, 204
zakāt (alms tax), 88

Zayd ibn ʿAlī, 168
Zaydiyyah (Zaydis), 143
Zayn al-Dīn al-ʿĀmilī, *see* al-Shahīd al-Thānī
Zaynab al-Shiʿriyyah, 200
Zaynab bint ʿAlī ibn Abī Ṭālib (A), 197
Zaynab bint Kaʿb, 196
Zaynab bint Nabīṭ al-Anṣāriyyah, 196
Zubaybah bint al-Nuʿmān, 196
al-Zuhrī, 56, 155
Zurārah ibn Aʿyan, 8, 44, 106, 110, 112, 115, 129, 198, 202-3